PENGUIN  CLASSICS

THE RAMCHARITMANAS 2

TULSIDAS (c.1532–1632), the most important of the saint-poets of the medieval bhakti movement in northern India, is also Hindi's greatest poet. Though very little is known about Tulsi's personal life, he left behind a considerable body of work, including his epic, the *Ramcharitmanas*, a retelling of the story of Ram in Avadhi. Tulsi was an ardent devotee of Ram, and his works have come to occupy almost a canonical status in the Ram tradition in northern India. His other important works include the *Gitavali*, the *Vinay Patrika* and the *Kavitavali*. In addition, the *Hanuman Chalisa*, a short devotional poem of forty verses in praise of Hanuman, is popularly ascribed to Tulsidas, and is considered by many to be his most important work after the *Manas*. Tulsidas's works continue to remain popular even today, more than four hundred years after their composition.

ROHINI CHOWDHURY is an established literary translator. Her primary languages are pre-modern (Braj Bhasha and Avadhi) and modern (Khari Boli) Hindi, and English. Her translations include the seventeenth-century Braj Bhasha text *Ardhakathanak*, widely regarded as the first autobiography in an Indian language, into modern Hindi and into English. She also writes for children, and has more than twenty books and several short stories to her credit. Her published writing, in English and Hindi, covers a wide spectrum of literary genres including novels, short fiction and non-fiction. Her literary interests include mythology, folklore, mathematics and history. She runs a story website at www.longlongtimeago.com.

THE
RAMCHARITMANAS
2

Tulsidas

Translated by Rohini Chowdhury

PENGUIN BOOKS

An imprint of Penguin Random House

PENGUIN BOOKS

USA | Canada | UK | Ireland | Australia
New Zealand | India | South Africa | China

Penguin Books is part of the Penguin Random House group of companies
whose addresses can be found at global.penguinrandomhouse.com

Published by Penguin Random House India Pvt. Ltd
4th Floor, Capital Tower 1, MG Road,
Gurugram 122 002, Haryana, India

First published in Penguin Books by Penguin Random House India 2019

Copyright © Rohini Chowdhury 2019
Introduction and Translation © Rohini Chowdhury 2019

All rights reserved

10 9 8 7 6 5 4 3 2

ISBN 9780143425885

Typeset in Adobe Caslon Pro by Manipal Technologies Limited, Manipal

Printed at Repro India Limited

www.penguin.co.in

Contents

Contents

Introduction

Amongst the most important of the saint-poets of the medieval bhakti movement in northern India, Tulsidas is also Hindi's most renowned poet. In 1574, he commenced the composition of his *Ramcharitmanas*, a retelling of the story of Ram, the legendary prince of Avadh. Tulsi's epic poem is unanimously regarded as the greatest achievement of Hindi literature, and is a significant addition to the Ramayana corpus. Composed in the vernacular Avadhi—a literary dialect of eastern Hindi—and therefore accessible to everyone without the need for learned intervention by the Brahmin, it became, and remains, the dominant and accepted version of Ram's story in the Hindi-speaking north.

My own engagement with Tulsidas began one crisp autumn night fifty years ago in a small town by the banks of the Ganga, when I saw my first performance of the *Ram Lila*. The sky was sprinkled with stars but I had eyes only for the drama unfolding upon the crude wooden stage before me, where the story had reached a critical point: Hanuman's tail was to be set on fire. The sets were crude, the costumes garish, the acting unsophisticated—but the story transcended all such concerns, such was its magic and power. I did not know it then, but that was also my first intimate encounter with the *Ramcharitmanas*, upon which the *Ram Lila* is based. Growing up, Tulsi's poem was always around me—chanted in the homes of friends or neighbours, sung on the radio, or the theme of plays and dance dramas. So when the opportunity came to translate it into English for Penguin India, I accepted it with alacrity—and the last five years that I have spent walking behind Tulsi, one of the greatest literary minds of all time, have been a pleasure and a privilege. My translation does not do justice to Tulsi's extraordinary poetic genius. His use of wordplay, his rhymes and alliteration, and the sheer musicality of his poem I have found impossible to capture in English. I have therefore contented myself with being as clear and accurate as possible in my translation, and to convey, to the best of my ability, the scale and grandeur of his great poem.

The Ramayana tradition

For at least the last two and a half thousand years, poets, writers, folk performers, and religious and social reformers have drawn upon the story of Ram as a source of inspiration. It has been told again and again in countless forms and dozens of languages, making it one of the most popular and enduring stories in the world. More than any other hero, Ram has been upheld as dharma personified, the epitome of righteousness, and his actions as the guide for right conduct. In recent times, the story has provided inspiration for films, novels, and in the late 1980s, a weekly television series watched by more than eighty million viewers.

The oldest and most influential surviving literary telling of the story of Ram is the Sanskrit epic called the Ramayana. Composed sometime during the first millennium BCE, and consisting of some 50,000 lines in verse set in seven kands or books, it is attributed to the poet Valmiki, and is widely regarded as the 'original'.[1] The influence of Valmiki's Ramayana has been so profound that the title of his epic has come to denote the entire tradition, from oral and folk performances to literary texts and translations. Within this rich and varied tradition also lie the Ramayana songs from Telangana, the folk performances of the *Ram Lila* in northern India, the eleventh-century Tamil *Iramavataram* ('The Incarnation of Ram') by Kamban, and Tulsidas's *Ramcharitmanas*.

The rise of bhakti

Scholars of the Ramayana tradition hold the view that Ram was originally a human hero and was only later raised to the status of avatar of Vishnu. In the five central books of Valmiki's epic, Ram is portrayed as an earthly prince: though endowed with godlike courage, fortitude and compassion, his exploits are those of a human being. It is only in the first and last books of the poem—which are considered to be later additions to Valmiki's epic—that Ram is explicitly declared to be an incarnation of Vishnu on earth.

Soon after the beginning of the Common Era, Ram began to be increasingly regarded as an avatar of Vishnu. At about the same time, a new attitude towards the divine began to replace austere monistic meditation, sacrificial rites and polytheistic practices. This was bhakti, or intense emotional attachment and love towards a chosen, personal god and his avatars—particularly Vishnu and his earthly incarnations, Ram and Krishna—and joyous and public worship of that god. Bhakti assumed a dualistic relationship between the devotee and his god, as opposed to the monistic ideal of the Advaita or non-dualistic school of philosophy. Its proponents considered the way of bhakti (bhakti-marg) superior to other means of achieving salvation such as knowledge or good works or ascetic disciplining of the body; it was also open to everyone, regardless of their caste, class or sex. With the advent of bhakti, Ram's transition from godlike prince to God became complete. This was a critical transformation of the Ram story—and it is within this bhakti tradition that Tulsi wrote his *Ramcharitmanas*.

The bhakti movement was characterized by its emphasis on the use of vernacular languages, making its teachings directly accessible to the common people, regardless of class or caste. This was in stark contrast to traditional practice, within which Sanskrit, regarded as the sacred language, was used for all important literary and religious texts. Sanskrit was thus the preserve of an elite few, typically high-caste Brahmins, who would study, interpret and explain the texts to the common people. The earliest bhakti texts to appear were in Tamil—these were devotional poems in praise of Shiv and Vishnu, composed by saint-musicians, the Nayanars and Alvars, of southern India between the seventh and the tenth centuries CE. Also written in Tamil was Kamban's *Iramavataram*. Composed in the eleventh century, it is amongst the earliest vernacular Ramayanas. It became, and still is, the definitive version of the Ram story in the Tamil-speaking areas of the subcontinent. The bhakti movement soon spread northwards, appearing in texts such as the *Bhagavata Purana*, composed in Sanskrit in the tenth century and celebrating devotion to Krishna. More vernacular Ramayanas were composed. Amongst the more noteworthy of these were the thirteenth-century Telugu Ramayana of Buddharaja and the fifteenth-century Bengali *Sriram Panchali* by Krittibas. In Hindi, the bhakti movement reached its zenith in the sixteenth century, with Tulsidas's *Ramcharitmanas*.

The *Ramcharitmanas*: spread and impact

From Tulsi's own writings we infer that his poem, written in the spoken tongue rather than in the sacred Sanskrit, was criticized and ridiculed by the religious establishment of his times. Despite this initial disapproval by the Brahmins (ironically complicated by the fact that the *Ramcharitmanas* itself is so pro-Brahmin), it became hugely popular amongst other groups, especially the merchant caste and lower orders of society, and soon acquired the status and religious authority usually enjoyed only by Sanskrit texts. Within a very short time, carried by wandering sadhus, recited and performed by travelling bards and musicians across towns and villages, it had spread across northern India, from Tulsi's native Banaras in the east to the Rajput kingdoms of Rajasthan in the west. It is worth noting that this initial circulation of Tulsi's poem took place before the advent of printing in India, in areas and times of exceedingly low literacy, its currency strongly dependent on the oral tradition and remarkable feats of memorization by its devotees. Such was the rapid spread and influence of Tulsi's poem that his contemporary, the poet Nabhadas, declares Tulsi to be Valmiki himself, born again to bring his epic once more to the world.[2]

In the late eighteenth century, the *Ramcharitmanas* found royal patronage in the courts of resurgent Hindu kingdoms in northern India who found it a convenient, authoritative and accessible text through which to assert their Hindu identity and legitimize their rule by invoking Ram as the ideal and perfect king. In the nineteenth century, the *Ramcharitmanas* gained even greater currency as north Indian mainstream Hinduism found within it not only an answer to the Christian Bible, but also a nationalistic response to British colonialism. The development of movable type in Indian scripts led to the growth of vernacular presses and the printing of popular books in Indian languages, including, in 1810 in Calcutta, Tulsidas's *Ramcharitmanas*. By the end of the century, printed versions of Tulsi's epic were available all across the north of India—from Calcutta, in Bengali translation, to Gurmukhi-script editions in Delhi and Lahore, and Gujarati and Marathi versions from Bombay.[3] Today, known to its audience as 'Tulsi's Ramayan', or simply the *Manas*, Tulsi's great poem is read, sung, recited and retold in almost every Hindu household in northern India as the accepted and dominant version of the story of Ram. It is also the basis of the *Ram Lila*, a tradition believed to have been started in Banaras almost 500 years ago by Tulsidas himself and still enthusiastically observed.

Tulsidas

We know very little about Tulsidas himself, except what can be pieced together from autobiographical references in his own writings and some contemporary and later, not entirely reliable, accounts of his life. His date and place of birth are uncertain—though it is now generally accepted that he was born in 1532, possibly in the town of

Sukarkhet in the present-day state of Uttar Pradesh. From some of his later works, we know Tulsidas was abandoned in childhood by his parents, and that he was rescued and looked after by sadhus who introduced him to the worship of Ram. Some scholars believe that Tulsidas then took up the life of a sadhu. It is probable, though, that Tulsidas did not become a sadhu at once, but went to Banaras and acquired the traditional Sanskrit education of a Brahmin. He then returned to the village of his birth, where he married. He began to live as a householder, but an altercation with his wife caused him to renounce home and family and take up the wandering life of a sadhu. He lived for a while in Ayodhya, where he composed the initial parts of his *Ramcharitmanas*. Tulsi later settled in Banaras where he wrote most of his other major works; there, he also instituted the *Ram Lila*. He died in Banaras, probably in 1632.[4]

A synopsis

In the beginning sections of his poem, Tulsidas tells us that he commenced this work in Ayodhya, on the ninth day of the Hindu month of Chaitra—the day of Ram's birth—in the year 1631 of the Vikram Era, i.e., 1574 CE.[5] This also makes the *Ramcharitmanas* the earliest of his major works. Consisting of approximately 12,900 lines of Avadhi verse set in seven kands or books, it is also Tulsi's longest work, and its composition probably took him several years. The fourth book of his poem opens with an invocation to the city of Banaras, suggesting that he completed the epic after moving there.

In the beginning of the *Ramcharitmanas*, Tulsi explains that he first heard the story of Ram from his guru in Sukarkhet when he was still a boy, and that this is the story that he now seeks to set down in the spoken tongue.[6] In outline, the story of the *Ramcharitmanas* is as follows:

King Dasharath of Koshal rules in splendour from his capital city, Avadh. The king has all that a man could desire, except a son.

So, upon the advice of his guru, the sage Vasishtha, he holds a great fire-sacrifice, as the result of which four sons are born to him: Ram, the eldest, to his chief queen, Kaushalya; Bharat to his favourite wife, Kaikeyi; and the twins Lakshman and Shatrughna to his third queen, Sumitra. Ram is no other than the great god Vishnu, who has become incarnate in human form in order to rid the world of Ravan, the powerful king of the Rakshasas, who cannot be killed except by a mortal man and who has overrun the earth and overwhelmed even the gods.

The four princes grow up to be brave and skilled warriors. One day, when the princes are still youths, the sage Vishvamitra arrives at Dasharath's court and requests that Ram and his brother Lakshman be sent with him to help protect his fire-sacrifices from the depredations of the Rakshasas. Dasharath protests that his sons are still too young, and offers the sage his whole army instead. But Vishvamitra insists that he wants only Ram and Lakshman to help him. Finally, Dasharath agrees.

The two young princes leave with Vishvamitra for the forest, where they successfully kill the Rakshasas disturbing his worship. Vishvamitra then takes the princes to the city of Mithila, to the court of King Janak. There, Ram sees and falls in love with the king's daughter, Sita, and wins her hand in marriage by breaking the great bow of Shiv. The wedding of Ram and Sita is celebrated with great splendour. Lakshman, too, is married to Sita's sister Urmila, and Bharat and Shatrughna to her cousins, the daughters of King Janak's brothers. The four princes and their brides return to Ayodhya, where they continue to live in harmony for several years.

The aging Dasharath then decides to appoint Ram his heir. As preparations for his investiture get under way, Kaikeyi's old nursemaid Manthara convinces her that Ram's investiture would mean the end of her position as the king's favourite, and would cause Bharat to languish in a prison cell while Ram ruled with the help of his favourite, Lakshman. Once, in return for saving his life on the battlefield, Dasharath had given Kaikeyi the gift of two boons: she could ask of him anything that her heart desired and he would fulfil it. Kaikeyi now demands that Bharat be made heir in place of Ram, and that Ram be banished to the forest for fourteen years. Bound by his word, the old king is unable to deny her requests. Realizing the situation, Ram cheerfully accepts his exile and leaves for the forest. Sita and Lakshman, who refuse to stay back, accompany him. Dasharath dies of a broken heart, and all of Avadh is plunged into mourning.

Bharat, who has been away all this while, is summoned back urgently by Vasishtha. He returns and is devastated to find his brother exiled and his father dead. He denounces his mother's actions, refuses the kingship and sets out in pursuit of Ram, determined to bring him back as the rightful king of Avadh. Ram, however, refuses to return, saying that he must honour their father's word, and requests Bharat to go back and rule as their father had desired. Bharat returns heartbroken to Avadh, and taking up an ascetic residence in the nearby village of Nandigram, rules as Ram's regent till the end of his period of exile.

Ram, Lakshman and Sita wander through the forest, encountering demons, ascetics and sages, including the sage Valmiki, who directs them to make their home amongst the hills and forests of Chitrakut. There, Supnakha, the sister of Ravan, sees and falls in love with Ram. Turning herself into a beautiful woman, she approaches Ram, who rejects her advances. Lakshman cuts off her ears and nose in order to teach her a lesson. Mutilated and humiliated, she appeals to her Rakshasa brothers, Khar and Dushan, who attack Ram with their entire army. While Lakshman protects Sita and hides her away in a mountain cave, Ram single-handedly kills the demons and destroys their army. Supnakha then runs in despair to Ravan, who is infuriated by her story, in particular the killing of Khar and Dushan. Ravan decides to kidnap Sita and enlists the help of Marichi, another Rakshasa. Marichi turns himself into a golden deer and manages to lure Ram and Lakshman into the forest. In their absence, Ravan carries Sita off to his island kingdom of Lanka, where he keeps her prisoner.

The vulture Jatayu sees Sita being carried off and tries to save her, but is fatally wounded by Ravan. Ram and Lakshman return to find the hermitage deserted and Sita missing; as they search for her, they find the wounded Jatayu, who lives just long enough to tell them of her abduction. Ram performs his last rites, and Jatayu receives liberation.

Ram and Lakshman search desperately for Sita, and reach the monkey kingdom of Kishkindha. There, Ram meets Hanuman, who becomes a staunch devotee. He also meets the displaced monkey prince Sugriv, who has also lost both wife and kingdom to his brother Baali. Ram kills Baali and installs Sugriv as king of the monkeys; in return, Sugriv agrees to help him and sends his warriors in every direction in search of Sita. They discover that she is being held prisoner in Lanka.

Hanuman leaps across the ocean, locates Sita and gives her Ram's ring. He lays waste the ashok grove in which Sita is being held, and allows himself to be captured. On Ravan's orders, his tail is set on fire, but Hanuman escapes and, after setting the city of Lanka ablaze, returns to Ram. Meanwhile, Ravan's brother, Vibhishan, who is a devotee of Vishnu and opposed to Ravan's abduction of Sita, also joins Ram's forces. The monkeys build a bridge across the ocean to Lanka, and after a long and bloody battle, Ram kills Ravan. Vibhishan is crowned king of Lanka, and Sita is rescued.

The kidnapped Sita proves to be a shadow replica of herself— Ram, as Vishnu, had foreseen her abduction, and at his behest, the real Sita had stepped into fire, leaving behind a shadow image of herself. It was this shadow Sita that Ravan had kidnapped, while the real Sita had remained hidden, safe from dishonour till Ravan had been killed and the purpose of the gods achieved. Ram now orders Lakshman to light a great fire, and demands that Sita step into it as a test of her chastity. The shadow Sita steps into the fire and is destroyed, and the real Sita steps out, unharmed.

The period of his exile almost over, Ram returns to Ayodhya with
Sita and Lakshman. There, he is crowned king amidst much joy
and celebration, and so begins his long reign, during which pain
or unhappiness were unknown, and all beings lived in harmony
and joy.

The influence of Valmiki's epic upon Tulsi cannot be denied: in
the initial verses of the *Ramcharitmanas*, Tulsi salutes Valmiki as
the author of the Ramayana,[7] thus acknowledging him as one of
the important sources for his own poem. Tulsi's epic, however,
differs from Valmiki's in one very important particular: Valmiki's
Ramayana was a secular text, whilst Tulsi's *Ramcharitmanas* is,
without question, a devotional text. Tulsi's Ram is unequivocally
divine. He is also Tulsi's chosen god, in whose worship the poet
is totally, completely and blissfully immersed—as he tells us in the
invocatory verses of the first book, he composed this story of Ram
for 'his own delight and satisfaction'.[8]

Tulsi's telling of the Ram story in the *Ramcharitmanas* is very
close to the version contained in the Sanskrit text known as the
Adhyatma-ramayana (or 'spiritual' Ramayana). Composed sometime
between 1450 and 1550, the *Adhyatma-ramayana* identifies Ram not
only as an incarnation of Vishnu, but also as the personification of
brahm, the ultimate Absolute of the Upanishads and the Advaita
school of philosophy. It also emphasizes bhakti rather than
knowledge, and recommends meditation on Ram's name as a means
to salvation. It is only through intense devotion to Ram, says the
Adhyatma-ramayana, that knowledge of the non-dual Self can arise
in the individual soul. This is reflected in Tulsi's own, more skilful,
amalgamation of the dualism of Vaishnav bhakti with Advaita
monism in the *Ramcharitmanas*, particularly in the sections where
Tulsi explains the reasons for Ram's actions and their significance.
Tulsi's Ram, as the avatar of Vishnu, also has the attributes of the
Supreme God—he is all-knowing and all-seeing, so that his actions
are predetermined by him to suit his purpose and all that he does or

causes to happen in his incarnate form is merely his *lila*, his divine play or pastime.

Tulsi's replacement of the kidnapping of Sita by the abduction of a 'shadow' or illusory Sita whilst the real Sita remains concealed in the abode of Agni, the fire god, is a major deviation from Valmiki and in keeping with the demands of bhakti. The idea of an illusory Sita arose as early as the eighth century and was further developed in the *Adhyatma-ramayana* where it became an integral part of the plot. Along with Ram's transformation from earthly prince to avatar of Vishnu, Sita acquired the status and attributes of Shri, Vishnu's divine consort. As the incarnation of the goddess upon earth, it became unacceptable that she be kidnapped and imprisoned by Ravan and defiled by his touch. Tulsi's substitution of the real Sita with a shadow replica of herself solved this problem and kept safe the purity and chastity of the goddess. In addition to protecting the sacred person of the goddess, it also justified Ram's demand that Sita prove her chastity after her long imprisonment in Lanka by stepping into the sacred fire. Sita's trial by fire thus becomes a device for the return of the real Sita rather than an unwarranted and unjust test of her purity as in Valmiki's epic.[9] Tulsi's poem ends on a 'happily-ever-after' note, with Ram ruling gloriously in Ayodhya, his beloved Sita by his side. Valmiki's epic does not stop there, but continues in the last book to describe Ram and Sita's later years, in particular the aspersions cast on Sita's chastity by the people of Ayodhya, and her consequent banishment by Ram to the forest. Though Tulsi does refer to this in passing in the first book—Ram, he says, has great affection for the people of Ayodhya, 'for although they maligned Sita, he freed them from all their sins and sorrows'[10]—his device of the shadow Sita precludes the need for him to include this in his version of the story.

Tulsi pays homage to the great and eminent poets who preceded him, as well as to the vernacular poets who told of the deeds of Ram in the spoken tongue.[11] The influence upon him of texts other than Valmiki's is evident in passages such as his delightful descriptions of Ram's childhood, which were probably inspired by the *Bhagavata Purana* and contemporary bhakti poetry in praise of Krishna, both of which celebrate the child Krishna. Tulsi's charming description of Sita's first meeting with Ram[12]—in a garden, where Ram has gone with Lakshman to gather flowers for his morning worship and Sita with her handmaidens to offer worship at a temple of the goddess Parvati—was possibly inspired by the fourteenth-century Sanskrit drama, *Prasannaraghava*, by Jaidev.[13]

In the *Ramcharitmanas*, Tulsi successfully brings together the many contrasting ideologies of his time—joyous, unrestrained Vaishnav bhakti and austere Advaita meditation, the worship of Vishnu and the worship of Shiv, the worship of the abstract, nirgun ('without attributes') Absolute and the adoration of the sagun ('with attributes') Incarnate endowed with form and beauty. Tulsi's Ram is the Supreme Being personified, and Sita is his Shakti, or primal energy. From Ram and Sita spring all the other gods, including Shiv and Parvati (whom Tulsi elsewhere calls 'the father and mother of the Universe'), and even Lakshmi and Vishnu. For Tulsi, Ram is the Supreme God, yet throughout the poem, Tulsi's Ram declares that without the worship of Shiv, no one can attain to his bhakti. Yet, the name of Ram is the high mantra chanted by Shiv, who declares it necessary for salvation even in his own holy city of Banaras. Tulsi takes every opportunity to describe the beauty of Ram's incarnate form in loving detail—his body dark as a rain-laden cloud, his radiant face and lotus eyes, the tilak upon his forehead—but reminds us at once that he is the all-pervading Spirit of the Universe, unborn, uncreated, without flaw, without form. Tulsi prostrates himself at the lotus-feet of the incarnate Ram and adores the name of Ram as borne by his chosen god. This integration of different ideologies in the *Manas* is one of Tulsi's most significant achievements.

Tulsi has been criticized in modern times for his apparent support of the caste system, his reverence for Brahmins and his characterization of women as inherently inferior to men. However, here too he brings together opposing views. While paying homage to

Brahmins as 'gods upon earth', he upholds the tribal woman Shabari, who waited in the forest for Ram, as the epitome of devotion and virtue.[14] So, while the social order must be upheld, within bhakti, the boundaries of caste, class and gender disappear. Tulsi's institution of the *Ram Lila* may be seen as an attempt at a degree of social integration, albeit within the Hindu framework—for everyone, regardless of caste, class and religion, was invited to take part in these performances, whether as actors or audience. This inclusivity remains, by and large, a feature of the *Ram Lila* even today.

Structure

The titles and line counts of the seven books of the *Ramcharitmanas* are as follows:

1. *Balkand* (Childhood)   4200 lines
2. *Ayodhyakand* (Ayodhya)   3300 lines
3. *Aranyakand* (The Forest)   750 lines
4. *Kishkindhakand* (Kishkindha)   400 lines
5. *Sundarkand* (The Beautiful)   750 lines
6. *Lankakand* (Lanka)   1700 lines
7. *Uttarkand* (Epilogue)   1800 lines

Each book begins with a *mangalacharan*, the traditional worship or salutation at the commencement of a written work, in which Tulsi calls upon various gods to bless his endeavour. In order to underline the sacred nature of what was to come, Tulsi chose to write these invocatory passages in Sanskrit.

Tulsi presents his story through a series of interwoven conversations between four narrator–listener pairs, whom he introduces at the beginning of his poem:[15]

- Shiv, and his wife, the goddess Parvati—the story arose in Shiv's heart and he revealed it to Parvati

- Kak Bhushundi, a sage in a crow's body, and Garud, king of the birds and Vishnu's divine steed—Shiv gave the same story to Bhushundi, who related it to Garud
- The sages Jagbalik and Bharadvaj—Jagbalik obtained the tale from Bhushundi and recited it to Bharadvaj
- And finally, Tulsidas and his audience—Tulsi heard the story from his guru and set it down in common speech for his audience

The narrative moves deftly, often unexpectedly, from one narrator to another and back again. The conversation between Bhushundi and Garud is contained mainly in, and takes up most of, the seventh book. Tulsi indicates the narrator–listener pairs sometimes directly, explicitly naming either the speaker or the listener ('Then said Mahesh [Shiv] with a smile . . .'),[16] or by frequent interjections that identify the listener ('O king of the birds' or 'O muni') and so, by extension, the speaker (Bhushundi in the first instance, and Jagbalik in the second). A fifth narrator is implied—just as Tulsi is relating the story to his listeners, in the same way, they too may tell this story to others.

The title of Tulsi's work deserves some attention.[17] The name 'Ram' needs little explanation. Not only is it the name of the hero of the epic, but it is also the name of Tulsi's chosen god, who is none other than the personification of the Supreme Spirit of the Universe. The word *charit* (from the root *char*, 'to move') means 'going, moving' and becomes by extension, 'movement or deeds'. Thus *Ram+charit* means 'the movements or doings of Ram'. The word *manas* is derived from the root word *man*, usually translated into English as 'heart' or 'mind', and means 'belonging to, or born from, the heart or mind'. 'Manas' is also the name of a lake in the Himalayas; lying at the foot of Mount Kailash, the abode of Shiv, the Manas lake, or Manasarovar, is considered to be sacred by many faiths and is used as a metaphor for the mind in its highest state of pure bliss. In the early sections of the first book, Tulsi tells us that this work arose in the mind of Shiv, who kept it within his heart, till, finding an auspicious moment, he revealed it to his wife, the goddess Parvati. And that is why, having seen this sacred story of the doings of Ram within his mind, Shiv called it 'Ramcharitmanas'. Inspiration, by the grace of Shiv, then gladdened his own mind, says Tulsi, and he composed his great work, making it as pleasing to the heart as his wit allowed.[18]

Tulsi also compares his epic, the *Manas*, to the holy Manas lake—it is the reservoir that contains within it the sacred story of the doings of Ram. Its four narrators are the four ghats that surround it, and the seven books seven staircases that lead down to the clear waters of Ram's fame.[19] He introduces the imagery of the lake in Stanza 36 of the first book and builds it up over the next seven stanzas. He describes the clusters of waterlilies and many-coloured lotuses that grow upon the lake—these are the poetic metres he has used in his poem, and their fragrance the elegant language. Swans of wisdom and detachment float upon the tranquil surface of the lake, while the fish that are wordplay and allusion shimmer beneath its clear waters. The songs in praise of Ram are rare and wonderful water birds, while lustful and evil men are storks and crows that dare not come near the lake. The pleasure derived from this tale, says Tulsi, is a garden watered by the heart with tears of love, and the bliss that wells up in his heart and pours out in a flood of love and joy is the Sarju, Ayodhya's sacred river. This stream of love flows into the glittering Ganga of devotion to Ram, and is joined by the majestic Sone, the great river that is the splendour of Ram and Lakshman in battle. Together, these three streams flow into the ocean that is Ram himself. Tulsi reaffirms the imagery of the Manas lake through his entire work. He calls each of the seven books a 'sopan' or 'descent' into the lake, and reintroduces the imagery of the lake in the seventh book, in the conversation between Bhushundi and Garud.[20]

Tulsi wrote for an audience which was familiar not only with the story of Ram, but also knew the dozens of 'backstories' that weave in and out of the main narrative, or to which Tulsi refers, either directly or obliquely. I am aware that many of those who read my translation will not have the same familiarity with these tales, and so I have attempted, in footnotes, endnotes and a glossary, to give as much background information as I could. Also, the Hindu gods all have more than one name, and Tulsi refers to them by these different names, with which, once again, his audience would have been familiar. Each distinct name or epithet for a god or goddess refers to a quality, characteristic or action of that deity. So, for instance the god of love, Kamdev, or 'lord of passion', may also be referred to as Hridayniket, 'one whose abode is the heart', Manmath, 'he who churns the heart', or Manobhav, 'mind-born'. Similarly, the god Shiv ('the auspicious, the fortunate'), the Destroyer, the great and powerful third deity in the Hindu triad, is, as the lord of all creation, also called Akhileshvar, and as the Destroyer, he is also called Har. While I am aware that these different names for the same deity may be confusing to modern readers, reducing the gods to a single name would, I felt, take away from the meaning and atmosphere of Tulsi's poem. So, for the most part I have kept the names as Tulsi has used them; to make it easier, I have given the most familiar name of the deity as a footnote at the first occurrence of another name for the same god or goddess (for instance, 'Hridayniket' has been footnoted as 'Kamdev'; 'Har' has been footnoted as 'Shiv'). I have also included the various names with their meanings under the glossary entry for the relevant god or goddess (so all of the names of Kamdev used in the text are given under the entry 'Kamdev' in the glossary).

Tulsi may have composed his poem in the 'common tongue', but his control of language, his mastery of rhythm and his deliberate and skilful use of literary devices throughout display a literary virtuosity that is nothing short of genius. He composed his poem mainly in two alternating metres, the *chaupai* and the *doha*. A chaupai is a quatrain consisting of four parts or 'feet'; each quarter verse is made up of sixteen *matras* or 'instants', which is the time required to pronounce a short vowel (a long vowel is twice the length of a short vowel, and thus is equal to two matras). A doha is a couplet, each line of which consists of two unequal parts, usually of thirteen and eleven matras respectively, separated by a caesura; the rhyme occurs at the end of the lines. Thus the doha, though a couplet, may also be thought of as consisting of four, even if unequal, parts. Sometimes Tulsi uses the *sortha* instead of, or along with, the doha. Also consisting of two lines, a sortha is a mirror image of the doha, with its half-lines transposed so its lines are divided into eleven- and thirteen-matra segments separated by a caesura; the rhyme falls at the caesura in the middle of the line. I have rendered each metre in four lines in English translation: each quarter part of a chaupai translates into a single line of verse in English as does each part of a doha or sortha; the lines of the doha and sortha are usually shorter than those of the chaupai.

Tulsi uses the measured and regular chaupai metre in which to tell his story and take it forward. Each series of four to eight chaupais is followed by a doha or dohas (or sometimes a sortha or doha/sortha mix). Many oral performances of the epic take the doha/sortha as a unit of closure. I have followed the same approach, and for the sake of easy reference, taken each chaupai set along with its concluding dohas/sorthas to represent a stanza—though the term 'stanza' has no equivalent in medieval Hindi poetry and Tulsi's text shows no such divisions. I have numbered only the concluding couplets, and matched this numbering to my source text, the popular and widely available Gita Press edition of the *Ramcharitmanas* with a commentary by Hanuman Prasad Poddar. A stanza could just as well be defined as beginning with a doha and some commentators prefer this approach.

A fourth metre that occurs with some frequency in the *Ramcharitmanas* is the *chhand*.

The most musical of the metres used by Tulsi, a chhand consists of four equal lines of twenty-six to thirty matras, with the rhyme at the end of each line. Tulsi uses the chhand to highlight moments of intense emotion, or to further describe and thus emphasize critical scenes or events. The chhand's flowing lyrical nature makes it particularly well suited for such use. Chhands are usually inserted between chaupais and their concluding dohas/sorthas, and so appear within 'stanzas' as defined above.

Other metres used by Tulsi include the hymns of praise or *stutis* spoken by various characters, and the invocatory Sanskrit shlokas of the mangalacharan at the beginning of each book.

It is impossible to reproduce the beat and rhyme schemes of these metres in English, and I have not attempted to do so. However, I have attempted to give the reader some idea, at least visually, of the structure of the poem. Therefore, the dohas/sorthas are indented; chhands, stutis and shlokas are in italics; and the chaupais form the main body of the text.

Other works

Tulsidas has left behind a considerable body of work. However, of the twenty-two works popularly attributed to him, only twelve, including the *Ramcharitmanas*, can be ascribed to him with certainty. The story of Ram is a recurring theme in Tulsi's writings and his works have come to occupy almost a canonical status in the Ram tradition in northern India. The *Gitavali* is his second-longest work; it presents incidents from the life of Ram in 328 songs. The *Vinay Patrika*, considered Tulsi's second-most important work after the *Ramcharitmanas*, consists of some 280 songs, in the form of a personal petition to Ram asking for deliverance from the age of Kali. Both these works are in the western-Hindi Brajbhasha, and were composed in the middle years of the poet's life. A major work of Tulsi's later years is the *Kavitavali*. Also in Braj, it tells the Ram story in some 325 verses. Other, lesser, works include two poems on mythological weddings: the *Parvati-mangal*, a description of the marriage of Shiv and Parvati, composed in 1586, and the *Janaki-mangal* on the marriage of Ram with Sita, which is undated; both these poems are in Avadhi. Another minor work is the *Barvai-ramayan*, an abridged rendition of the Ram story in sixty-nine stanzas in the barvai metre; this is also in Avadhi. A large collection of verses in the doha and sortha metres, called *Dohavali*, is also ascribed to Tulsidas.

In addition, the *Hanuman Chalisa*, a short devotional poem of forty verses in praise of Hanuman, is popularly ascribed to Tulsidas. Though the poem begins with a doha from the second book of the *Ramcharitmanas*[21] and contains several lines that seem to have been taken from the epic, it remains doubtful that it was composed by Tulsidas. However, it is considered by many to be his most important work after the *Manas*. It is recited daily by millions of Hindus and is one of the most popular devotional poems of all time.

Tulsidas was a man of deep spiritual insight and a poet of extraordinary talent. His bhakti is joyous and intense, and very soon, his audience too is drawn into exuberant devotion to the 'feet of Ram'. He charms and moves his audience with his delicate descriptions and enthrals them with the intellectual force and clarity of his discourses on points of doctrine. His achievements are significant: not only did he successfully recast the ancient story of Ram in the mould of bhakti, but by composing it in the vernacular he took away forever the need for its interpretation by the Brahminical elite. His synthesis of contrasting ideologies and points of view in the *Manas* made it acceptable to a wider audience and led to greater integration within the Hindu community. Nothing that can be said about the beauty of his great poem or the significance of its contribution to the religious and social landscape of northern India is enough. Thus, it is perhaps best that we now 'listen' to this great story in the manner that Tulsi asks—with our full attention. I hope, despite its many shortcomings, my translation will give my readers an appreciation of this great work.

Book II

AYODHYAKAND
(AYODHYA)

Mangalacharan

He in whose lap shines the mountain's daughter, Parvati,
Upon whose head is held the gods' river, Ganga,
Upon whose brow is the new moon, in whose throat is held poison,
Upon whose breast is resplendent the serpent king, Sheshnag,
He whose ornaments are ashes,
The greatest of all gods, the eternal Lord of all,
The complete, the all-pervading Shiv, of auspicious form,
As fair and radiant as the moon, the Lord Shankar—
May he protect me always. (1)

The beauty of the lotus face of Raghunandan—
Which neither brightened with the joy of being anointed heir
Nor dimmed with the sorrow of exile in the forest—
May it ever bring me sweet prosperity and well-being. (2)

He whose limbs are as dark and as soft as the blue lotus,
Who has Sita resplendent to his left,
And holds in his hands a mighty arrow and a beautiful bow—
I salute him, Ram, lord of the Raghu dynasty. (3)

Cleansing the mirror of my heart
With the dust of my revered guru's lotus feet,
I sing of Raghubar's unblemished fame
Which gives the four fruits of this existence.   (0)

From the moment that Ram returned home wedded,
There were daily new festivities, and constant rejoicing
    and celebrations.
Upon the mighty mountains that were the fourteen spheres,
Clouds of virtue rained down showers of bliss.
The sparkling rivers of prosperity and spiritual accomplishment
Swelled and grew, and flowed into the ocean that was Avadh.
The well-born men and women of the city were like fine jewels,
Flawless, priceless and beautiful in every way.
The splendour and magnificence of the city is beyond telling—
It seemed as though Viranchi's art had reached its pinnacle here.
Gazing upon the moon of Ramchandra's countenance,
All the people of the city were, in every way, content and happy.
The royal mothers and all their friends and companions were delighted
To see the vine of their hearts' desire bearing fruit.
The king was overwhelmed with joy to see and hear about
Ram's beauty, virtue and gracious good nature.

In everyone's heart was this longing
Which they uttered in their prayers to Mahesh—
'May the king himself in his lifetime give Ram
The title of Jubaraj[i], and make him heir-apparent.'   (1)

Once, the king of the Raghus, with all his courtiers
Sat resplendent in the royal court.
Himself the embodiment of every virtue, the lord of men
Rejoiced exceedingly to hear of Ram's glorious fame.

---

[i]   The heir apparent

All the kings longed for his favour,
Even the divine guardians of the three worlds loved him, keeping
    in mind his wishes.
In all the three worlds, in all the three times, past, present and future,
No one was as fortunate as Dasharath,
Whose son was Ram, the source of all blessing.
Whatever one might say about him is not enough!
The king chanced to pick up a mirror in his hand,
And, while straightening his crown, glanced at his face.
Near his ears his hair had grown white
As though old age was giving him this counsel:
'King, why not declare Ram the Jubaraj,
And take the reward of your birth and your life?'

    With this thought in his heart,
    The king found an auspicious day and opportune time.
    Then, overcome with love and with a rejoicing heart,
    He went to his guru, Vasishtha, and declared his
        intention to him.   (2)

The king said, 'Hear me, king of the munis,
Ram is now accomplished and able in every way.
Attendants, ministers, the residents of the city,
Our enemies, our friends, and those indifferent to us—
Ram is as dear to them all as he is to me.
It is as though your blessing, lord, is embodied in his glorious form.
The Brahmans with their families, sire,
All love him as much as you do, lord.
Those who bear the dust of their guru's feet upon their heads
Acquire dominion over all glory—
No one knows this as well as I do,
For I have attained all by worshipping the dust of your feet.
Now only one desire remains in my heart,
And that too, lord, by your grace will be attained.'

The muni was pleased to see the king's sincere love
And said, 'Tell me what you wish, lord of men. Give me your
     royal command.

> King, your name and glory,
> Themselves give all that is desired,
> And fulfilment, jewel amongst kings, follows
> Every longing of your heart.'   (3)

Seeing the guru so pleased in every way,
The king, smiling, spoke in gentle tones,
'Lord, make Ram the Jubaraj,
Utter the words by your grace, so that the necessary preparations
     may be made.
Let this joyous event take place in my lifetime
So that all my people may derive the full profit of their eyes.
By your grace, lord, Shiv has fulfilled all my wishes,
So that only this one longing remains in my heart.
After it is fulfilled, I will have no concern if my body thrives
     or fades,
And no regrets later.'
The muni was pleased to hear Dasharath's noble words,
The root of all well-being and joy.
'Hear me, king—that same Lord, turning away from whom
     causes regret,
And without whose worship the burning distress of the heart is not
     soothed,
Has taken birth as your son,
For Ram follows where there is pure and sincere love.

> Now, king, do not delay,
> But quickly make all preparations.
> The day and hour are auspicious
> Whenever Ram is proclaimed Jubaraj.   (4)

Delighted, the king returned to his palace
And summoned his attendants and the minister Sumantra.
Crying 'Victory and long life!' they bowed their heads,
And the king gave them the glad news.
'Today, to my great delight, my guru said to me,
"King, make Ram the Jubaraj."
If the council likes this proposal,
Rejoice in your hearts and place upon his forehead the tilak
    of investiture.'
The minister was overjoyed to hear these pleasing words
Which fell like rain upon the tender shoot of his own
    heart's desire.
With folded hands, he prayed,
'May you live ten million years, lord of the world!
You have thought of an act that will benefit the world,
So make haste, lord, do not delay.'
The king was pleased to hear his minister's encouraging words,
Like a growing vine that finds a sturdy branch.

        The protector of the earth said,
        'Carry out with all speed
        Whatever orders the king of sages gives
        For Ram's royal investiture.'   (5)

The great muni, rejoicing, said in sweet tones,
'Bring water from all the holy places of pilgrimage.'
He enumerated by name
Everything appropriate for a king's coronation—
Medicinal herbs, roots, flowers, fruits and leaves
Of many auspicious kinds,
And fly whisks, deerskins, raiment of many kinds,
Innumerable kinds of woollen and silken cloths,
Precious stones, and many other auspicious objects.
He explained all the rites and ceremonies as laid down in the Vedas

And said, 'Put up canopies and pavilions of all kinds in the city,
And plant in every direction in the lanes and street of the town
Mango, areca and banana trees bearing fruit.
Make auspicious patterns of sacred squares with precious jewels,
And quickly decorate all the marketplaces.
Worship Ganpati, your guru, and your family deity,
And in every way serve the Brahmans, gods on earth.

> Flags, pennants, strings of flowers to festoon doors and
>   gateways, and sacred pitchers
> Make ready, and horses, chariots and elephants too.'
> Reverently obedient to the great muni's words,
> All became busy with their respective tasks.   (6)

Whatever order the great muni gave,
Was fulfilled with such speed it seemed it had been accomplished
    before the command.
The king offered worship to the Brahmans, the sages and the gods,
And performed all the auspicious rites for Ram's well-being.
Hearing the glad news of Ram's investiture,
All Avadh resounded with the sound of celebration.
Good omens declared themselves in Ram and Sita's bodies
As their auspicious sides began to twitch.
Delighted, they said lovingly to each other,
'This presages Bharat's return!
Many days have passed, and we are so very anxious to see
    him again.
These good omens assure us of a meeting with someone
    beloved—
And who in the world is as dear to us as Bharat?
These good omens can have no other meaning!'
Ram worried about his brother day and night
As constantly as a turtle whose heart is fixed upon her eggs
    far away.

At the same time, hearing these most auspicious tidings of
    Ram's investiture,
The women of the royal household were overwhelmed
    with joy
As the waves of the ocean swell with delight
Upon beholding the waxing moon. (7)

Those who went first with the news to the queens' apartments,
Received rich gifts of jewels and raiment.
Their bodies trembling with joy, their hearts filled with love,
The queens began to make ready the sacred pitchers for
    the celebrations.
Sumitra drew beautiful sacred squares,
And filled them with lovely jewels of various kinds.
Ram's mother, Kaushalya, steeped in joy,
Summoned Brahmans and gave them many gifts.
Worshipping the presiding goddess of the town, the gods and
    the serpents,
She pledged them future offerings,
'In whatever lies Ram's well-being,
By your mercy, grant me as a boon.'
Doe-eyed women, with faces radiant as the moon
And voices sweet as the kokil's, began singing songs of blessing
    and celebration.

Hearing of Ram's proposed royal investiture,
    Men and women rejoiced in their hearts,
And all began to prepare for the celebration,
Believing providence to be in their favour. (8)

Then the lord of men summoned Vasishtha,
And sent him to Ram's palace to instruct and advise him.
Raghunath, hearing the approach of the guru,
Went to the door, and bowed his head at his feet.

Reverently welcoming him with sacred libations, he led him into
     the palace
And paid him respectful homage in all the sixteen ways.
With Sita, Ram touched his feet again,
And folding his lotus hands, spoke.
'A master coming to his servant's home
Is a source of blessing and destroys all evil.
It would have been more fitting to lovingly summon your servant
For your purpose, lord—such is the prescribed way.
Instead, setting aside your prerogative, master, you show me love,
And today this house is sanctified.
Whatever be your command, sire, I will carry out,
For a servant's gain lies in serving his lord.'

    Hearing these words steeped in love,
    The muni praised Raghubar, and said,
    'Ram, you could not but have spoken thus,
    For you are the jewel of the solar line!'   (9)

Praising Ram's virtues and his courteous disposition,
The chief of munis said, overcome with love,
'The protector of the earth has made preparations for your investiture,
For he wishes to give you the title of Jubaraj.
So today, Ram, practise all restraint,
That Vidhi may ensure the fulfilment of this ceremony in the
     proper way.'
The guru, having instructed Ram, returned to the king,
But Ram's heart was filled with dismay.
'All of us brothers were born together,
We ate, slept and played together in our boyhood.
The piercing of our ears, our investiture with the sacred thread,
     marriage—
All the ceremonies and celebrations, we went through together.
In this unblemished dynasty, there is this one unbecoming practice—

That the eldest alone is crowned, without his younger brothers.'
May the Lord's gracious regret, so full of love,
Remove doubt and suspicion from the hearts of his devotees.[1]

> At that very moment came Lakshman,
> Full of love and joy.
> Ram, moon to the water-lilies of the line of Raghu,
> Welcomed him with loving words.   (10)

Many kinds of musical instruments played—
The city's joy was beyond description.
All prayed for Bharat's return, saying,
'May he come quickly and receive his eyes' reward.'
In marketplaces, streets, homes, alleyways and every place where
    people gathered,
Men and women asked each other,
'At what time tomorrow will that auspicious hour begin
When Vidhi shall fulfil our longing,
When upon a golden throne, with Sita,
Ram shall sit, satisfying the yearnings of our hearts?'
All asked, 'When will tomorrow come?'
But the scheming gods regarded this as an obstacle.
Avadh's festive celebrations did not please them,
As a moonlit night does not please a thief.
The gods invoked Sharada and pleaded with her
Falling again and again at her feet.

> 'Behold our great difficulty, Mother,
> And contrive it so today
> That Ram gives up the kingdom and leaves for the forest,
> So that the purpose of the gods may be fulfilled.'   (11)

Hearing the plea of the gods, she stood, sadly reflecting,
'I will be the winter's night that blights the lotus clusters!'

Seeing her thus, the gods again pleaded with her,
'Mother, no blame will be yours at all.
The lord of the Raghus is beyond sorrow and joy—
But you know well his might and glory.
As for the others, souls in karma's grip partake of happiness and grief.
So go to Avadh for the sake of the gods.'
Again and again they clasped her feet, embarrassing her,
Till she left, thinking, 'The gods have mean and contemptible minds!
Their abodes up high, their actions lowly,
They cannot bear to see another's glory.'
But reflecting again on the work that lay ahead, she thought,
'Talented poets will seek my favour!'
And rejoicing in her heart, she came to Dasharath's city,
Like some evil star that causes intolerable grief.

> Kaikeyi had a dull-witted bondswoman
> Whose name was Manthara.
> Choosing her as a receptacle of infamy,
> Gira perverted her good sense and left.   (12)

Manthara saw the city being decorated,
And heard the sweet and joyous music of celebration.
She asked the people, 'What is this rejoicing?'
Hearing of Ram's investiture, her heart began to burn.
She began to plot and scheme, that wicked, low-born wretch,
How this might be undone that very night,
Like a crafty tribal woman who sees a hive of honey
And, looking longingly upon it, schemes how to get hold of it.
Weeping loudly, she went to Bharat's mother.
'What's wrong?' asked the queen with a smile.
She did not reply, but sighed deeply,
And, using the wiles of women, shed copious tears.
The queen laughed and said, 'You are very impudent,
And it seems to me that Lakshman has taught you a lesson!'

Even then the wicked bondswoman would not speak,
But only hissed like a venomous snake.

> The queen, alarmed, asked, 'Why do you not speak?
> Is all well with Ram and the king,
> With Lakshman, Bharat and Ripusudan?'
> To hear this was as painful as a thorn in the
>   hunchback's heart.   (13)

'Why would anyone teach me a lesson, mistress?
With whose encouragement would I be impudent?
And who is well today but Ram,
To whom the lord of men is giving the title of Jubaraj?
Fate has favoured Kaushalya greatly,
And, perceiving this, she cannot contain her pride within her heart.
Why don't you go and look at all the splendour,
Seeing which has so tormented my mind?
Your son is away in a foreign land, yet you are not concerned,
For you believe the king is in your power.
You are too fond of sleep upon your quilted bed,
And do not see the king's deceitful cunning.'
Hearing the glad tidings and knowing her servant's base and
    evil mind,
The queen rebuked her angrily and said, 'Now, be silent!
If you ever speak like this again, you troublemaker,
I will have your tongue pulled out!

> The one-eyed, the lame and the hunchbacked,
> Know them to be crooked and malicious,
> Especially women—and what's more, a bondswoman!'
> So said Bharat's mother, and then smiled.   (14)

'Sweet-spoken one, I have said this only to instruct you—
I cannot be angry with you even in my dreams.

The best and most auspicious day will be the one
Upon which your words come true.
The eldest the lord, the younger brothers his servants—
This is the noble custom of the solar line.
If Ram is truly crowned tomorrow,
Ask of me anything your heart desires, my dear, and I will
    give it to you!
Like Kaushalya, all the mothers
Are innately dear to Ram.
He holds a special affection for me—
I have tested his love and know this.
If Vidhi by his grace should give me another birth,
Let Ram be my son, Sita my daughter-in-law.
Ram is dearer to me than my life's breath,
So why then your distress at his investiture?

    On Bharat I swear—speak the truth,
    Give up your deceit and your secrets!
    You grieve at a time of rejoicing—
    Tell me the reason why!'   (15)

'All my hopes were fulfilled by speaking once,
Now if I will speak it will be with a different tongue!
My unfortunate skull deserves to be broken,
For even my well-intentioned words make you unhappy.
Those who make up tales and lie,
Only they are dear to you, mistress, while I seem bitter
    and distasteful.
Now I, too, will speak words of flattery,
Or just keep silent, day and night.
By making me ugly and deformed, providence made me dependent
    on others—
But I must reap as I have sowed, and receive as I have given.
Whoever becomes king, what do I have to lose?

Will I cease to be a slave and now become a queen?
My nature deserves to be cursed,
For I cannot bear to see your misfortune.
That is why I said a few words.
Forgive me, mistress—I have made a great mistake.'

> Hearing these deceitful, flattering words, full of
>   hidden meaning,
> The queen, with a woman's weak mind and inferior
>   understanding,
> And, in the grip of divine maya,
> Believed this enemy to be her friend, and trusted her.   (16)

Again and again she humbly questioned her,
Like a doe bewitched by a savage huntress's song,
Her good sense perverted as had been ordained.
Seeing her chance, the slave-woman rejoiced.
'You ask me, but I am afraid to speak,
For you have already named me a troublemaker.'
Trimming and shaping her words in every way to increase her trust,
Avadh's evil star then spoke.
'You say Sita and Ram are dear to you, queen,
And you are dear to Ram—these words were true,
That is how it used to be, but now those days are over.
When times change, even dear ones become foes.
The sun nourishes a cluster of lotuses,
But without water, the same sun burns them to ashes.
Your co-wife, Kaushalya, wants to pull you out by the root—
So protect yourself, build a strong fence of stratagems.

> Secure in your husband's love, you have had no care,
> Thinking the king to be under your sway.
> The king is dark of heart though sweet of tongue,
> And you are simple-natured.   (17)

Ram's mother is clever and devious.
Finding an opportunity, she used it for her own ends.
The king sent Bharat away to your father's home—
You know it was Ram's mother's suggestion.
She thinks "All the other wives serve me well,
Only Bharat's mother is proud and arrogant, because of our
    husband's love."
You are the thorn in Kaushalya's side, mistress,
But she is deceitful and clever, so it is difficult to see.
The king has special love for you,
Which your rival co-wife naturally cannot bear to see.
So she schemed and plotted and won over the king,
And made him set the date for Ram's investiture.
That Ram should be crowned is in accordance with family custom,
It pleases everyone, and I like it very much too.
What frightens me is the thought of what will follow!
May fate give her back the fruit of this mischief!'

> Devising countless crafty lies,
> Manthara deceitfully persuaded her,
> And told her hundreds of stories about rival wives
> To fuel her animosity.   (18)

In the grip of destiny, the queen was convinced.
Making her swear an oath, she questioned Manthara again.
'What is it you ask? Have you still not understood?
Even a beast knows what is good or bad for it!
A fortnight has passed with preparations every day,
But you only got the news from me today!
I am fed and clothed by your royal generosity,
So commit no wrong by speaking the truth.
Were I to make up lies and utter untruths,
Vidhi would punish me.
If Ram's investiture takes place tomorrow,

Fate will have sown the seed of calamity for you.
I draw a line and most strongly declare—
Mistress, you have become a fly in the milk.
Only if you and your son serve Kaushalya,
Will you stay in this house—there is no other way.

> Kaushalya will inflict on you
> The misery that Kadru had inflicted on Vinata.[2]
> Bharat will languish in a prison cell,
> While Lakshman will be Ram's second-in-command.   (19)

When Kaikeya's daughter heard these bitter words,
She grew faint with fear and could not say a word.
Her body was bathed in perspiration, she trembled like a
    plantain tree.
The hunchback then bit her tongue.
Then, relating again and again countless deceitful tales,
She comforted the queen, 'Be calm, take courage!'
Instigating her into evil ways, she hardened her
Till she became as unbending as a piece of dead wood.
Kaikeyi's destiny was reversed, so that the wicked Manthara
    became dear to her,
And she began to praise that stork as if she were a swan.
'Listen, Manthara, your words are true,
For my right eye twitches incessantly.
Every night I have had bad dreams,
But overcome by my own delusions, I did not tell you.
Oh my dear, what shall I do? I am direct by nature
And do not know right from left.

> As long as it was in my power, I have never
> Harmed anyone to this day.
> For what crime has fate given me
> So much intolerable sorrow all at once?   (20)

I will go back to my father's house to spend the rest of my life,
But as long as I live, I will not serve my co-wife.
Dying is better than living for one
Whom fate condemns to live under a rival's sway.'
Many such wretched words did the queen speak,
Hearing which the hunchback employed all the cunning artfulness
     of woman, and said,
'Why do you speak thus, with so much sorrow and despair in
     your heart?
Your happiness and wedded bliss will yet double every day!
She who has wanted to do you such harm
Will herself reap its fruit at the end.
From the moment I heard of this wrong, mistress,
I've had no appetite by day or sleep at night.
I asked the astrologers, who made their calculations.
"Bharat shall be king, it is certain," they declared.
Mistress, if you are willing to act upon it, I will tell you the way,
For the king is still bound by your service to him.'

      'I would throw myself down a well at your word,
      Or abandon my son and my husband.
      You see my great distress—so how can I not do
      What you tell me for my own good?'   (21)

The hunchback, thus convincing Kaikeyi and receiving her assent,
Sharpened the knife of deceit upon the whetstone of her heart.
The queen did not see her impending doom—
She was as oblivious as a sacrificial beast grazing upon green grass.
Manthara's words were sweet to hear, but cruel and terrible in
     their consequences,
As though she were offering the queen honey laced with poison.
Said the slave woman, 'Do you or do you not remember, mistress,
The tale you had once told me?[3]
The two boons he promised you still rest with the king—
Ask for them today and soothe the distress in your breast.

Give the kingdom to your son, exile in the forest to Ram,
And take for yourself all the joy of your rival queen.
Ask only when the king swears an oath upon Ram,
So that he cannot go back on his word.
If this night passes, it will be a calamity—
So hold my words dearer to you than life.'

> Having thus put her treacherous plan into action,
> The vile wretch said, 'Go into the sulking-room,[4]
> Carry out your purpose carefully and with caution,
> And do not suddenly start believing him.   (22)

The queen thought the hunchback as dear as life,
And praised her great wisdom again and again.
'I have no well-wisher like you in the world—
I was being swept away, but you became my support.
If Vidhi fulfils my heart's desire tomorrow,
I will cherish you like the pupil of my eye, my dear.'
Showing the bondswoman her respect in many ways,
Kaikeyi went into the sulking-room.
Calamity was the seed, the slavewoman the season of rains,
And Kaikeyi's perverse mind the soil
In which, watered by treachery, the seed took root and sprouted—
The two boons were its leaves, and sorrow its final fruit.
Arranging about her all the signs and tokens of anger,
    Kaikeyi lay down,
Destroying her sovereignty by her own perversity.
Meanwhile, there were tumultuous celebrations in the palace and
    the town,
For no one knew of these evil doings.

> The men and women of the city, overjoyed,
> Were all preparing for the auspicious ceremony.
> People continuously went in and out—
> There was a great crowd at the king's palace door.   (23)

Ram's boyhood friends heard the news and rejoiced,
And went in groups of five or ten went to visit him.
Acknowledging their love, the Lord received them kindly
And in sweet tones asked after their welfare.
Returning home with their dear friend's permission,
They praised Ram to each other as they went.
'Who in the whole world is like Raghubir,
Always courteous and loving,
Wandering through existence in karma's grip, in whatever
    form we may be born,
Oh God, give us only this—
May we be the servants, Sita's lord our master,
And may this relationship endure to the end.'
This was the longing of everyone in the city,
But in Kaikeyi's heart there burnt a great fire,
For who is not destroyed by bad company?
Under the counsel of the vile, good sense does not stay.

    At dusk, the lord of men went
    To Kaikeyi's palace full of joy,
    Like love in bodily form
    Approaching cruelty personified.   (24)

Hearing that she was in the sulking-room, the king
    shrank back, alarmed,
And, overcome by fear, could not take a step forward.
He, by the might of whose arms the king of gods held sway,
And whose aspect was guardedly watched by all the kings of men,
Withered hearing of a woman's anger—
Look how mighty is the power of lust!
He who endured upon his body the blows of trident, thunderbolt
    and sword,
Was slain by Ratinath's flowery arrow.
Timidly, the king approached his beloved,

And was deeply distressed to see the state she was in.
She lay on the ground in garments that were old and coarse,
And had cast off the many jewels that had adorned her body.
This wretched attire befitted the perverse-minded Kaikeyi
As though heralding her imminent widowhood.
Drawing near, the king said in sweet and gentle tones,
'Beloved, tell me, why are you angry?'

'Tell me, my queen, why are you angry?' asked the king
And touched her with his hand. She shook it off and recoiled.
It was as though the woman was an angry serpent—she glared at
  her husband
Like a venomous cobra,
Her two wishes its forked tongue,
The boons its fangs as she searched for a vulnerable spot to bite.
But, says Tulsi, bound by what was ordained to be,
The king saw it all as love's sport.

> Again and again the king asked,
> 'My beautiful and bright-eyed one, with your voice as sweet as
>   a kokil's,
> And gait as graceful as an elephant's—
> Tell me the reason for your anger.   (25)

Who has wronged you, beloved?
Who has a head to spare? Who does the god of death yearn to take?
Tell me what pauper I should make king,
Or what king banish from his realm.
I could kill even an immortal were he your enemy,
So what of men and women, who are but miserable worms?
You know how I feel, my beautiful one—
My heart is the chakor to the moon of your face.
Dearest, my life, my sons, everything that I possess,
My household, my subjects—all are under your sway.

If you think I say all this to deceive you,
Know, my beloved, I swear it a hundred times upon Ram's name.
Smile, ask of me whatever your heart desires,
And adorn your lovely body with jewels.
Understanding the difference between an auspicious and
      inauspicious hour,
Abandon, beloved, this unbecoming attire.'

Hearing this and thinking of the king's great oath by Ram,
The foolish queen rose up with a laugh,
And began adorning herself with her jewels
Like a huntress seeing a deer and preparing a snare.   (26)

Thinking her placated and loving once more, the king spoke again,
Trembling with love, in tones that were tender and soft,
'Beloved, your heart's desire has come to be,
And there is rejoicing and celebration in every home in the city.
I will give Ram the title of Jubaraj tomorrow.
So, my pretty-eyed love, adorn yourself in festive attire.'
Hearing this, her cruel heart shook
As though a ripe boil had been touched.
Even such great agony she hid with a smile,
Like a thief's wife who hides her tears.
The king did not perceive her deceit and cunning,
For she had been taught by a jewel amongst ten million rogues.
Though the king was accomplished in statecraft,
Women's wiles are a fathomless sea.
Then, with an even greater show of deceitful love,
She averted her eyes and her face, and smiling, said,

'You keep saying "Ask, ask!", beloved,
But never do you actually give.
You had promised me two boons,
But I doubt I will get even these.'   (27)

'Now I understand the mystery,' the king said with a laugh.
'You are very fond of quarrelling.
You saved up the boons and never asked for them,
While I, absent-minded as I am, also forgot.
But do not accuse me of a lie—
In place of the two, ask for four!
For this has ever been the rule of the Raghu line—
We may give up our lives, but we don't break our word.
No multitude of crimes is equal to a lie—
Can ten million gunj seeds equal a mountain?
Truth is the root of all good and virtuous actions,
As is known in the Vedas and the Puranas and as Manu declares.
Moreover, I have unwittingly taken an oath upon Ram,
Lord of the Raghus, and the pinnacle of virtue and love.'
Thus firmly binding him to his word, the deluded queen laughed
      and spoke,
As though unhooding the bird of prey that was her dreadful plot.

      The king's longing was a charming forest,
      And happiness a flock of beautiful birds,
      Upon which, like a savage huntress, she wished to let loose
      The cruel hawk of her words.   (28)

'Listen, my beloved, to what pleases my heart—
Grant me one boon, that Bharat be crowned Jubaraj.
And, with folded hands, I ask my second boon—
Fulfil, lord, my heart's desire—
That, in the garb of an ascetic, and renouncing the world,
Ram dwell in the forest for fourteen years.'
Hearing her words, so sweetly spoken, the king was filled
      with grief,
As a kok becomes distressed at the touch of a moonbeam.
Overcome with terror, he could not say a word,
Like a quail in the forest attacked by a falcon.

The lord of men lost all colour and grew utterly pale,
Like a palm tree struck by lightning.
With his head in his hands, and both eyes shut,
The king began to grieve like grief personified,
'The divine Kalpataru of my heart's desire had burst into flower,
But about to bear fruit, it has been uprooted by this
    she-elephant.
Kaikeyi has laid waste Avadh,
And laid the foundation for everlasting calamity.

What an occasion this is, but look what has happened!
I have been destroyed by trusting a woman,
Like a yogi about to receive the reward for his penance,
Destroyed by ignorance.'   (29)

In this way the king silently lamented.
Seeing his sad condition, the wicked Kaikeyi grew furious.
'Is Bharat not your son?
And am I not your wife? Did you buy me for a price?
If my words pierce you like arrows,
Why did you give your word so carelessly?
Answer me—say yes, or say no!
You are sworn to truth, famed for honouring your word amongst
    the Raghus,
You said you would give boons, now don't give them,
Abandon truth and take upon yourself the world's disgrace.
Praising truth, you had given me the boons,
Thinking, no doubt, that I would ask for nothing more than
    parched grain!
Shibi, Dadhichi and Bali fulfilled
Whatever they promised, giving life and wealth to keep
    their word.'[5]
Sharp and biting words did Kaikeyi speak,
As though rubbing salt upon a burn.

The king, upholder of dharma,
Composed himself and opened his eyes.
Beating his head, he heaved a deep sigh,
'She has struck me in my weakest spot!'   (30)

He saw her standing before him, burning with rage,
Like a sword of wrath unsheathed,
Its hilt her folly, its edge cruelty,
Sharpened upon the whetstone that was the hunchback.
The protector of the earth saw her terrifying harshness
And wondered, 'Will she in truth take my life?'
Steeling himself, the king spoke
In gentle tones to please her,
'Beloved, how can you utter such harsh words,
Destroying modesty, trust and love?
Bharat and Ram are my two eyes—
I swear this to be true, with Shankar as my witness.
I will definitely send messengers in the morning,
So that the two brothers may return as soon as they hear the news.
Then, choosing an auspicious day and making all the required
    preparations,
I will give Bharat the kingdom, proclaiming it joyously by beat
    of drum.

Ram does not covet the kingdom
And has great love for Bharat.
I was but following royal custom,
Considering that he is older.   (31)

I swear by Ram a hundred times and tell you sincerely,
Ram's mother never said anything to me on this matter.
But I arranged everything without consulting you,
And so my heart's desire could not be realized.
Now give up your anger and adorn yourself in festive attire—

In a few days, Bharat will be crown prince.
Only one thing distresses me—
That the second boon you seek is unreasonable.
My heart burns even now with its fire.
Was it anger, or jest, or was it really true?
Without anger, tell me Ram's offence,
For everyone says he is most noble and good.
You too praise and love him,
But now hearing this, I have become uncertain.
How could one who by nature is kind even to an enemy
Do anything against his mother?

> So dearest, abandon jest and anger,
> Reflect and ask for a sensible boon,
> That I may gladly fill my eyes
> With the sight of Bharat's royal investiture.   (32)

A fish may survive without water,
And even a wretched cobra may continue a miserable existence
          without its crest-jewel.
But I declare sincerely, with no deceit in my heart,
That my life will end without Ram.
Consider in your heart, my wise love,
That my life depends upon seeing Ram.'
Hearing his gentle words, the vindictive queen flared up
Like a sacred fire on which an offering of ghee is poured.
She said, 'You may try ten million stratagems,
But your trickery will not work here.
Give me my boons, or say no and be disgraced—
I do not like all this copious talk.
Ram is a saint, you are saintly and wise,
Ram's mother is so virtuous—I understand you all!
Just as Kaushalya has sought my good,
So I will pay her back in a way she will never forget!

When morning breaks, and donning an ascetic's garb,
Should Ram not go into the forest,
My death and your disgrace will ensue,
King—understand this well.'   (33)

So saying, the cruel queen rose and stood erect
Like a river of wrath rising in flood.
It rushed forth from a mountain of sin,
Its furious waters too terrible to behold.
The two boons were its banks, her harsh insistence its fierce current,
Its eddies and whirlpools were impelled by the hunchback's words.
Tearing up by its roots and bringing down the tree that was the
    lord of the earth,
It rushed towards the ocean of calamity.
The king realized that it was really true—
Death in the form of his wife was dancing upon his head.
Clasping her feet, he persuaded her to sit, and humbly pleaded,
'Do not be the axe that brings down the tree of the solar dynasty.
Ask for my head—I will give it to you right now,
But do not kill me with the grief of separation from Ram.
Let Ram remain here, in any way that you will,
Or your heart will burn with anguish for the rest of your life.'

Realizing that her disease was incurable,
The king fell upon the ground, and, beating his head,
Cried out in tones of deepest distress,
'Ram! Ram! Raghunath!'   (34)

The king was distracted with grief, his body limp with sorrow—
He was like the divine Kalpataru felled by a she-elephant.
His throat was dry, no words came to his lips,
He was as distressed as a pathin fish without water.
Kaikeyi again spoke biting, bitter words,
As though pouring poison into his wounds,

'If you meant to act thus in the end,
On what basis did you say, "Ask, ask"?
Can one do two things at once, king?
Laugh unrestrainedly, and sulk and pout?
Call oneself bountiful, and be miserly?
Or be a hero in battle and remain unhurt?
Either abandon your promise or take courage,
But do not weep and wail like some weak and helpless woman.
Life, wife, son, home, wealth, land,
Are said to be but worthless blades of grass to a man who keeps
    his word.'

    Hearing her wounding words, the king said,
    'Say whatever you wish to, it is not your fault.
    My death has possessed you like a fiend,
    And it is that which makes you speak thus.   (35)

Bharat does not want the kingship even by mistake,
But destiny's grip has caused these perverse and evil sentiments to
    dwell in your heart.
It is all the result of my sins,
That fate has turned against me at this evil hour.
Beautiful Avadh will flourish and prosper again,
And Ram, abode of all virtues, shall be its king.
His brothers all will do him service,
And his fame will spread through all the three worlds.
But your disgrace and my remorse
Shall not be effaced even when we die, or ever go away.
Now do whatever you please,
But hide your face and get out of my sight.
For as long as I live, I beseech you with folded hands,
Do not speak to me again!
You will regret it at the end, unfortunate woman—
You are slaughtering a cow for a few strings of sinew!'

The king fell to the ground, lamenting in innumerable ways,
'Why are you destroying me?'
But the queen, adept in deceit, said nothing,
But sat as though keeping watch in a cremation ground.[6]   (36)

'Ram! Ram!' repeated the grief-stricken king,
As wild and inconsolable as a bird without wings.
He prayed in his heart, 'Let morning never come,
Let no one go and tell Ram of this!
Rise not, Sun, father of the dynasty of Raghu,
For to see Avadh will fill your heart with anguish!'
The king's love and Kaikeyi's cruelty—
Vidhi had created each at its extreme.
While the king was still lamenting, morning came.
The music of vina, flute and conch was heard at his door,
Bards recited his glory, and singers sang his virtues.
Hearing them, the king felt as though pierced by arrows.
All these auspicious celebrations were as repugnant to him,
As ornaments to a widow who accompanies her dead husband to
     his funeral pyre.
No one had slept for a moment that night
In their eagerness to behold Ram.

At the door, a crowd of servants and ministers
Saw the risen sun and said,
'The lord of Avadh has not awakened yet—
Is there any special reason for this?   (37)

The king awakens during the last watch of the night—
We find it very strange that he hasn't today.
Go, Sumantra, go wake him up—
Upon receiving the king's orders, we can begin our work.'
Sumantra then entered the royal palace.
Seeing it desolate, he was afraid to continue.

Its gloom seemed ready to run and devour him and was unbearable
    to see—
It was as though the palace had become the home of calamity
    and grief.
He inquired after the king, but no one answered him,
So he went to the apartments where the king was with Kaikeyi.
Wishing him 'Long life and victory', he bowed his head in homage
    and sat down,
But seeing the king's condition, he was struck with fear.
Tormented and pale with grief, he lay on the floor,
Like a lotus flower pulled out by its roots.
The terrified minister dared ask no questions,
But Kaikeyi, full of evil and empty of all good, spoke.

    'The king has not slept all night—
    God alone knows the reason!
    Repeating "Ram, Ram", the lord of the earth has ushered
       in the dawn,
    But has not told me his secret.   (38)

Go quickly and fetch Ram here,
You can ask what the matter is when you return.'
Perceiving this to be the king's wish from the look on his face,
    Sumantra went,
But he had understood that the queen had done something evil.
Uneasy with worry, he could barely walk, and wondered,
'Summoning Ram, what will the king say to him?'
Steadying his heart, taking courage, he went to the palace gate.
Seeing him so despondent, everyone began to question him.
Reassuring and comforting them all,
He went to the crest-ornament of the solar dynasty.
When Ram saw Sumantra approaching,
He paid him homage, treating him like his father.
Looking at Ram's face, Sumantra told him the king's royal order,

And returned, taking with him the light of the Raghu dynasty.
Seeing Ram leave so unceremoniously with the minister,
People everywhere grew deeply worried.

> The jewel of the Raghu line came and saw
> The lord of men in a wretched and dishevelled state,
> Like an aged king-elephant
> Prostrate with fear at the sight of a lioness.   (39)

His lips were dry, and his whole body burned,
Like a hapless cobra bereft of its jewel.
Beside him he beheld the wrathful Kaikeyi,
Like death counting the hours.
Ram, by nature compassionate and gentle,
Saw now, for the first time, grief such as he had never heard
     of before.
Even so, heedful of the situation, he composed himself,
And inquired in soft words of his mother,
'Tell me, Mother, the cause of my father's grief,
So that we may endeavour to remove it.'
'Listen, Ram, the cause is only
That the king has great affection for you.
He had promised to give me two boons,
And so I asked for whatever I pleased.
Hearing this, the king's heart filled with sorrow,
For he cannot let go his attachment to you.

> On one side, his love for his son, on the other, his promise—
> The king has fallen into a quandary!
> If you are able, uphold his order,
> And remove his dreadful anguish.'   (40)

She sat there, speaking these sharp words without hesitation,
Hearing which cruelty itself was distressed.

Her tongue was her bow, her words her many arrows,
And the lord of the earth her easy target.
It seemed as though harshness had assumed the body
Of a great warrior and was practising archery.
Relating all the circumstances to Raghupati,
She sat there like heartlessness personified.
The sun of the solar dynasty,
Ram, the accumulation of innate joy, smiled to himself,
And spoke words free of all censure,
So gentle and sweet that they were the ornaments of speech itself.
'Listen, Mother, he alone is a fortunate son
Who cherishes his father's and mother's word.
A son who pleases his mother and father,
Is very hard to find in this world, Mother.

> In the forest I will meet ascetics and sages,
> Which will be beneficial to me in every way—
> That too, as I fulfil my father's wish,
> And with your approval as well, Mother—   (41)

While Bharat, dear as my life's breath, will get the kingdom.
Providence, in every way, favours me today.
If I do not go to the forest for such ends,
Count me first in the assembly of fools!
Those who abandon the celestial Kalpataru to tend a worthless
    castor-oil plant,
Or refuse amrit to ask for poison in its stead—
Even they will not miss such an opportunity as this!
Reflect on this in your heart, Mother.
But, Mother, one especial sorrow troubles me:
To see the lord of men in such great distress.
That such a small matter should so deeply grieve my father—
I am unable to believe that, Mother,
For the king is brave and resolute, and an ocean of infinite virtue.

I must have committed some great offence,
That the king says not a word to me.
Upon my life, tell me the truth.'

> Raghubar's words were simple and honest,
> But the wicked Kaikeyi thought them scheming and devious,
> For a leech in water moves in a crooked manner,
> Even if the water is smooth and still.   (42)

The queen smiled at Ram's acquiescence,
And said with a false show of affection,
'I swear upon you, and upon Bharat, too,
I know of no other cause for the king's distress.
You are incapable of giving offence, dear son,
You who give such joy to your mother, father and brothers.
Ram, whatever you say is all true—
You are devoted to your father and mother's command.
I beseech you, explain to your father, make him understand,
So that he does not incur disgrace in his old age.
The merit that gave him a son like you,
It is not right that it be dishonoured now.'
These virtuous words in her false mouth
Seemed like Gaya and other holy sites in impure Magadh.[7]
But all his mother's words pleased Ram,
Like waters of all kinds when they flow into the purifying Ganga.

> Recovering from his swoon, the king
> Turned on his side and called Ram's name.
> His minister respectfully informed him of Ram's arrival,
> With the reverence appropriate to the moment.   (43)

When the lord of the earth heard that Ram had come,
He composed himself and opened his eyes.
His minister carefully helped the king sit up,

And the lord of men saw Ram prostrate at his feet.
With anguished affection, he clasped him to his bosom,
As though a serpent had found again its lost jewel.
The lord of men remained gazing at Ram,
While tears streamed from his eyes.
Overcome by grief, he could not speak,
But again and again clasped him to his heart.
Inwardly, he prayed to the Creator
That Raghunath not go to the forest.
Invoking Mahesh, he humbly pleaded,
'Hear my prayer, eternal Shiv!
You who are easily pleased, and give without being asked—
Take away my anguish, knowing my distress.

> You direct the hearts of all,
> So inspire Ram
> To disregard my promise and stay at home,
> Abandoning duty and his love for me.   (44)

Let me be disgraced in the world, my good name destroyed,
Let me fall into hell and heaven be lost to me,
Make me suffer every unendurable agony,
But do not let Ram be taken from my sight.'
Thus prayed the king, but did not speak,
His heart trembling like a pipal leaf.
Raghupati, seeing his father overpowered by love,
And suspecting that his mother might again say something,
Spoke after careful thought, words that were modest and courteous,
And in accordance with the place, the time and the occasion.
'Father, I make bold to speak—
Forgive this offence, knowing my youth.
You have suffered so much grief over a most trifling matter,
About which no one told me before.
Seeing my lord's condition, I asked Mother,

And learning the circumstances from her, my fear subsided and I
    grew calm.

    At this time of celebration, Father,
    Abandon this brooding worry born of love,
    And give me your command with a happy heart,'
    Joyfully said the Lord.   (45)

'His birth alone upon this earth is blessed,
Whose deeds, when he hears of them, cause his father great joy,
And life's four rewards are in the palm of his hand,
Who loves his father and mother as he loves his life's breath.
Obeying your order and receiving my birth's reward,
I will soon come back—so give me your command.
Taking leave of my mother, I will return
And touching your feet again, I will leave for the forest.'
So saying, Ram departed.
The king, overwhelmed with grief, did not reply.
This painful news spread through the city as quickly
As venom through the whole body at a scorpion's sting.
Hearing it, men and women all grew distraught,
Like vines and trees upon seeing a forest fire.
Whoever heard it beat his head, no matter where he was,
The grief so great that no one was able to stay calm.

    Their faces were strained, their eyes streaming with tears,
    Their grief could not be in contained in their hearts.
    It was as though sorrow's legions, with beat of drum,
    Had descended upon Avadh.   (46)

'It had all fallen into place, but providence ruined it!'
They cried, and everywhere cursed Kaikeyi.
'What came into this sinful woman's head
To set fire to a house newly thatched?

Tearing out her own eyes, she wants to see,
Throwing away nectar, she wants to taste poison.
Cruel, stubborn, perverse, unfortunate,
She is a fire in the bamboo forest of the Raghu line.
Perched on a branch, she has cut down the tree,
In the midst of joy, she has raised an edifice of sorrow.
Ram was always as dear as life to her—
So why did she become bent upon such cruelty?
Truly speak the poets that woman's nature
Is in every way incomprehensible, unfathomable and mysterious!
We might even manage to catch our own shadow,
But it is impossible to know the ways of women, my brother!

> What can fire not burn?
> What can the ocean not hold within itself?
> Though called weak, what can a woman, if powerful,
>   not accomplish?
> Who in this world does death not devour?   (47)

What had fate proclaimed, but what does it tell us now?
What plan had it first conceived, but what does it show us now?'
Said some, 'The lord of the earth did not do right.
He did not think before giving boons to this wicked woman.
Through her stubbornness, he has himself become the source
      of all sorrow,
As though, in her clutches, his wisdom and virtue have fled.'
Others who were wiser, discerned the bounds of dharma,
And did not blame the king.
They related to each other
The stories of Shibi, Dadhichi and Harishchandra.[8]
One said that this plan had Bharat's approval,
Another, hearing this, grew sad, but stayed silent,
While another stopped his ears and bit his tongue
And declared, 'This is a lie!

By speaking thus, you lose all the merit of your deeds,
For Ram is as dear to Bharat as life itself!

> The moon may rain sparks of fire,
> Or nectar turn to poison,
> But never, not even in dream,
> Would Bharat do anything against Ram.'   (48)

One blamed Vidhata,[ii]
Who had promised nectar but given poison.
There was turmoil in the city, and all were sad and anxious,
Their hearts burning with intolerable anguish, all their joy destroyed.
The Brahman wives, the respected, elder women of the family,
And all who were most dear to Kaikeyi,
Began instructing her, praising goodness—
But their words pierced her like arrows.
'"Even Bharat is not as dear to me as Ram"—
So you have always said, as the whole world knows,
And you love Ram naturally and spontaneously.
So for what offence do you send him to the forest today?
You have never been jealous of the king's other wives,
Your love and trust are known throughout the land.
So now how has Kaushalya harmed you,
That you have hurled this thunderbolt at the city?

> Can Sita desert her beloved?
> Can Lakshman remain at home?
> Can Bharat enjoy his dominion?
> And can the king live without Ram?   (49)

Reflecting upon this, banish anger from your heart,
Do not become a storehouse of grief and disgrace.

[ii] Brahma

By all means give Bharat the title of Jubaraj—
But what is the need to exile Ram to the forest?
Ram is not hungry for the kingdom,
He is an upholder of dharma and indifferent to worldly pleasures.
Let Ram leave home to go and live in his guru's house—
Ask this of the king as your second boon.
If you do not listen to our advice,
You will gain nothing at all.
And if this is some joke that you have played,
Say so clearly and let us know!
Does a son like Ram deserve exile in the forest?
Hearing this, what will people say about you?
Get up at once and do what is needed
To end this grief and disgrace.

Do whatever is needed to end this grief and disgrace,
And to protect your family.
Stop Ram as he leaves for the forest, insist upon it,
And raise no other matter!
Like a day without sun, a body without breath,
And night without the moon,
Will Avadh be, says Tulsidas, without its lord.
Think about this carefully, gracious lady!'

Thus did her friends instruct her,
With words sweet to hear and beneficial in their consequence.
But she gave no ear to them,
Tutored as she was by the cunning hunchback.   (50)

She gave no reply, but harsh with intolerable rage,
Glared at them like a hungry tigress at a herd of does.
Recognizing her malady as incurable, they left,
Declaring her foolish and ill-fated as they went.
'Fate has destroyed her, even while she ruled the land,

For she has done what no one else would do!'
Thus the men and women of the city lamented,
And heaped countless curses upon the evil Kaikeyi.
Burning with the violent fever of grief, they sighed deeply and said,
'Without Ram, what hope of life is there?'
The people were as distraught at their long separation from him
As water-creatures in a drought.
All men and women were in the grip of intense sorrow.
But Lord Ram went to his mother,
His face joyful, and great eagerness in his heart,
For his worry that the king would hold him back had disappeared.

> Raghubir's heart was like a newly captured elephant,
> Fettered by the chains of kingship.
> Learning that he must go to the forest, he knew himself
>   to be free,
> And his heart filled with great joy.   (51)

That ornament of the Raghu line folded both his hands
And happily bowed his head at his mother's feet.
She gave him her blessing and clasped him to her heart,
And gave alms of raiment and jewels for his well-being.
Again and again, his mother kissed his face,
Her eyes full of tears of love, her body trembling.
She held him in her lap, and hugged him once more to her heart,
And her beautiful breasts overflowed with the milk of motherly love.
Her love and delight are impossible to describe—
Like a pauper suddenly appointed to be the god of wealth.
Gazing reverently at his beautiful face,
His mother spoke sweet and tender words.
'Dear son, tell me,' asked his devoted mother,
'When will come the happy and auspicious moment,
The glorious culmination of my good deeds, virtue and joy,
And the fulfilment of my life's purpose,

The moment for which all men and women yearn
As anxiously as
The thirsty chatak and chataki
Long for the autumn rain of Svati?   (52)

But, dear son, I entreat you—go and quickly bathe,
Eat something sweet, whatever you like,
And then, dear child, go to your father,
For it is already very late.' So spoke his loving mother.
Hearing his mother's affectionate words,
Like flowers on the celestial Kalpataru of her love,
Filled with the nectar of joy, and the source of all good fortune,
The bee of Ram's mind did not lose its way.
The upholder of dharma, and knowing dharma's ways,
He said to his mother in tones very sweet and gentle,
'Father has given me the kingdom of the forest,
Where lies in every way my greatest purpose.
Give me your permission, Mother, with a joyous heart,
So that my journey to the forest be happy and blessed.
Do not, bound by love, be afraid for me even by mistake,
For all will be happy, Mother, by your grace.

When I have lived fourteen years in the forest,
And made true my father's promise,
I will return to behold your feet once more.
So do not darken your heart with grief.'   (53)

Raghubar's sweet and humble words,
Pierced his mother's heart like arrows and lodged painfully there.
Hearing his gentle words, she grew afraid and wilted
Like a javas in the first shower of the rains.
Her heart's grief is impossible to describe—
She was like a doe that has heard the lion's roar.
Her eyes filled with tears, and her body trembled violently,

Like a fish made mad by swallowing the foam of the waters of the
     early rains.[9]
Composing herself, gazing at her son's face,
His mother said in a voice choking with emotion,
'My son, you are as dear as life to your father,
He watches your doings with constant delight.
He had himself fixed an auspicious day to give you the kingdom,
So for what crime has he ordered you to the forest?
My son, tell me the real reason for this—
Who has become the fire destroying the sun's dynasty?'

> With a glance at Ram's expression,
> The minister's son explained the reason.
> Hearing the circumstances, she was struck dumb—
> Her condition cannot be described.   (54)

She could not keep him back, nor could she tell him to go.
In both situations her heart would burn with anguish.
'He began to write "moon" but wrote "Rahu" instead—
Vidhi's ways are ever hostile to all.'
Duty and love both laid siege to her mind,
And her state became that of a snake that has caught a muskrat.[10]
'If I insist and keep my son by my side,
Dharma will be lost and there will be conflict between
     the brothers.
But if I tell him "Go to the forest", it will be a terrible loss.'
Caught between these two great griefs, the queen grew helpless.
Then reflecting once more upon a wife's dharma,
And deeming Ram and Bharat to be equally her sons,
The wise Kaushalya, Ram's mother, by nature sincere and honest,
Composed herself and calling up all her courage, spoke.
'My son, I swear by my love for you, that you have acted rightly,
For obedience to one's father's command is the highest of
     all duties.

He promised the kingdom but gave the forest instead—
That does not cause me the least sorrow.
But without you, Bharat, the king himself,
And all our people will suffer intolerable anguish.   (55)

If it were only your father's command, my son,
You should not go, knowing that a mother's wishes come first.
But if both father and mother say that you must go to the forest,
The forest will be like a hundred Avadhs for you.
The gods of the forest will be your father, the goddesses
     your mother,
And the birds and beasts will serve your lotus feet.
Dwelling in a forest is appropriate for a king towards
     the end of life,
But looking at your tender years, I am grieved and troubled in
     my heart.
Blessed is the forest, and unfortunate is Avadh
That you, ornament of the line of Raghu, have given up.
If I say, "Take me with you," my son,
Uncertainty will arise in your heart.
My son, you who are supremely beloved to us all,
The breath of our life's breath, the life of our hearts,
Is saying, "Mother, I am going to the forest,"
And I, hearing these words, sit here and lament.

     Thinking this, I do not insist
     Or falsely exaggerate my love.
     Yet I ask, by my love for you, that you honour our bond of
          mother and son,
     And do not forget me.   (56)

May all the gods and ancestors, Lord,
Protect you as the eyelids do the eyes.
The period of your exile is the water, your dear kinsfolk the fish,

And you the compassionate upholder of dharma.
Keeping this in mind, make it so
That we all may live to greet you on your return.
May I take all your misfortunes upon me! Go in peace to the forest,
Leaving your people, your family and the whole town without
    their lord.
Today, the reward of everyone's good deeds is exhausted,
And cruel fate has turned against us.'
Lamenting thus in many ways, she clung to Ram's feet,
Regarding herself to be the most unfortunate of women.
Intolerable anguish pervaded her heart—
The magnitude of her grief cannot be described.
Ram raised his mother and held her to his heart,
And consoled her again with sweet and tender words.

At that moment, Sita heard the news
And rose, anxious and greatly agitated.
She went to her mother-in-law, paid homage to her
    lotus feet,
And sat down, her head bowed.   (57)

Her mother-in-law gave her blessings in gentle tones,
And grew even more distressed to see her extreme youth and
    delicate beauty.
Sita, her face lowered, sat lost in thought,
Accumulation of beauty, unblemished in her love for her husband.
'The lord of my life wants to go to the forest,
Which of my meritorious deeds will let me accompany him?
Will it be with my body and my life, or with my life's breath alone?
Fate's intentions cannot be known.'
With her beautiful toenails, she scratched the earth,
Her anklets tinkled sweetly—as though, say the poets,
Overcome by love, they were imploring,
'Let Sita's feet never abandon us.'

Sita's lovely eyes streamed with tears.
Seeing her, Ram's mother said,
'Dear son, listen. Sita is young and very delicate,
Dear to her father- and mothers-in-law, and to all our family
    and household.

Her father, Janak, is the jewel of earth's protectors,
Her father-in-law, sun of the solar line,
And you, her lord, are the moon to the lilies of the
    sun's dynasty,
And the abode of virtue and beauty.   (58)

And I, I have found a beloved daughter-in-law,
Beautiful, accomplished, virtuous and good-natured.
I have treasured her above all others with ever-increasing love—
My life's breath resides in Janaki.
I have cherished her in many ways, like a celestial creeper,
Nurturing her with the water of my affection,
But just as she has begun to blossom and bear fruit, fate has turned
    against me—
There is no knowing what the outcome will be.
Leaving bed, chair, lap, or swing,
Sita has never set foot on hard ground.
I guard her like the life-giving Sanjivani herb,
And have never even asked her to trim the wick of a lamp.
This same Sita now wants to go with you to the forest.
What is your command, Raghunath?
How can a chakori, who takes delight in the nectar of moonbeams,
Turn her eyes towards the sun's blazing face?

Elephants, lions, night-wandering demons,
And many other evil creatures roam the forest.
My son, how can a garden of poisonous plants
Suit the lovely Sanjivani?   (59)

For the forest, Viranchi fashioned tribal maidens, Kols and Kirats
Who know nothing of physical comfort and worldly delights.
They are by nature as hardy as insects that burrow in stone—
For them the forest presents no hardship.
Or then, the wives of ascetics are fit for the forest,
Who have, for the sake of penance, renounced all worldly pleasures.
Son, how will Sita live in the forest,
She who gets frightened by a monkey's picture?
Is a young swan who wanders amidst the lovely lotus clusters of the
	divine Manas lake,
Fit to live on a pond?
Reflect upon this, and then, as you command,
I will instruct Janaki.
But should Sita remain home,' his mother added,
She will be a great support to me.'
Raghubir, hearing his mother's loving words,
Steeped in the nectar of grace and affection,

	Spoke affectionate words full of discernment,
	To console and comfort his mother.
	He began to instruct Janaki,
	Explaining clearly to her the virtues and faults of the forest.	(60)

He hesitated to speak to her in front of his mother,
But understanding the need of the moment, he said,
'Princess, listen to my instructions,
And do not consider any other way in your heart.
If you want your own good and mine,
Listen to my words and remain at home—
You will fulfil my wishes and serve your mother-in-law.
In staying home, beloved, there is every kind of benefit.
To worship with reverence the feet of your mother- and father-in-law—
There is no other dharma greater than this.
Whenever Mother begins thinking of me,

And distracted by her love for me, forgets herself,
At such moments, relate to her old tales and legends
In your sweet voice, my beautiful one, and thus comfort and
    console her.
Sincerely and honestly I say to you and confirm with a
    hundred oaths—
It is only for my mother's sake, lovely one, that I leave you at home.

    This dharma is according to your guru and the Vedas,
    And its fruit you will obtain without sorrow.
    In the grip of their stubbornness,
    Galav and King Nahush suffered every hardship.[11]   (61)

I shall make true my father's word
And quickly come back, my wise and lovely one.
It will not take long for these days to pass,
So heed my advice, my beautiful one.
If, from love, my pretty wife, you insist on accompanying me,
You will find sorrow as the outcome.
The forest is cruel and exceedingly dangerous,
With terrible heat, and cold and rain and wind.
The paths have sharp grass and thorns and stones
And you will have to walk barefoot.
Your lotus feet are soft and beautiful,
And the road is difficult, the mountains huge.
The chasms and caverns, rivers, streams and torrents
Are impassable and deep, and terrible to behold.
Bears, tigers, wolves, lions and elephants
Roar so fearsomely that resolve and courage run away.

    The ground will be your bed, the bark of trees your clothes,
    And tubers, fruits and roots your food—
    Even these you will not find always or every day,
    But only in their proper season.   (62)

Night-wandering demons who eat men roam there,
Assuming deceptive forms of innumerable kinds.
The mountain water is extremely unwholesome,
And the travails of the forest are beyond all telling.
There are huge serpents and terrifying wild birds in the woods,
And hordes of night-wandering demons who steal men
    and women.
Even the bravest are terrified at the thought of the forest,
And you, my doe-eyed one, are by nature timid and afraid.
My graceful one with the gait of a swan, you are not meant for
    the forest—
Hearing of it, people will heap disgrace upon me.
Can a swan-maiden, reared upon the nectar of the waters
    of Manasarovar,
Survive in the salt sea?
Can a kokil that rejoices amongst mango groves laden with new fruit,
Ever be suited to a forest of thorny karila bushes?
Reflect on all this in your heart and remain home,
My moon-faced one, for there is great hardship in the forest.

    She who does not follow with reverence
    The advice of a sincere friend, guru, or husband,
    Repents deeply later,
    And comes to definite harm.'   (63)

Hearing her beloved's sweet and charming words,
Sita's beautiful eyes filled with tears.
His calm and soothing advice burned her
As a moonlit autumn night burns the chakwi.[iii]
The anguished Vaidehi could find no answer, thinking,
'My noble, loving husband wants to abandon me!'
Determinedly holding back her tears,

[iii] The female kok bird

The daughter of the earth[iv] took courage.
Throwing herself at her mother-in-law's feet, and folding her
    hands, she said,
'Forgive me, lady, my great presumption and want of modesty—
My beloved lord has given instruction
Most beneficial for me.
But looking into my heart, I see that there is
No grief in the world as great as separation from one's beloved.

        Lord of my life, abode of compassion,
        Beautiful, wise, the giver of happiness and joy—
        Without you, moon to the lilies of the Raghu dynasty,
        Even the city of the gods would be like hell.   (64)

Mother and father, sisters and dear brothers,
Beloved kinsfolk, a crowd of friends,
Mother-in-law, father-in-law, guru, dear companions and one's
    own people,
Even a son, handsome, accomplished and the source of joy—
Whatever the bonds of kinship and affection, my lord,
For a woman without her love, they are as fiercely scorching as
    the sun.
Body, wealth, house, land, city, kingdom,
For a woman bereft of her husband, these are but a horde
    of sorrows.
Luxury is like an illness, ornaments a burden,
And the world is like the torments of Yama's hell.
Lord of my life, without you, there is nothing in this world
Anywhere to give me joy.
A body without life, a river without water—
Just so, my lord, is a woman without her man.
Lord, for me, all happiness is with you,

[iv] Sita

In looking upon your face, bright and unblemished as
    the autumn moon.

Birds and deer will be my kin, the forest my city,
And the bark of trees my spotless raiment of fine silk.
And with my husband, a hut of leaves will be
As delightful as a palace of the gods.   (65)

The benevolent forest goddesses and gods,
Will take care of me like my mother- and father-in-law.
My pretty mat of kush grass and tender new leaves,
With my lord, will be Kam's own soft mattress.
Tubers, roots and fruit will be food as sweet as amrit,
And mountains like a hundred glittering mansions of Avadh.
Gazing every moment upon my lord's lotus feet,
I will remain as joyous as a chakwi in the daytime.
You have recounted, husband, the many hardships of the forest,
Its numerous terrors, sorrows and torments.
But, abode of mercy, all these combined do not equal the
    tiniest part
Of the grief of separation from my lord.
Knowing this in your heart, wisest of all men,
Take me with you, do not leave me.
How more may I beseech you, husband?
You are compassionate and tender-hearted, and pervade
    the hearts of all.

If you keep me in Avadh for the period of your exile,
Know that my life's breath will leave me,
Friend of the helpless, beautiful, and giver of joy,
The abode of kindness and love!   (66)

Walking along the path will not tire me,
When every instant I see your lotus feet.

In every way I will serve my beloved,
And take away all your fatigue of the road.
Seated in the shade of a tree, I will wash your feet
And fan you, my heart full of delight.
Beholding your dark body beaded with perspiration,
Gazing at the lord of my life, what time will I have to dwell
    upon hardships?
Spreading a bed of grass and leaves upon even ground,
This slave will massage and rub your feet all night.
As I constantly gaze upon your sweet form,
Hot summer winds will not hurt me, my dearest.
Who, when I am with my lord, would dare raise his eyes to
    look at me,
Like a hare or jackal on a lion's bride?
Am I fair and delicate, and you, my lord, fit for the forest?
Is penance proper for you, and only luxury for me?

        But since my heart did not break
        Even upon hearing such cruel words,
        Lord, it seems my base and miserable spirit
        Can endure even the terrible grief of separation from you!'   (67)

So saying, Sita grew most distraught,
She could not say the word 'separation'.
Seeing her condition, Raghupati understood in his heart,
'If I insist that she remain behind, she will not survive.'
Said the compassionate lord of the sun's lineage,
'Abandon grief, and come with me to the forest—
Today there is no occasion to lament.
Quickly now, make your preparations to leave for the forest.'
With these loving words he consoled his beloved,
And touching his mother's feet, received her blessings.
'Return quickly to remove your subjects' sorrow,
And do not forget this hard-hearted mother.

Will the circumstances of my life ever change, O God,
So that I may, with my own eyes, behold this lovely pair again?
When will that blessed day and auspicious hour come, my son,
When your mother, in this life, sees the moon of your face again?

> When will I again say "my darling child", "my beloved boy",
> "Raghupati", "Raghubar", "my son",
> And calling you, hold you to my heart,
> To gaze, rejoicing, upon your form?'   (68)

Seeing his mother so distraught with love
And so agitated that she could not speak,
Ram consoled her in many ways—
The love in that moment is impossible to describe.
Then Janaki fell at her mother-in-law's feet.
'Listen, mother, I am the most unfortunate of women—
When it is time to serve you, fate has given me exile in the forest,
And refused to fulfil my heart's desire.
Abandon your anguish, but do not let go your affection for me—
Fate is cruel, but I am not at fault.'
Hearing Sita's words, her mother-in-law was deeply distressed—
How can I describe her state?
Again and again she clasped Sita to her heart,
And, composing herself, instructed and blessed her.
'As long as the streams of the Ganga and the Jamuna flow
May your state of wedded bliss, unbroken, endure.'

> Thus did her mother-in-law give Sita
> Countless blessings and advice.
> And Sita, with great affection, bowed again and again
> At her lotus feet and took her leave.   (69)

When Lakshman heard the news,
He came rushing, his face grief-stricken,

His body trembling, his eyes full of tears.
He clasped Ram's feet, agitated by his love for his brother.
He could not speak, but gazed unblinking,
Helpless as a fish pulled out of water.
His heart was full of worry—'Dear God, what will happen now?
All my happiness and the rewards of my past good deeds are
    gone forever.
What will Raghunath say to me?
Will he leave me at home or will he take me with him?'
Ram saw his brother, his hands folded,
Having broken all ties with body and home.
Then Ram, ocean of grace, love, sincerity and bliss,
Who knew well the rules of life and correct conduct, spoke,
'Brother, under the sway of love, do not distress yourself,
But know in your heart that the end of all this is joy.

> By simply following and observing with reverence
> The advice of our mother, father, guru and master,
> We obtain the full benefit of our birth—
> Otherwise our birth in this world has been in vain.   (70)

Know this in your heart and listen to my instruction, brother—
Serve the feet of our mothers and father.
Bharat and Ripusudan are not at home,
And the king is old and his heart is full of grief over me.
If I go to the forest taking you with me,
Avadh will be without a master in every way.
Our guru, father, mother, subjects and family,
Upon them all will fall an immense weight of intolerable grief.
So stay and comfort them all,
Otherwise, dear brother, it will be a great mistake.
A king in whose realm the beloved subjects are unhappy,
Is most certainly deserving of hell.
Stay behind, dear brother, bearing this doctrine in mind.'

Hearing this, Lakshman grew deeply distressed,
And shrivelled at these cool and calm words,
As a red lotus when touched by frost.

> Overwhelmed by love, he could not reply,
> But clasped his brother's feet in anguish.
> 'Lord, I am the servant, you the master—
> If you abandon me, what will I do?   (71)

You have given me sound advice, Lord,
But because of my own cowardice, it seems impossible.
Only those noble, resolute men, who steadfastly uphold dharma,
Have the right to be instructed in the Vedas and moral doctrine.
I am but a child, Lord, nurtured by your love—
Can a young swan lift Mandar or Meru?
I know no other guru, mother, or father—
I say this sincerely, Lord, believe me.
Whatever bonds of love there be in this world,
Of affection and trust, of which the Vedas themselves do sing,
For me, master, they all are you and you alone,
Friend of the humble, who pervades all hearts.
Lectures on duty and moral conduct are given to one
Who holds dear fame, glory and greatness.
But one who, in heart, deed and word, is devoted to your feet—
Should he, gracious Lord, be abandoned?'

> That ocean of compassion heard
> The sweet and modest words of his beloved brother,
> And, knowing him to be afraid because of love,
> The Lord clasped him to his heart and reassured him.   (72)

'Go, take leave of your mother,
And quickly return to go to the forest, brother.'
Lakshman was overjoyed to hear Raghubar's words—

Great was his gain, and his immense loss disappeared.
With a glad heart he came to his mother,
Like a blind man who has regained his eyes.
He went to his mother and bowed his head at her feet,
Though his heart was with Raghunandan and Janaki.
Seeing him troubled and distracted, his mother asked
    the cause,
And Lakshman told her the whole story at length.
Hearing the cruel words, she grew afraid,
Like a doe who sees wildfire all around her.
Seeing this, Lakshman despaired, 'This may all go wrong now!
This very love of hers will ruin all my plans!'
Afraid, he hesitated to take her leave—
'Oh God, will she let me go with them?' he worried.

> Sumitra, thinking of Ram and Sita's beauty
> And gentle, courteous natures,
> And knowing the king's love, beat her head—
> 'That sinful woman has dealt a mortal blow!'   (73)

But realizing that it was an unpropitious time,
    and composing herself,
The gentle and kind-hearted Sumitra sweetly said,
'My son, Vaidehi is your mother now,
And Ram, who loves you in every way, is your father.
Avadh is there where Ram resides,
Just as it is day there where is the sun's light.
If Sita and Ram leave for the forest,
You have no work here in Avadh.
Guru, father, mother, brothers, gods and master,
Should be served like your life's breath,
And Ram is dearer than life itself, the life of our hearts,
Selfless and unselfish and a friend to all.
All those in this world most worthy of adoration and love,

Are revered only because of their association with Ram.
Knowing this in your heart, go with him to the forest,
And receive, my son, the reward of your existence in this world.

> You will receive supreme good fortune,
> And I, your devoted mother, along with you,
> If your heart abandons all guile,
> And makes its home at Ram's feet.   (74)

In this world, that woman alone is considered blessed
Whose son is a devotee of Raghupati.
It is better she were barren, who considers herself fortunate
In a son hostile to Ram, for she has given birth in vain.
It is only for your sake that Ram is going to the forest—
There is no other reason for it, my son—
For the highest reward for all good deeds
Is innate love for Ram and Sita's feet.
Desire, wrath, envy, pride and delusion—
Do not fall under their sway even in your dreams.
Discarding every kind of imperfection,
Serve Ram and Sita in thought, act and word.
For you there will be every safety and comfort in the forest,
For Ram and Sita will be with you as your father and mother.
And make sure, son, that Ram does not suffer
In the forest. This is my advice.

This is my advice, dear son, that with you
Ram and Sita may find happiness,
And be able to forget, in the forest, all the comforts of
Father, mother, beloved family and city.'
Having thus instructed Lakshman, Tulsi's Lord,[12]
She gave him her permission and her blessing again,
'May your love for the feet of Sita and Raghubir
Be constant, pure and renewed afresh each day.'

Bowing his head at his mother's feet, Lakshman
Rushed away at once, but with a heart full of apprehension,
Like a deer escaping, by good fortune,
From a perilous trap and taking flight.   (75)

Lakshman went at once to Janaki's lord,
His heart rejoicing to find again his beloved company.
Paying homage to Ram and Sita's lovely feet,
He went with them to the king's palace.
Said the men and the women of the city to each other,
'Fate made a wonderful plan, then ruined it!'
Their bodies wasted, their hearts sad, their faces downcast,
They were as distraught as bees robbed of their honey.
They wrung their hands, beat their heads and lamented,
Agitated as birds without wings.
A great crowd had assembled at the royal gate,
And their boundless grief was beyond description.
The minister raised the king and helped him sit,
And spoke the dear words, 'Ram has come.'
Seeing his two sons accompanied by Sita,
The lord of the earth was deeply distressed.

Gazing at his two handsome sons with Sita,
The king grew ever more troubled,
And overcome with love,
Clasped them again and again to his heart.   (76)

The distraught king could not speak a word,
As in his heart burned the terrible fire of grief.
Then, bowing his head at his feet with profound love,
Raghubir arose and asked permission to depart.
'Father, give me your blessing and your command.
At this time of joy, why do you despair?
By neglecting duty out of love for a beloved one, dear father,

One's reputation in this world is lost and disgrace incurred.'
Hearing this, the lord of men rose, overwhelmed with love,
And taking Raghupati by the arm, made him sit down.
'Listen, dear son—of you the munis say,
"Ram is master of all created beings, animate and inanimate."
In accordance with our virtuous and wicked actions,
The Supreme Being, after reflecting upon them in his heart, gives
    their reward.
As each one does, so does he receive the fruit of his actions—
This is the law of the Vedas, and so all affirm.

But here, one commits the offence,
And another suffers its consequences.
Strange and surprising are the ways of God.
Who in the world can understand them?'   (77)

To keep Ram from leaving for the forest, the king,
Tried every expedient, abandoning all pretence.
But seeing Ram's face, he realized he would not stay,
He, the upholder of dharma, steadfast and wise.
Then the king held Sita to his heart,
And affectionately counselled her in many ways.
He told her of intolerable hardships in the forest,
And explained to her the joys of remaining with her in-laws
    or her father.
But Sita's heart was devoted to Ram's feet,
And home did not seem easy, nor the forest arduous, to her.
Then everyone else, too, tried to convince Sita,
By telling her again and again of the terrible hardships
    of the forest.
The minister's wife and the guru's wife, wise women both,
Said lovingly to her in gentle tones,
'You were not the one given exile,
So do as your parents-in-law and your guru tell you.'

This advice, though soothing, well-meant, gentle and sweet,
Did not please Sita,
Just as the touch of the autumn moon's light
Distresses the chakwi.   (78)

Sita, overcome by modesty, did not reply,
But Kaikeyi, hearing these words, flew into a passion,
And fetching an ascetic's robes, accoutrements and utensils,
Placed them before Ram and said in a soft voice,
'You are as dear as life to the king, Raghubir.
But that weak and timid man can't let go virtue or love.
He will ruin his good works, honour and happiness in
        the next world,
But he will never tell you to go to the forest.
So reflect upon this and do what pleases you.'
Ram was glad to hear his mother's advice,
But her words pierced the king like arrows—
'Why does my wretched life-breath not leave?'
The people were agitated, the king in a faint,
And no one knew what to do.
Ram at once donned the ascetic garb,
Bowed to his father and mother, and departed.

        Having made all preparation for the forest,
        With his wife and his brother, the Lord
        Paid homage to the feet of the Brahmans and his guru
        And set out, leaving them all numb and confused.   (79)

Leaving the palace, he stopped at Vasishtha's door,
And saw the people burning in the fire of separation.
With sweet words he consoled them all.
Then Raghubir summoned the Brahmans.
He asked his guru to arrange food for them for the duration of
        his exile,

And won them over with humility and courteous gifts.
He satisfied the mendicants with alms and respect,
And delighted his friends with love pure and unblemished.
Then, summoning his serving men and women,
He entrusted them to his guru, and said with folded hands,
'Master, look after them all and protect them
Like a father or mother would do.'
Again and again, and with folded hands,
Ram said to them all in gentle tones,
'He alone in every way will be my friend and well-wisher
Who ensures that the king remains well and happy,

> And that all my mothers, suffering separation from me,
> Do not become sad and miserable.
> Make it so, all of you,
> My supremely wise people of Ayodhya.' (80)

In this way Ram consoled them all
And happily bowed his head at his guru's lotus feet.
Then, having worshipped Ganpati, Gauri and Girish,
And received the blessings of his guru, Raghurai departed.
As soon as Ram left, there arose great lamentation,
And the sound of the city's grief was terrible to hear.
There were bad omens in Lanka, deep sadness in Avadh,
And the realm of the gods was overwhelmed with joy mingled
     with sorrow.[13]
When the king awoke from his faint,
He called Sumantra, and began to speak thus:
'Ram has left for the forest, but my life's breath has not left me—
What joy does it hope to find by remaining in my body?
What pain greater than this
Can I ever suffer to cause my breath to leave this body?'
Then, composing himself, the lord of men spoke again,
'Take your chariot, dear friend, and go with them.

The two princes are young and tender,
And young and delicate is the princess, Janak's daughter.
Take them up into your chariot, show them the forest
For three or four days, and then return with them.   (81)

And should the two brothers, determined, do not return,
For Raghurai is true to his word and steadfast in his resolve,
Then plead with him with folded hands,
"Send back, Lord, the king of Mithila's daughter."
When Sita, seeing the forest, becomes frightened,
Take the opportunity and convey to her my instruction,
"Your mother- and father-in-law have sent this message:
Daughter, return home, the forest is full of hardship.
Stay sometimes in your father's home, sometimes with your
     husband's parents,
As it pleases you."
In this manner, try all and every means,
For if she returns, my life will have some support.
Otherwise, my death will be the result.
But nothing is in one's control once fate turns hostile.'
The king fell senseless upon the ground, crying,
'Bring back Ram, Lakshman and Sita to me!'

     Receiving the king's royal command, Sumantra bowed
     And quickly readying a swift chariot,
     Went to that place outside the city,
     Where the two brothers and Sita were.   (82)

Then Sumantra related to them the king's words,
And entreated Ram to ascend the chariot.
The two brothers, with Sita, climbed into the chariot
And set out, bowing their heads to Avadh.
Seeing Ram depart, leaving Avadh orphaned,
The grief-stricken people began to follow him.

Ram, that ocean of compassion, reasoned with them in many ways,
And they turned back—but, overcome with love, they came
    back again.
Avadh appeared most terrifying,
As though it was the dark night of death.
The men and women of the city were like dreadful beasts,
Frightened at the sight of each other.
Homes were like cremation grounds, kinsfolk like ghosts,
And sons, well-wishers and friends like the messengers of Jam.
In gardens, trees and vines withered,
While streams and ponds were too dismal to behold.

    The millions of horses and elephants, and deer kept for sport,
    The town's cattle, the chataks, peacocks,
    Kokils, geese, parrots, mynahs,
    Saras cranes, swans and chakors,   (83)

Confounded at the separation from Ram, stood still
Everywhere, as though images in a painting.
The city was a great fruit-laden forest, dense and mighty,
And all the men and women, its many birds and animals.
But Vidhi made Kaikeyi a tribal Kirat woman,
Who set it fiercely ablaze in all the ten directions.
Unable to bear this fire of separation from Raghubar,
The people fled running to him in their distress.
All thought to themselves,
'Without Ram, Lakshman and Sita, there is no happiness.
Wherever Ram is, there we should all live,
For without Raghubir, Avadh is of no use to us.'
Having thus firmly concluded, they set off with him,
Abandoning comfortable homes filled with luxuries denied even to
    the gods.
After all, can they who hold dear the lotus feet of Ram,
Ever be overpowered by worldly pleasures?

Leaving children and the elderly at home,
   The rest of the people all joined Ram.
   At the end of the first day, Raghunath made camp
   On the banks of the Tamasa river.   (84)

When Raghupati saw his subjects so overpowered by love,
Great sorrow arose in his kind heart.
The Lord, Raghunath, is full of compassion,
And quick to take upon himself the pain of others.
Speaking sweet words full of love,
He consoled and reasoned with them in many ways,
Giving them many lessons on dharma.
But the people, overcome with love, refused to turn back.
Unable to abandon kindness and affection,
Raghurai found himself in a quandary.
The people, exhausted with grief and fatigue, fell asleep;
A little divine illusion, too, served to beguile their minds.
When two watches of the night had passed,
Ram affectionately said to the minister,
'Drive the chariot, respected sir, so as to efface the tracks of
    its wheels,
For there is no other way to accomplish our objective.'

Bowing their heads at Shambhu's feet,
   Ram, Lakshman and Sita mounted the chariot.
   The minister swiftly drove it away,
   Driving now in this direction, now in that, thus
      concealing the tracks of its wheels.   (85)

When dawn broke, the people all awoke,
And a great cry broke out, 'Raghunath has gone!'
They searched but could find no trace of the chariot,
And calling 'Ram, Ram!' they ran in all directions.
They were as frantic as a company of merchants,

When a ship sinks at sea.
They said to each other,
'Understanding our distress, Ram left us.'
They reproached themselves and praised the fishes,[14] crying,
'Fie upon our lives without Raghubir!
If the Creator has separated us from our beloved,
Why does he not give us death upon our asking?'
In this manner the crowd wailed and lamented,
And, burning with grief, returned to Avadh.
Their pain at the separation was terrible beyond telling,
And only the hope that Ram's exile would end kept them alive.

> In the hope of seeing Ram again,
> Men and women began to fast and practice penance,
> Wretched as the kok and koki,
> Or lotuses, bereft of the sun.   (86)

With Sita and the minister, the two brothers
Reached Shringberpur.
Seeing the river of the gods, Ram alighted from the chariot,
And joyfully prostrated himself.
Lakshman, the minister and Sita also paid it homage,
And, together with Ram, were filled with gladness,
For the Ganga is the root of all joy and well-being,
The bringer of every happiness and the remover of all pain.
Repeating countless stories and legends,
Ram gazed upon the waves of the Ganga,
And explained to the minister, his brother and his beloved
The sublime glory of the river of the gods.
Bathing in the river, the fatigue of their journey disappeared,
And drinking its pure water, their hearts grew joyful.
For him, merely remembering whom removes the profound fatigue
    of birth and rebirth,
This weariness was merely in accordance with worldly conduct.

The root of pure being, consciousness and bliss,
The banner of the Sun's dynasty,
Performed actions like those of an ordinary man,
As a bridge over the ocean of mundane existence.   (87)

When Guha, chief of the Nishad tribe, heard this news,
He was delighted and summoned his beloved kinsfolk
        and friends.
Taking with him great baskets of fruits and tubers as gifts,
He went to meet Ram, boundless joy in his heart.
Laying down his gifts, he prostrated himself before Ram,
And gazed with great love at the Lord.
Raghurai, who is won over by simple love,
Seated him beside him and asked after his well-being.
'Lord, in looking upon your lotus feet is well-being,
And I can now count myself amongst the fortunate.
Lord, my land, wealth, and home are yours
And I, together with my family, your lowly servant.
Show us your favour and set foot in our village,
Mark me your servant and make all envious of my good fortune.'
Ram replied, 'You speak truly, my wise friend,
But my father has commanded me otherwise.

        For fourteen years I must live in the forest,
        In ascetic robes, following ascetic vows and diet,
        So for me to stay in a village is not right.'
        Hearing this, Guha was deeply grieved.   (88)

Seeing Ram, Lakshman and Sita's beauty
The village men and women lovingly wondered,
'Tell me, my friend, what sort of father and mother are they,
Who have sent such children to the forest?'
But one said, 'The king did well,
For God has given us this reward for our eyes.'

Then the Nishad chieftain reflected in his heart,
And thinking of a beautiful sinsupa tree,
Took Raghunath and showed him the place.
Ram declared it to be suitable and pleasant in every way.
The villagers paid him homage and returned home,
And Raghubar went to perform the evening rites.
Guha carefully made a bed, soft and pretty,
Of kush grass and fresh new leaves,
And fruits and roots, pure and sweet and tender,
He placed there with his own hand in leaf-cups filled to the brim,
    with water.

> After dining on the tubers, roots and fruits
> With Sita, Sumantra and his brother,
> The jewel of the Raghu line lay down to rest.
> His brother massaged his feet.   (89)

When he saw that the Lord was asleep, Lakshman rose,
And in a soft voice told the minister to sleep.
At a little distance, he made ready his bow and arrows,
And sat awake in a warrior's stance, to keep watch.
Guha summoned his trusted guards,
And with great love for the Lord, stationed them at
    different points.
He himself went to sit beside Lakshman,
With his quiver at his waist and an arrow fitted to his bow.
The Nishad, seeing the Lord sleeping,
Was overcome with love, and his heart filled with grief.
His body trembling, his eyes flowing with tears,
He spoke loving words to Lakshman.
'The king's palace is inherently beautiful,
Even Indra's abode cannot compare to it.
Its charming, jewel-encrusted pavilions
Seem fashioned by Kamdev's own hands.

Bright and clean, of rare and handsome construction, they are
 filled with luxuries,
And fragrant with the sweet perfume of flowers.
With soft beds and jewelled lamps,
They have every kind of comfort,   (90)

And coverlets, cushions and quilts of many kinds,
As soft and white and pleasing as froth on milk.
There Sita and Ram would lie down to rest each night,
Their radiant beauty destroying Rati and Kamdev's pride.
The same Ram and Sita now sleep upon a mat of grass and leaves,
Exhausted, without sheets and coverlets—it is a sight intolerable
 to behold.
He whom mother, father, kinsfolk and the citizens of Avadh,
Devoted friends, servants and handmaidens,
Would protect and cherish as their own life's breath,
The same Lord Ram now sleeps upon the ground!
And she whose father is mighty Janak, renowned throughout
 the world,
Whose father-in-law is Indra's friend and the lord of the Raghus,
Whose husband is Ramchandra—the same Vaidehi
Sleeps upon the ground! Whom does fate not turn against?
Are Sita and Raghubir fit for exile to the forest?
Men do rightly say that destiny is supreme!

 Kaikaya's foolish daughter,
 Through cruel, devious means,
 At a time of joy, brought grief
 Upon Raghunandan and Janaki.   (91)

That foolish, vicious woman became an axe to the tree of the
 sun's dynasty,
And plunged the whole world into grief.'
The Nishad was profoundly sad

To see Ram and Sita sleeping upon the ground.
Then Lakshman spoke in tones sweet and soft,
And steeped in the essence of wisdom, detachment and faith.
'No one is a giver of joy or sorrow to another,
All suffer the results of their own actions, brother.
Union and separation, the experiencing of joy or grief,
Friends, enemies, and those in between—all are snares of delusion.
Birth and death, anywhere in the entangled net of this
      illusory world,
Prosperity and adversity, destiny and time,
Land, home, wealth, city, family,
Heaven and hell, and the extent of all human affairs,
All that you can see and hear or imagine in your mind—
Are rooted in delusion, and not the supreme truth.

      Just as in a dream a beggar becomes a king,
      Or the lord of paradise, a pauper,
      But awakening, finds neither gain nor loss—
      So must you look, in your heart, upon this delusory world.   (92)

Reflecting thus, do not be angry
Or uselessly blame anyone.
All of us sleep in the night of delusion
And see dreams of many kinds.
In the night that is this world, only the yogis are awake,
Seekers of the highest truth, free from delusion.
Know a soul to be truly awake in this world
Only when it has renounced all sensual pleasure.
With discernment, delusion and attachment flee,
And then comes love for Raghunath's feet.
Friend, the supreme, most sublime truth is only this:
Devotion to Ram's feet in thought, word and deed.
Ram is brahm, the Supreme Reality embodied,
Inconceivable, imperceptible, incomparable,

Without beginning, free of all flaws, indivisible,
Whom the Vedas ever describe as "Not this".

> The compassionate Lord, for the sake of devotees,
> The earth, Brahmans, cows and gods,
> Takes the form of a man and performs wondrous deeds,
> Hearing of which, the snares and tangles of birth and
>   rebirth in this world disappear.   (93)

Understanding this, friend, abandon delusion
And be devoted to Sita and Raghubir's feet.'
In speaking of Ram's virtues, day broke,
And he who brings joy and bliss to the world awoke.
After performing all the purificatory rites, Ram bathed;
Then he, the pure and wise, called for the milk of the banyan tree
And together with his brother, matted his hair.
Seeing this, Sumantra's eyes filled with tears.
His heart burning with anguish, his face sorrowful,
He spoke, utterly wretched, his hands folded,
'Lord, the king of Koshal said thus to me:
"Take a chariot and go with Ram.
Show them the forest, let them bathe in the divine Ganga,
And then quickly bring the two brothers back.
Bring back Lakshman, Ram and Sita,
Settling all their doubts and hesitation."

> The king so commanded me, master.
> But now, upon my life, I will do whatever you say.'
> Thus entreating him, he fell at Ram's feet,
> Weeping like a child.   (94)

'Beloved son, in your mercy act so that
Avadh is not left without a master.'
Ram raised up the minister and consoled him,

'Sir, you have studied and investigated all the aspects of dharma.
Shibi, Dadhichi and King Harishchandra
Endured innumerable hardships for the sake of dharma.
The wise kings Rantidev[15] and Bali
Upheld dharma even whilst bearing many afflictions.
There is no dharma equal to truth,
As the Vedas, the Shastras and the Puranas all declare,
And I have attained that dharma with ease.
If I abandon it, my disgrace will spread across the three worlds,
And to men of honour, disgrace
Is like the burning anguish of ten million deaths.
What more can I say to you, respected sire?
In answering you, I only take sin upon myself.

> Clasp my father's feet, salute him ten million times
> And with folded hands, entreat him from me,
> "Do not be anxious in any way, Father,
> On my account."   (95)

You, too, seek my well-being like my own father,
And so, revered sire, with folded hands I entreat you,
Make it your duty in every way to ensure
That my father does not suffer with anxiety about us.'
Listening to this conversation between Raghunath and
      the minister,
The Nishad and his people grew distressed.
Then Lakshman spoke some bitter words,
But the Lord stopped him, regarding them most unseemly.
Embarrassed, Ram made the minister swear upon him
That he would not repeat Lakshman's words.
Sumantra then gave the king's message:
"'Sita will not be able to bear the hardships of the forest,
So whatever will persuade Sita to return to Avadh,
That is what you, Raghubar, must do.

Otherwise, left completely without support,
Like a fish without water, I will not survive.

> In her father's home and with her husband's parents, there is
>   every comfort.
> Sita can live happily
> Wherever her heart desires,
> Until these troubles pass."   (96)

The manner in which the king made this plea,
His anguish and his love—I cannot describe.'
Hearing his father's message, the abode of compassion,
Tried to persuade Sita in innumerable ways:
'Your mother- and father-in-law, our guru, our beloved kinsfolk—
If you go back, all their grief will vanish.'
Hearing her husband's words, Vaidehi replied,
'Listen, most loving lord of my life,
You are compassionate, Lord, and most discerning—
Abandoning its body, can a shadow remain?
Without the sun, where will its radiance go,
Or where the moonlight, abandoning the moon?'
Having made this entreaty full of love to her husband,
She spoke to the minister in a voice sweet and gentle:
'You are my well-wisher, like my father and father-in-law,
So to answer you back is most unseemly of me.

> But, in the grip of sorrow, I oppose you,
> So do not be offended, revered sire.
> Without the lotus feet of my noble lord,
> All relationships are meaningless to me.   (97)

I have seen my father's magnificence and grandeur,
His footstool kissed by jewelled crowns of kings.
Such an abode of bliss is my father's home,

Yet, without my beloved, it does not please my heart even in a
    moment of forgetfulness.
My father-in-law is the emperor, Koshal's king,
Whose glory is manifest in all the fourteen spheres,
And whom the king of the gods, Indra himself, rushes forward
    to welcome,
Giving him half his own throne as a seat.
Such is my father-in-law, and Avadh my home,
Beloved is my family, and my mothers-in-law each like a mother
    to me—
But without the pollen-dust of Raghupati's lotus feet,
None of these give me joy even in dream.
Inaccessible paths, forests and mountains,
Elephants, lions, impassable lakes and rivers,
Kols, Kirats, kurang deer and wild birds—
With my beloved lord, all are delightful to me.

Falling at the feet of my mother- and father-in-law
Entreat them on my behalf,
"Do not worry about me at all,
For I am inherently happy in the forest.   (98)

With the lord of my life and beloved brother-in-law,
The greatest of heroes, bearing bows and quivers,
I will know no fatigue on the road, nor any apprehension or sorrow
    in my heart.
So do not, even unwittingly, be anxious about me.'"
Sumantra, hearing Sita's calm and soothing words,
Grew as distraught as a cobra bereft of its crest-jewel,
And his eyes could not see, nor his ears hear.
He could not utter a single word, so deeply distressed was he.
Ram consoled him in many ways,
But his troubled heart could not be calmed.
He begged in countless ways to go with them,

But Raghunandan gave an appropriate reply each time.
Ram's command could not be disobeyed—
The ways of fate are cruel and beyond control.
Bowing his head at Ram, Lakshman and Sita's feet,
He turned back, like a merchant who has lost his capital.

> He tried to drive his chariot away, but the horses
> Kept looking back at Ram and whinnying.
> Seeing this, the Nishads were overwhelmed by grief—
> They beat their heads, and lamented,   (99)

'When even animals are so distressed at being separated from him,
How will his people and his mother and father survive?'
Resolutely, Ram sent Sumantra away,
Then came to the banks of the sacred Ganga.
He called for a boat, but the boatman would not bring it,
Saying, 'I know your secret—
Everyone says that the dust of your lotus feet
Is some magical herb that can turn things into people.
At its touch, a rock became a beautiful woman!
Wood is not as hard as stone,
And if my boat turns into a muni's wife
And flies off, I will be ruined.
This boat is the mainstay of my whole family,
And I know no other trade.
If you are determined to go across, Lord,
First allow me to wash your lotus feet.

Only after I have washed your lotus feet will I let you board
    my boat—
I seek no other fee from you, Lord.
I swear by you, Ram, and by Dasharath too,
That I am speaking truly.
Let Lakshman shoot his arrows at me,

But until I wash your feet—till then,
Compassionate lord of Tulsidas,
I will not ferry you across!'

Hearing the boatman's words,
So rough and clumsy and wrapped in love,
The abode of mercy laughed,
Glancing at Janaki and Lakshman.   (100)

The ocean of compassion replied with a smile,
'Do that by which your boat is not lost,
Quickly fetch some water and wash my feet—
It is getting late, take us across.'
He whose name, remembered once,
Takes men across the boundless ocean of this existence,
And for whose three strides the universe was too small—[16]
That same merciful Lord obliged a boatman.
Gazing upon the Lord's toenails, the divine river rejoiced,
For his words had confused and bewildered her.[17]
The boatman, having received Ram's royal permission,
Brought a wooden basin full of water.
With great joy and his heart brimming with love,
He began to wash Ram's lotus feet.
The gods, raining flowers upon him, were all envious and declared,
'There is none so full of merit as him!'

Washing Ram's feet, he drank of that water,
Together with his family,
Thus ferrying the souls of his ancestors across the ocean of
    rebirth to salvation.
He then joyfully took the Lord across.   (101)

Disembarking, they stood upon the sands of the sacred river,
Sita and Ram, with Guha and Lakshman.

The boatman stepped out of his boat and prostrated himself
    in homage,
And the Lord felt embarrassed that he had given him nothing.
Sita, who knew her beloved's heart,
Gladly removed her jewelled ring,
And the compassionate Lord said, 'Take your fare for ferrying
    us across.'
But the boatman clasped his feet in distress,
'Lord, what have I not already received today?
The fires of sin, sorrow and poverty have been extinguished.
I have laboured for my living a long time,
And today God has given me a good and abundant wage in return.
Now I want for nothing, master,
By your grace, merciful Lord.
But at the time of your return, I will accept,
Whatever you give, and cherish that gift with all my heart.'

    The Lord, Lakshman and Sita tried their best to persuade him,
    But the boatman would take nothing.
    So the abode of mercy dismissed him,
    Bestowing upon him the boon of pure, unblemished
        devotion.   (102)

Then the lord of the Raghu dynasty bathed in the river,
And bowing his head, worshipped a shivaling made of clay.
Sita, with folded hands, said to the divine river,
'Mother, fulfil my heart's desire,
That with my husband and his younger brother, I may return safe
    and well
To worship you again.'
Hearing Sita's prayer steeped in love,
A gracious voice came from the clear water.
'Listen, Vaidehi, Raghubir's beloved,
Who in creation knows not your power and glory?

Those at whom you merely glance become rulers of the celestial quarters,
And all the mystic powers wait upon you with folded hands.
By entreating me so humbly,
You have bestowed your grace upon me and exalted me.
Even so, divine goddess, I will give you my blessing,
To make true my own words.

    With the lord of your life and his younger brother,
    You will come back safe and well to Koshal.
    All your heart's desires will be accomplished,
    And your fair renown will spread throughout the world.'   (103)

Hearing Ganga's words, source of joy and well-being,
And finding the sacred river so well-disposed towards her, Sita rejoiced.
Then the Lord said to Guha, 'Return home.'
Hearing this, Guha's face grew pale, and burning anguish arose in
    his heart;
With folded hands, he spoke in sad and pleading tones,
'Listen to my prayer, jewel of the Raghu line—
Let me stay with you, Lord, to show you the road,
And for a few days, to serve at your feet.
In whichever forest, Raghurai, you may make your home,
I will build you a beautiful hut of leaves,
And after that, whatever you command me,
I swear by you, Raghubir, I will do.'
Ram, seeing his simple love,
Agreed to take him along. Guha rejoiced in his heart,
And calling together all his kinsmen,
Reassured them, and took his leave of them.

    Invoking Ganpati and Shiv,
    The Lord bowed his head to the sacred river.
    Then, with his friend, his younger brother and Sita,
    Raghunath proceeded towards the forest.   (104)

That day they halted beneath a tree,
And Lakshman and Guha made all arrangements for their rest.
At dawn, Raghurai performed all the morning rites,
And went to visit Prayag, the king of pilgrimage sites.
This king's minister is truth, piety his beloved wife,
And Madhav his dear friend and well-wisher.
His storehouse is filled with the four rewards of life,
And that pure and sacred realm is his beautiful kingdom.
His land is an unassailable, strong and handsome fort
That enemies cannot conquer even in dream.
All pilgrimage sites are his army of chosen and valiant warriors,
Steadfast in battle, crushing the forces of sin.
The confluence of the rivers is his magnificent throne,
His umbrella the imperishable banyan tree that charms the hearts
    of sages.
His fly whisks are the waves of the Jamuna and the Ganga—
Merely looking upon them destroys sorrow and poverty.

> Pure and pious sadhus wait upon him,
> And attain all that their hearts desire.
> The Vedas and the Puranas are his host of bards,
> Who sing of his clear and stainless virtues.   (105)

But who can relate the power and glory of Prayag,
A lion against the elephant herd of accumulated sin?
On beholding this glorious lord of pilgrimage sites,
The ocean of bliss, Raghubar, himself attained bliss,
And recounted to Sita, Lakshman and his friend,
With his own lovely lips, the greatness of this king of holy sites.
Making obeisance to the holy site, gazing at its groves and gardens,
And praising its grandeur with deep devotion,
He came and beheld the triveni,
Merely remembering which confers all happiness and well-being.
Bathing in it with deep joy, he worshipped Shiv,
And propitiated the gods of the sacred site according to custom.

Then came the Lord to Bharadvaj,
And, as he prostrated himself before him, the muni clasped him to
    his breast.
The joy in the muni's heart was beyond description,
As though he had found a treasury of ultimate bliss.

> The king of sages blessed him
> With great joy in his heart, knowing that it was
> As though God, by bringing before him Ram, Lakshman
>   and Sita,
> Had made visible to his eyes the reward of all his
>   good deeds.   (106)

Asking after their well-being, he seated them,
Pleasing them with loving homage.
The muni then brought and offered them
Sweet tubers, roots, fruits and sprouts as delicious as amrit.
With Sita, Lakshman and his devoted friend,
Ram ate with great pleasure those roots and fruits.
His fatigue disappeared and Ram relaxed, content.
Then Bharadvaj addressed him in sweet words.
'Today, my penance, pilgrimages and renunciation have borne fruit,
Today, my worship, yogic meditation and detachment have
    been rewarded.
All my spiritual practices have been successful
By looking upon you, Ram, today!
There is no gain beyond, no happiness greater than this—
Seeing you, all my desires are fulfilled.
Now by your favour grant me the boon
Of spontaneous love for your lotus feet.

> Till the time a man does not become your devotee,
> Abandoning deceit in act, speech and thought,
> He cannot find happiness even in his dreams,
> Not even by resorting to a crore of contrivances.'   (107)

Though joyfully satisfied and content by his devotion,
Ram grew embarrassed hearing the muni's words.
Then Raghubar related to all who were there,
The muni's glorious renown, in countless ways.
'Exalted is he, and in him reside all virtues,
Whom you choose to honour, lord of sages.'
The muni and Raghubir thus honoured each other,
And experienced inexpressible joy.
When they heard this news, the residents of Prayag—
Young students, ascetics, sages, siddhas, hermits who had
     renounced the world—
All flocked to Bharadvaj's ashram
To see Dasharath's handsome sons.
Ram reverently greeted them all,
And they rejoiced to receive their eyes' reward.
Supremely glad, they gave their blessings,
And returned home, praising his beauty.

     Ram rested there for the night,
     And at dawn, after bathing in the sacred confluence,
     He set out with Sita, Lakshman and his devoted friend,
     Bowing his head to the muni with joy.   (108)

Ram affectionately said to the muni,
'Master, tell us, which path should we take?'
The muni smiled to himself and said to Ram,
'All paths are easy for you.'
Then he called for his disciples to go with them,
And hearing his summons, fifty or more came rejoicing.
All of them had boundless love for Ram,
And all declared, 'We know the way!'
The muni picked four students—
Who had, throughout many births, performed every virtuous act—
To accompany them.

Then, bowing to the rishi, and receiving his permission,
Raghurai set forth with a happy heart.
Whenever they passed by a village,
The women and men rushed out to look at them.
Finding their protector, and so receiving the fruit of their birth,
They returned home, sad, sending their hearts with him.

> Ram courteously dismissed the students,
> Who turned back, having attained their heart's desire.
> After crossing the Jamuna, he bathed in its waters,
> Dark like his own body.   (109)

Hearing of his arrival, the men and women who lived along
    the riverbank,
Came rushing, abandoning whatever they were doing.
Beholding Lakshman, Ram and Sita's beauty,
They praised their own good fortune.
Though in their hearts they yearned to know,
They hesitated to ask their names and village.
But those amongst them who were old and wise,
Were able to deduce Ram's identity.
They related to all the others the whole story
Of his going to the forest at his father's command.
They heard this with deep sorrow, and all sadly lamented,
'The queen and king have not done right!'
At that very moment, an ascetic arrived,
Fiery, handsome and young in years,
A poet unknown, in hermit's guise,
And in thought, act and word, utterly devoted to Ram.[18]

> His eyes full of tears, and his body trembling with love,
> He recognized his own chosen Lord,
> And fell prostate like a stick upon the ground—
> His state was beyond description.   (110)

Ram, delighted and full of love, clasped him to his heart,
As ecstatic as a pauper who has found the philosopher's stone.
'It is as though love and supreme truth have both
Taken form and are embracing each other!' said everyone.
Then he threw himself at Lakshman's feet,
Who, too, raised him up, brimming with love.
The ascetic then placed the dust of Sita's feet upon his head,
And the mother, considering him her child, blessed him.
The Nishad prostrated himself before the ascetic,
Who embraced him joyfully, knowing him to be dear to Ram.
With the cups of his eyes, he drank the nectar of Ram's beauty,
As delighted as a starving man who finds a delicious meal.
'Tell me, my dear, what sort of father and mother are they,
Who have sent such children to the forest?' asked the women of
    each other.
Seeing the beauty of Ram, Lakshman and Sita,
The men and women grew agitated with love.

> Then Raghubir, in many ways,
> Urged his friend to return.
> In obedience to Ram's royal command,
> Guha turned back towards home.   (111)

Then, with folded hands, Sita, Ram and Lakshman
Paid homage to the Jamuna once more,
And, accompanied by Sita, the two brothers set forth, rejoicing,
Praising the daughter of the Sun.[v]
They met many travellers along the road,
Who, seeing the two brothers, affectionately said,
'The marks of royalty are on your every limb—
Seeing this, there is great anxiety in our hearts.
You travel along the road on foot,

---

[v] The Jamuna

So that it seems to us that astrology must be false.
This road is difficult, with mountains and dense forests,
Moreover, you have a young woman with you.
Full of elephants and lions, the forest is too dreadful to contemplate.
But if you permit us, we will escort you,
Take you where you wish to go,
And then, bowing our heads to you, return.'

 In this manner they begged to help, overcome with love,
 Their bodies trembling, their eyes full of tears.
 But the ocean of compassion sent them away
 With soft and courteous words.   (112)

The cities of the Nagas and the gods envied
The towns and villages that lay along their road—
'Which virtuous man, in what auspicious hour, settled them,
That they are so blessed, full of virtue and supremely beautiful?'
Even Amaravati could not compare to the places
Where Ram's feet trod.
And those living near his path were storehouses of virtue,
Praised even by the inhabitants of heaven,
For they could gaze upon Ram, filling their eyes with him,
Dark as a storm cloud, with Sita and Lakshman.
The lakes and rivers of the gods envied
The ponds and streams where Ram bathed.
And the celestial Kalpataru praised
Any tree under which the Lord sat down.
Touching the dust of Ram's lotus feet,
Earth considered herself most fortunate.

 The clouds gave him shade, and the multitude of gods
 Rained down flowers upon him and praised him,
 As, gazing at mountains, forests, birds and beasts
 Ram continued along that road.   (113)

Whenever Raghurai, with Sita and Lakshman,
Passed near a village,
Hearing of his arrival, old and young, men and women,
All came at once, abandoning household chores.
Seeing the beauty of Ram, Lakshman and Sita,
They received their eyes' reward and were happy.
Their eyes full of tears, their bodies trembling with joy,
All were enraptured upon seeing the two heroes.
Their state cannot be described—
It was like those of paupers who find a pile of wish-fulfilling jewels.
Calling out, they advised each other,
'Take, this very moment, your eyes' reward.'
Some, seeing Ram, became so enamoured
That they followed him, gazing.
Others, through the path of their eyes, drawing his radiant beauty
    into their hearts,
Became still in body, mind and speech.

> Some, seeing the cool shade of a banyan,
> Spread soft grass and leaves
> And said, 'Rest here for a moment, let your fatigue disappear,
> Then move on—now, or at dawn.'   (114)

Some brought pitchers filled with water,
And softly said, 'Sip a little, Lord.'
Hearing their affectionate words, seeing their great love,
Ram, compassionate and exceedingly good-natured,
And knowing that Sita was tired,
Rested for a while in the banyan's shade.
Delighted, the men and women gazed upon his shining beauty,
Their eyes and hearts captivated by his incomparable form.
Radiant in their rapture, they gazed unblinking from every side,
Like chakors at the moon of Ramchandra's face.
His comely body was as dark as a young tamal tree—

A mere look enchants the hearts of countless Kamdevs.
Lakshman, bright as lightning, handsome
From head to toe, looked most charming, delighting the heart.
Clad in ascetic garb, with quivers tightly fastened at their waists,
Bows and arrows resplendent in their lotus hands,

> Crowns of matted locks upon their shapely heads,
> They had broad chests, long arms and large eyes,
> And upon their lovely faces, bright as the full moon
> of autumn,
> Glittered tiny drops of perspiration.   (115)

That heart-enchanting pair surpasses description,
For their beauty is great and my intellect small.
All gazed at the beauty of Ram, Lakshman and Sita,
Completely absorbed, souls, hearts and minds.
The men and women, thirsty for love, were as still
As stags and does transfixed by lamplight.
The village women approached Sita,
Full of love, but too shy to ask questions.
Again and again they touched her feet,
And spoke words that were simple and sweet.
'Princess, we have a question,
But our womanly natures make us afraid to ask.
Forgive our rudeness, mistress,
And do not take offence, knowing we are but village women.
But these two young princes, so naturally handsome
That emerald and gold must draw their brilliance from them,

> One dark, the other fair-complexioned, both young
> and comely,
> Abodes of charm and beauty,
> With faces as radiant as the autumn moon,
> And eyes like autumn lotuses,   (116)

Who put to shame countless gods of love—
Tell us, beautiful lady—who are they to you?'
Hearing their soft and loving words,
Sita felt embarrassed and smiled to herself.
Glancing at them, and then at the ground,
Fair-complexioned Sita shrank with a twofold diffidence.
Shyly and lovingly, the fawn-eyed princess,
Replied in a voice as sweet as a kokil's.
'That one, easy in manner, handsome and fair-bodied—
His name is Lakshman, he is my young brother-in-law.'
Then, covering the radiant moon of her face with the end of her sari,
And arching her eyebrows, she glanced towards her beloved.
With a sidelong look of her lovely eyes, as quick as a wagtail,
Sita indicated to them that he was her husband.
The village women all became as joyful
As paupers who have looted a king's pile of riches.

> With great love they fell at Sita's feet,
> And gave her countless blessings.
> 'May your wedded life last as long
> As earth rests upon Shesh the serpent's hood,   (117)

And may you be, like Parvati, forever your lord's beloved.
Divine lady, never take away your love from us.
Again and again, we beseech you with folded hands,
If you return by this same road,
Let us look upon you, knowing us to be your servants.'
Sita saw that they were all thirsty for love,
And reassured them again and again with sweet words,
Like moonlight nourishes water-lilies.
Then Lakshman, perceiving Raghubar's wish,
Sweetly asked the people the road they should take.
As soon as they heard this, the men and women grew sad,
Their limbs trembled, and their eyes filled with tears.

Their joy disappeared, and their hearts grew heavy,
As though providence had given them a treasure only to snatch it back.
But, accepting it as the ways of fate, they composed themselves,
And deciding upon the easiest road, explained it to them.

> Then, with Lakshman and Janaki,
> Raghunath proceeded on his way,
> Sending the people back with loving words,
> But taking their hearts with him.   (118)

The men and women turned back, lamenting,
And blaming destiny in their hearts.
With great sorrow they said to each other,
'Perverse are the ways of the Creator,
Utterly uncontrolled, cruel and remorseless.
It is he who made the moon sickly and stained,
The Kalpataru a mere tree and the ocean salt,
And it is he who has sent these young princes to the forest!
If he has given them exile in the forest,
The Creator made luxury and pleasure in vain.
If they must wander the road without shoes,
In vain did he create all sorts of vehicles.
If they must lie on the ground, spreading kush grass and leaves,
Why did he fashion comfortable beds?
If the Creator decreed that they should live under trees,
He laboured uselessly to build one glittering palace after another.

> If these most handsome and tender youths
> Wear the rough garb and matted hair of ascetics,
> In vain has the Creator made
> So many different kinds of clothes and ornaments.   (119)

If they eat wild tubers, roots and fruits,
Nectar and other delicious foods are useless in this world.'

One said, 'They are so innately beautiful,
They must have appeared on earth themselves, not created
    by Vidhi.
In all that the Vedas say of Vidhi's creations,
Perceptible to our ears, eyes and minds,
In all the fourteen spheres—search them all and see for yourself—
Where is such a man, where such a woman?
Seeing them, Vidhi was greatly enamoured,
And began to fashion others like them.
He worked very hard, but could not make any to match them,
And so, out of jealousy, he hid them in the forest.'
Others said, 'We don't know much,
But consider ourselves supremely fortunate.
It seems to us that they too are abodes of virtue
Who see, have seen, or will see them.'

> Thus they said these loving words,
> Their eyes overflowing with tears.
> 'How will they travel such difficult roads,
> These youths with their delicate forms?'   (120)

Overcome by love, the women grew distraught,
Like beautiful chakwis at dusk.
Thinking of their soft lotus feet and the rough road ahead,
They spoke gentle words from troubled hearts.
'At the touch of their soft and rosy feet,
The very earth must shrink, just like our hearts.
If the lord of the universe had to give them exile in the forest,
Why didn't he strew their path with flowers?
If we can truly get what we ask from God,
Dear friend, let us keep them forever in our eyes!'
Those men and women who had not come in time,
Were unable to see Sita and Ram.
Hearing of their beauty, they asked anxiously,

'How far must they have gone by now, brothers?'
Those who could, went running to see them,
And returned full of joy, having received their birth's reward.

Women, children and the old
Wrung their hands and lamented.
Thus it was that wherever Ram went,
People were overcome by love.   (121)

In village after village there was similar rejoicing
On seeing that moon to the lilies of the solar line.[19]
Those who heard something of the circumstances of Ram's exile,
Blamed the king and queen.
But others said, 'The lord of men was very kind,
For he gave us our eyes' reward.'
So men and women conversed amongst themselves,
In simple, loving, pleasing words.
'Fortunate are the father and mother who gave them birth
And blessed is the city from whence they came.
Fortunate is the lands, the hills, forests, villages,
And every place they go—they are all blessed.
Even Viranchi found joy in creating anyone
Who feels love for them in every way.'
The charming story of Ram and Lakshman's travels,
Spread all along their path and through the forest.

In this manner, the sun to the lotuses of the Raghu line,
Gave joy to the people along the way,
As he proceeded, looking at the forest,
With Sita and Sumitra's son.   (122)

Ram walked ahead, Lakshman behind,
Shining in their ascetic's robes,
And between the two Sita was as resplendent

As maya between the Absolute and the soul.
I describe again her radiance, as it dwells in my heart:
Like Desire shining between Love and Spring.
And searching my heart, I give another simile—
Like Rohini resplendent between Mercury and the moon.[20]
Placing her feet between her lord's footprints,
Sita walked fearfully along the path.
Guarding the marks of both Sita and Ram's feet,
And always keeping them to his right, Lakshman walked
    the road.[21]
The beauty of Ram, Lakshman and Sita's love
Is beyond words—how can I describe it?
Even birds and beasts were enraptured by its radiance,
For Ram the wayfarer had stolen their hearts as well.

    Whoever saw these beloved travellers—
    The two brothers with Sita—
    Joyfully and without effort attained
    The end of rebirth's difficult path.   (123)

Even today, one in whose heart the travellers
Lakshman, Sita and Ram abide, even in dream,
Finds the way to Ram's abode—
A path that even munis only sometime find.
Then Raghubir, knowing Sita was tired,
And seeing a banyan close by and cool water,
Halted there, eating tubers, roots and fruits.
After bathing at dawn, Raghurai continued his journey.
Seeing beautiful forests, lakes and mountains along the way,
The Lord came to Valmiki's ashram.
Ram saw the muni's beautiful abode,
With its beautiful mountains, forests and streams of clear water.
There were lotuses upon the lakes, and groves of trees in the forest
    in full flower,

While honeybees, drunk upon their nectar, softly hummed.
Birds and beasts made a great clamour,
As they grazed with happy hearts, without enmity.

> Seeing this sacred and beautiful ashram,
> The lotus-eyed Ram rejoiced,
> And hearing of Raghubar's arrival,
> The muni came out to welcome him.   (124)

Ram prostrated himself in homage before the muni,
And the illustrious sage gave him his blessing,
The sight of Ram's radiant beauty gladdening his eyes,
And with every honour, he led him to his ashram.
The great muni, receiving such guests, as dear as his life,
Called for sweet tubers, roots and fruits.
Once Sita, Saumitri and Ram had eaten,
The muni gave them a pleasant place to rest.
Valmiki's heart was full of great joy,
As his eyes gazed upon the embodiment of bliss.
Then, Raghurai, folding his lotus hands,
Spoke words that pleased the muni's ears.
'Greatest of munis, you know the past, present and future,
The world is a *ber* fruit in the palm of your hand.'
So saying, the Lord related to him the whole tale,
Of how the queen had banished him to the forest.

> 'To be able to honour my father's command, please my mother,
> Let a brother like Bharat be king,
> And receive the grace of your presence, lord—
> All these must be the rewards of my past acts.   (125)

Seeing your feet, king of munis,
All our virtuous deeds have borne fruit.
Now we shall go where we have your permission,

A place where no sage or muni will be troubled.
For kings who bring distress to sages and ascetics,
Are burned to ashes even without fire.
The happiness of Brahmans is the root of well-being,
And the anger of these gods on earth burns countless generations.
Keeping this in mind, tell me a place
Where I may go with Sita and Sumitra's son,
And, building a pleasant abode of grass and leaves,
May live there for a while, compassionate lord.'
Hearing Raghubar's sincere and simple words,
The all-knowing muni declared, 'Quite right, excellent!
How else would you speak but thus, banner of the dynasty
　　of Raghu,
You who guard the perpetual bridge of divine knowledge?

Guardian of the bridge of divine knowledge, Ram,
You are the Lord of creation, and Janaki your maya
Who creates, preserves and destroys the universe
At your wish, abode of compassion.
The thousand-headed king of the serpents, who bears the earth upon
　　his crest,
Is Lakshman, lord of all created beings, animate or inanimate.
To fulfil the purpose of the gods, you have assumed the bodies of princes,
And go forth to crush the wicked demon army.

　　Ram, your true being,
　　Is beyond words and intellect,
　　Imperceptible, inexpressible, infinite,
　　　Of which the Vedas ever declare, "Not this, not this!"　　　(126)

The world is a spectacle, and you the spectator,
Who makes Vidhi, Hari and Shambhu dance to your will.
Even they do not know your mystery,
So who else could ever know you?

He alone can know you to whom you give knowledge of yourself,
And knowing you, he at once becomes you.
It is by your grace alone, Raghunandan,
That your devotees know you, soothing sandalwood to their hearts.
Your body, imbued with pure intelligence and bliss,
Is without flaw, as the knowledgeable ones know,
But assuming the body of a man for the sake of saints and gods
You speak and act like an ordinary king.
Seeing and hearing of your doings, Ram,
The dull are confused, but the wise grow blissful.
All that you say and do is true—
For as is the role one has assumed, so must be the dance.

> You ask of me, "Where should I live?"
> But I, in awe, ask you,
> Tell me a place where you are not,
> Only then can I show you where.'   (127)

Hearing the muni's words so steeped in love,
Ram grew shy, but inwardly smiled.
Then Valmiki laughed and spoke again,
Sweet words steeped in nectar.
'Listen, Ram, I will now tell you the places
Where you may reside with Sita and Lakshman.
Those whose ears are like the ocean,
Which the many diverse and beautiful streams of your story
Constantly fill, but never to the full—
Their hearts are pleasing abodes for you.
Those who have made their eyes into chataks
And yearn for the raincloud of your presence,
Scorning great rivers, seas and lakes
To quench their thirst with a single drop of your beauty—
In the pleasing palaces of their hearts, Raghunayak,
Dwell with your brother and Sita.

> One whose tongue is the swan
> Of the clear Manas lake of your renown,
> Pecking up the pearls of your myriad virtues—
> Ram, reside in his heart!   (128)

Those whose nostrils with reverence daily breathe,
The pure and fragrant offerings made to you, Lord,
Who eat only food that has been offered to you,
Wear clothes and ornaments received as your grace,
Whose heads bow at the sight of god, guru, or the twice-born
With love and great humility,
Whose hands daily worship Ram's feet,
Whose hearts depend on Ram and no other,
And whose feet walk to Ram's holy places—
Ram, reside in their hearts.
Those who ever chant your supreme mantra,
And worship you along with their family,
Who offer libations and perform the sacrificial rites in diverse ways,
Who feast the Brahmans and bestow upon them alms and
       many gifts,
Who consider their guru greater even than you in their hearts
And serve and honour him with complete devotion,

> And who, having done all this, ask only one reward:
> That they find love for Ram's feet—
> In the temple of their hearts, reside
> You two who are the delight of the Raghus, with Sita.   (129)

Those without lust, anger, arrogance, pride, delusion,
Or greed, of equable temperament, without passion or hatred,
With no subterfuge, hypocrisy, or deceit—
Reside in their hearts, Raghurai.
Those who are beloved by all, benefactors of all,
For whom joy and sorrow, praise and abuse are the same,

Who speak only true and loving words, after due reflection,
Who, waking or sleeping, find refuge only in you,
Who have no other way to salvation but you—
Ram, abide in their hearts.
Those who consider another's wife their mother,
Another's wealth more poisonous than poison,
Who rejoice to see another's prosperity
And grow sorrowful at their misfortune,
And to whom, Ram, you are as dear as their own life-breath—
Their hearts are auspicious abodes for you.

> Those for whom, son, you are everything—
> Master, friend, father, mother, guru—
> In the shrine of their hearts abide,
> You two brothers, with Sita.					(130)

Those who ignore the vices of others and seize upon their virtues,
Endure hardships for the sake of Brahmans and cows,
Who have established their reputation in the world by
	moral conduct—
Their noble minds are fitting homes for you.
One who regards virtue as arising from you, and considers his
	faults his own,
Who places his trust in you in every way,
And who holds dear the other devotees of Ram—
Dwell, with Vaidehi, in his heart.
He who renounces caste, community, wealth, faith and fame,
Beloved friends and comfortable home,
And lives holding you alone in his heart—
Live in his heart, Raghurai.
One for whom heaven, hell and liberation from rebirth are equal,
Who sees you everywhere, bearing bow and arrows,
Who is your servant in act, word and thought—
Ram, take up abode in his heart.

One who never desires anything,
And has innate love for you—
Abide without end in his heart,
For it is your very own home.'   (131)

In this way did the great muni show him an abode,
With words full of love that pleased Ram's heart.
Then the muni said, 'Listen, lord of the solar line,
I will tell you of an ashram that will be pleasant and comfortable
    for now.
Make your home on Mount Chitrakut,
For you will have every comfort there.
It is a charming hill with beautiful forests,
Where elephants, lions, deer and birds frolic.
Through the power of her penance, Atri's wife
Brought there a sacred river, praised in the Puranas.
A stream of the divine Ganga, it is called Mandakini,
A witch who devours all the children of sin.[22]
Atri and other great munis live there,
Engaged in profound meditation and prayer, punishing their
    bodies through intense penance.
Go there, Ram, and make all their labour fruitful,
And bestow grandeur and dignity on that noble mountain.'

The great Muni Valmiki praised at length
The boundless glory of Mount Chitrakut,
And the two brothers with Sita
Came there and bathed in its sacred river.   (132)

Raghubar said, 'Lakshman, this is a good ghat on the river—
So now make arrangements to stay somewhere here.'
Lakshman surveyed the north bank of the Payasvini[vi] river:

[vi] The River Mandakini

'A ravine shaped like a bow runs all around it—
The river is its bowstring, the trees and branches its arrows,
And the many wild animals, all the impurities of Kaliyug.
Thus armed, Mount Chitrakut is like a resolute huntsman,
Whose aim never misses and who strikes from the front at
    close range.'
With these words, Lakshman showed him the site,
And Raghubar, seeing the place, was delighted.
When the gods learnt that Ram's heart was captivated by the place,
They left for Chitrakut with their chief architect, Vishvakarma.
They all came disguised as Kols and Kirats,
And built lovely dwellings of leaves and grass.
The beauty of these two huts cannot be described—
One was charming and small, one more spacious.

        With Lakshman and Janaki, the Lord,
        Shone glorious in his charming abode,
        Like Madan resplendent in ascetic's garb,
        Accompanied by Rati and Spring.   (133)

Gods, Nagas, Kinnaras and the guardians of the quarters of
    the world
Came to Chitrakut at that time.
Ram saluted them all,
And the delighted gods took their eyes' reward.
Raining down flowers, the assembled gods declared,
'Master, we have found a protector today!'
Humbly, they told him of their intolerable suffering,[vii]
Then joyfully departed for their own abodes.
Hearing the news that Raghunandan had arrived
To dwell in Chitrakut, ascetics and sages came.
When he saw the rejoicing company of sages approaching,

---

vii Caused by Ravan's doings

The moon of the Raghu dynasty prostrated himself before it.
The munis raised Raghubar and clasped him to their hearts,
Giving him their blessings for success.
Seeing the beauty of Sita, Ram and Saumitri,
They considered all their spiritual practices rewarded.

> The Lord, paying due homage to the sages,
> Bade them farewell,
> And they, practising yogic meditation, prayer, sacrifices
>   and penance,
> Now lived freely and happily in their own ashrams.   (134)

When the Kols and the Kirats heard the news,
They were overjoyed as though the nine treasures of Kuber had
    come to their homes.
With leaf-cups filled to the brim with tubers, roots and fruits,
They set off eagerly, like paupers to loot gold.
Those who had already seen the two brothers,
Were questioned by the others along the way.
Telling and hearing of his goodness,
They all came and beheld Raghurai.
Placing their offerings before him, they fell at his feet,
Gazing upon the Lord with profound love.
They stood still where they were, like figures in a painting,
Bodies trembling with joy, eyes overflowing with tears.
Ram, knowing them to be overwhelmed with love,
Spoke sweet words, and honoured them all.
Paying the Lord homage again and again,
They spoke humble words, with folded hands.

> 'Master, we have all found a protector,
> Now that we have seen your feet, Lord.
> It is our good fortune that you came here,
> King of Koshal!   (135)

Fortunate are the earth, forests, roads and mountains,
Wherever you have placed your feet, Lord.
Fortunate are the birds and deer that wander in the forest,
Whose births have been fulfilled upon seeing you.
And blessed are we all, together with our families,
That we have looked upon you, filling our eyes with your presence.
You have chosen a good spot to set up your dwelling,
You will be comfortable here in all seasons.
We will serve you in every way,
Chasing away elephants, lions, snakes and tigers.
These dense forests, mountains, caves and caverns, Lord—
We have explored every step of them all.
We will take you hunting to various spots,
And show you the lakes and streams and waterfalls.
We and our families are your servants,
Lord, so do not hesitate to command us.'

> He whom the Vedas cannot describe, nor the hearts of munis
>   comprehend,
> That same Lord, the abode of compassion,
> Listened to the words of the Kirats
> As a father to the words of his children.   (136)

It is only love that Ram holds dear—
Know this, those who wish to know.
Then Ram pleased all the forest-dwellers,
Speaking sweet words filled with love.
He bade them farewell, and they, bowing their heads, departed,
And relating and listening to the Lord's perfections, returned home.
In this manner, the two brothers and Sita
Lived in the forest, pleasing gods and sages.
From the moment that Raghunayak came to live there,
The forest became a source of abundance and happiness.
Trees of many kinds flowered and bore fruit,

And pretty, twisting vines formed charming canopies.
As graceful and beautiful as the divine Kalpataru,
They seemed to have come there abandoning the forest of the gods.
Swarms of honeybees sweetly hummed,
While pleasing breezes, soft, cool and fragrant, blew.

> Blue-throats, sweet-voiced kokils, parrots,
> Chataks, chakwas and chakors—
> Various kinds of wild birds called,
> Pleasing the ear and captivating the heart.   (137)

Elephants, lions, monkeys, boars and kurang deer,
Abandoning enmity, wandered together.
Seeing Ram's beauty as he roamed the forest, hunting,
The herds of animals felt special delight.
All the divine forests anywhere in the world,
Grew envious looking upon Ram's forest.
The divine Ganga, the Sarasvati, the sun's daughter Jamuna,
Mekal's daughter Narmada, and blessed Godavari,
All the lakes and seas, and all the various streams and
    mighty rivers,
Praised the River Mandakini.
Udayagiri, Astagiri, Kailash,
Mandar, Meru, all the abodes of the gods,
Snow-clad Himalaya, and all the mountains that exist,
Sang the glory of Chitrakut.
The Vindhya range was delighted and could not contain
    its happiness[23]
For having achieved such great renown without effort.

> 'The birds and animals of Chitrakut,
> Its vines, trees and grasses,
> Are all blessed and full of merit!'
> So proclaimed the gods day and night.   (138)

Beholding Raghubar, those who had eyes
Received their birth's reward and became free of sorrow.
Touching the dust of his feet, the inanimate beings rejoiced
And became entitled to the supreme state.
That forest and hill, naturally pleasing
And exceedingly auspicious, purified even the pure.
How may the glory of that place described,
Where the ocean of bliss made his home?
Renouncing the Ocean of Milk, abandoning Ayodhya,
There where Sita, Lakshman and Ram came and dwelt—
The beauty of that forest cannot be told,
Even by a hundred thousand thousand-headed serpent kings.
So how, then, can I describe it?
Can a turtle living in a pond raise up Mount Mandar?
Lakshman served Ram in act, thought and speech—
His goodness and love cannot be described.

> Gazing every moment upon Sita and Ram's feet,
> Knowing their love for him,
> Not even in his dreams did Lakshman miss
> His brothers, mother, father and home.   (139)

With Ram, Sita lived happily,
Forgetting city, family and home.
Gazing every moment upon the moon of her beloved's face,
She was as joyful as a young chakori.
Seeing her lord's love for her daily increasing,
She lived in joy, like a kok in daytime.
Sita's heart was so in love with Ram's feet,
That the forest seemed as dear as a thousand Avadhs.
The hut of leaves was dear in the company of her dearest.
Kurang deer and birds were her beloved family,
The great munis and their wives were like her parents-in-law,
And her diet of tubers, roots and fruits was like amrit.

With her lord, a pretty mat of leaves and grass
Was as comfortable as a hundred of Kamdev's beds.
But could she whose mere glance confers the guardianship of the
    celestial quarters,
Ever be deluded and enticed by sensual delights?

    When, upon merely remembering Ram, his devotees discard
    Worldly pleasures like blades of grass,
    It is not surprising that Sita, Ram's beloved and the
        world's mother,
    Gave up all comforts.   (140)

Raghunath would do and say
Whatever made Sita and Lakshman happy.
He would relate ancient legends and stories,
To which Lakshman and Sita would listen with great delight.
Whenever Ram remembered Avadh,
His eyes would fill with tears.
Thinking of his mother and father, his kinsfolk and his brothers,
Of Bharat's love, goodness and devotion,
The compassionate Lord would grow sorrowful,
But then would take courage, reflecting that times were unpropitious.
Seeing this, Sita and Lakshman would grow distressed too,
As a man's shadow behaves like him.
Perceiving the state of his beloved and his brother, Raghunandan,
Who is steadfast, merciful and as soothing as sandalwood paste to
    his devotees' hearts,
Would begin to relate some sacred stories,
Listening to which Lakshman and Sita would find consolation.

    Ram, with Lakshman and Sita,
    Was as resplendent in that hut of leaves
    As Basav, king of the gods, dwelling in Amarpur
    With Shachi and Jayant.[24]   (141)

The Lord looked after Sita and Lakshman
As eyelids protect the eyes,
While Lakshman served Sita and Raghubir
As an unenlightened man indulges his own body.
In this manner, the Lord lived contentedly in the forest,
The benefactor of birds, beasts, gods and ascetics.
I have told of Ram's lovely journey to the forest—
Now listen how Sumantra returned to Avadh.
When the Nishad chief returned after escorting the Lord,
He saw the minister with the chariot.
Beholding Sumantra distraught with grief,
The anguish that Guha felt is impossible to describe.
Crying 'Ram! Ram! Sita! Lakshman!'
Sumantra fell to the ground, utterly overcome,
While the horses looked towards the south and whinnied,
As frantic as birds that have lost their wings.

> They would neither graze, nor drink water,
> Their eyes shed copious tears.
> All the Nishads grew distressed,
> Seeing Raghubar's horses.   (142)

Then, composing himself, the Nishad chief said,
'Now, Sumantra, abandon grief,
You are a learned man, one who knows the supreme truth.
So steady yourself, knowing that fate has turned its face away.'
Relating various stories in gentle tones,
He firmly took the minister to his chariot and seated him.
But, weak with grief, Sumantra could not drive it,
For separation from Raghubar was a sharp pain in his heart.
The horses reared and bucked and would not move,
As though wild beasts from the forest had been yoked to
    the chariot.
They would fall and stumble, or turn to look behind,

Distressed by the sharp grief of separation from Ram.
If anyone mentioned Ram, Lakshman, or Vaidehi,
They would neigh and whinny and look affectionately at him.
The state of the horses in their grief for Ram cannot
 be described—
They were as distraught as cobras bereft of their crest-jewels.

> Seeing the minister and the horses,
> The Nishad was overcome with grief.
> He then summoned four of his best men,
> And sent them with the charioteer.   (143)

Guha returned after seeing off the charioteer—
His grief at the parting is impossible to describe.
The Nishad men drove the chariot towards Avadh,
Though, every moment, they too were immersed in sorrow.
Sumantra, miserable and distraught with grief, thought,
'Shame upon a life without Raghubir!
This wretched body will not survive forever,
So why did it not win glory by dying when it parted
 from Raghubir?
These breaths of mine have become vessels of disgrace and sin,
So why do they not just leave?
Ah, my dull and stupid soul missed its chance,
And even now my heart does not break in two!'
Wringing his hands and beating his head, he lamented
Like a miser who has lost his hoard of treasure;
Or like a hero, armed for war, proclaims himself a valiant warrior,
Sets off to fight, but then flees the field of battle.

> As though a Brahman, discerning and learned in the Vedas,
> Respected by the virtuous and high-born,
> Was tricked into drinking—
> Such was the minister's remorse.   (144)

As though a woman of good family, virtuous and wise,
Whose husband is her god in deed, thought and speech,
But who, in the grip of destiny, is forced to leave her lord—
Such was the terrible anguish that burned in the minister's heart.
His eyes were full of tears, his sight grew dim,
His ears could not hear, his mind was distracted with grief,
And his lips and mouth had grown dry.
But his life-breath, held back by the closed doors of the term of
    Ram's exile, did not depart.[25]
His face had lost all colour and was impossible to look upon,
As though he had killed his father and mother.
The great weariness of loss filled his heart,
He was like a sinner on his way to Jam's domain.
He could find no words, but inwardly grieved,
'When I reach Avadh, what will I see?
Whoever sees this empty chariot, without Ram,
Will shrink from even looking at me.

> When the distraught men and women of the city,
> Run to question me,
> I will answer them all,
> Hardening my heart like adamant.   (145)

When the sad and grieving mothers question me—
Dear God! What shall I say to them?
When Lakshman's mother questions me,
What happy message can I give her?
When Ram's mother comes running,
Like a cow that has just given birth thinking of her new-born calf,
And questions me, I will reply,
"They have gone into the forest—Ram, Lakshman, Vaidehi."
Whoever questions me, I will give them this same reply—
This is the joy that will be mine when I reach Avadh.
And when the king, wretched with grief,

And whose life depends on Raghunath, questions me,
With what face will I answer him saying
That I have returned safely, having escorted the princes to
    the forest?
The moment he hears the news about Lakshman, Sita and Ram,
The lord of men will abandon his body like a worthless blade of grass.

> My heart, bereft of my beloved Ram, did not break—
> Like clay when drained of water cracks.
> So now I know that Fate has given me
> A body able to endure the torments of hell.'[26]   (146)

Thus lamenting and sorrowing on the way,
His chariot soon reached the banks of the Tamas.
There he courteously dismissed the Nishads,
Who fell at his feet and turned back, grief-stricken.
The minister shrank from entering the city,
As though he had killed his guru, a Brahman, or a cow.
He passed the day sitting under a tree,
And it was only at dusk that he took his opportunity.
He entered Avadh in darkness,
And went into the palace, leaving his chariot at the gate.
All who heard the news
Came to the king's door to look at the chariot.
Recognizing the chariot, and seeing the restless horses,
Their bodies grew weak with apprehension like hailstones melting
    in the heat.
The men and women of the city were distraught
Like schools of fish in receding water.

> Hearing of the minister's arrival,
> All the royal women grew troubled.
> To him, the palace appeared desolate and terrifying,
> Like an abode of ghosts and spirits.   (147)

Deeply distressed, the queens all questioned him,
But he could not answer, his voice failed him.
His ears could not hear, his eyes could not see,
And he asked everyone, 'Tell me, where is the king?'
The serving women, seeing the minister's confusion,
Led him to Kaushalya's apartments.
Entering, Sumantra beheld the king as wan and listless
As the moon without nectar.[27]
Forsaking throne and couch, and bereft of ornaments,
The king lay upon the ground, utterly wretched.
Heaving deep sighs he grieved and lamented,
Like Yayati hurled down from heaven.[28]
He heaved deep sighs full of grief every moment,
Like Sampati fallen from the sky with burned wings.[29]
'Ram! Ram! My beloved Ram!' he called,
And then, 'Ram! Lakshman! Vaidehi!'

> The minister, seeing him, cried, 'Victory and long life!'
> And fell prostrate before him.
> Upon hearing this, the king rose at once, and bewildered,
>   asked,
> 'Tell me, Sumantra, where is Ram?'   (148)

The king drew Sumantra to his bosom,
Like a drowning man who has found some support.
Affectionately, he seated him by his side,
And with his eyes full of tears, asked,
'Tell me, how is Ram, dear friend?
Where are Raghunath, Lakshman and Vaidehi?
Have you brought them back or did they leave for the forest?'
Hearing these words, the minister's eyes filled with tears.
Restless with sorrow, the king asked again,
'Give me news of Sita, Ram and Lakshman.'
Remembering Ram's beauty, virtue, and gentle nature

Again and again, the king grieved in his heart.
'I proclaimed him king, then gave him exile in the forest,
And hearing this, his heart remained unmoved by joy or grief.
Separated from such a son, my life's breath did not leave me—
Who is a sinner greater than I?

> Dear friend, take me there,
> Where Ram, Sita, Lakshman are.
> Otherwise, I tell you truly,
> My life's breath now wants to depart.'   (149)

Again and again, the king asked his minister,
'Tell me news of my beloved son,
And, dear friend, quickly devise some way
To bring Ram, Lakshman and Sita before my eyes.'
The minister composed himself and replied in gentle tones,
'Maharaj, you are learned and wise,
A mighty warrior, foremost amongst the steadfast, lord,
And you have always served sadhus and sages.
But birth and death, the experience of joy and sorrow,
Loss and gain, union and separation from those we love,
Are all subject to time and destiny, lord,
And as inexorable as night following day.
Fools rejoice in happiness and weep in adversity,
But the steadfast regard both the same in their hearts.
So, considering this matter sensibly and wisely, take courage
And abandon grief, you who are the benefactor of all.

> Their first halt was by the Tamasa,
> The second, on the banks of the divine Ganga.
> There they bathed and drank only water,
> The two heroes and Sita.   (150)

The boatman rendered great service to them,
And they passed that night at Singraur.[viii]
As soon as day broke, they called for the milk of the banyan tree
And matted their hair into a crown upon their heads.
Ram's friend, Guha, then called for a boat.
After helping his beloved wife on it, Raghurai climbed in,
And Lakshman, carefully placing their bows and arrows in the boat,
Also climbed aboard upon the Lord's command.
Seeing me distraught with sorrow, Raghubir
Composed himself and spoke sweet words to me.
"Respected sir, convey to my father my salutations,
And clasp again and again his lotus feet.
There, at his feet, again entreat him,
'Father, do not be anxious about me.
In the forest and on the road, we will fare happily and well,
By your grace, your love and the merit of your good actions.

By your love, Father, I will receive
Every happiness in going to the forest.
Then, after fulfilling your orders, I will safely return
To behold once more your feet.'
Consoling all my mothers, and falling
Again and again at their feet, implore them—
Says Tulsi—'Make every effort to ensure
The king of Koshal remains happy.'

Give this message to my guru, Vasishtha,
Clasping his lotus feet again and again,
'Give only such counsel to the lord of Avadh
That he no longer grieves for me.' (151)

_____

viii Shringberpur

Bow to the townspeople and my kinsfolk all,
And place before them my humble entreaty,
'He alone will be my benefactor in every way
Whose actions ensure the happiness of the lord of men.'
And give my message to Bharat, when he returns,
'Do not give up what is moral and right upon attaining kingly status,
Protect your subjects in action, thought and speech,
And serve our mothers, regarding them all the same.
Honour our bond of brotherhood till the end, brother,
By serving our father, our mothers and our kin.
And, dearest brother, look after the king in such a manner
That he never, in any way, grieves for me.'"
Lakshman spoke some harsh words,
But Ram forbade him to speak, and then implored me,
Making me swear again and again in his name,
"Sire, do not repeat Lakshman's childish talk there."

> Sita saluted me and began to say something,
> But was overwhelmed with love.
> Her voice faltered, her eyes filled with tears,
> And her body trembled with emotion.   (152)

At that very moment, at a sign from Raghubar,
The boatman began to guide the boat to the other side.
In this way the crown-jewel of the Raghu line departed,
While I stood looking on, a stone upon my heart.
But how can I describe my own anguish
In returning alive, bearing Ram's message?'
Saying this, the minister could speak no more—
He was overcome by loss, remorse and grief.
The king, when he heard the charioteer's words,
Fell to the ground, with grief a raging fire in his heart.
A deep sorrow filled his heart, and distraught, he writhed in agony,
Like a fish caught in the foam of the first rains.

The queens all wailed and wept and lamented—
How can their great misfortune be described?
Hearing their lamentation, even sorrow grew sorrowful,
And fortitude itself lost courage.

> Upon hearing the uproar in the royal apartments,
> A great tumult arose in Avadh,
> As though a cruel bolt of thunder had fallen in the night
> Upon a vast forest full of birds.   (153)

The king's life-breath flew up into his throat—
The lord of the earth was as distraught as a serpent bereft of
    its jewel.
All his senses grew troubled and uneasy,
Like a cluster of lotuses in a lake without water.
Kaushalya, seeing the king so feeble and sorrowful,
Knew in her heart that the sun of the solar dynasty was setting.
Composing herself, Ram's mother
Spoke words appropriate to the moment.
'Lord, ponder in your heart and understand
That separation from Ram is the boundless ocean,
You are the helmsman, and Avadh the ship,
Upon which have climbed aboard as passengers, all those dear to us.
If you take courage and compose yourself, the ship will reach the
    other shore,
If not, our whole family will drown.
If you take this entreaty of mine into your heart, my beloved
    husband,
You will see Ram, Lakshman and Sita again.'

> Hearing the gentle words of his beloved queen,
> The king opened his eyes and looked up,
> Like a fish writhing in agony,
> Which is sprinkled with cool water.   (154)

Taking courage, the lord of the earth sat up.
'Tell me, Sumantra, where is compassionate Ram?
Where is Lakshman? Where is my beloved Ram?
And where is my dear daughter-in-law, Vaidehi?'
The king, distraught, wept and lamented in many ways,
And that night became like an aeon and would not end.
The curse of the blind ascetic came back to his mind,
And he told Kaushalya the whole story.[30]
He grew deeply distressed as he narrated the story.
'Fie on the hope of a life bereft of Ram!
What will I gain by holding on to a body
That failed to honour my vow of love?
Hai Raghunandan, dear as my life's breath!
Too many days have passed, living without you!
Hai Janaki, Lakshman! Hai Raghubar,
Rain-bearing cloud that gladdened the chatak that is your
        father's heart!'

        Crying 'Ram! Ram!' and again 'Ram!'
        And then once more, 'Ram! Ram!' and 'Ram!'
        The king gave up his body in the grief of separation
                from Raghubar
        And went to the abode of the gods.   (155)

In life and death, Dasharath reaped his full reward,
And his bright renown spread across countless universes.
Living, he gazed upon the radiant moon of Ram's countenance,
And made glorious his death by making separation from Ram his
        reason for it.
Distracted with grief, the queens all wept and wailed,
Recounting his beauty, amiability, strength and glory.
They wept and lamented in many ways,
Falling to the ground again and again.
Distraught, the menservants and waiting-women wept,

And in every house in the city, the people wailed and cried.
'Today the sun of the solar line has set,
The pinnacle of dharma, the accumulation of virtue and beauty.'
All reviled Kaikeyi and called her names,
She, who had deprived the world of its eyes.
In this way, the night passed in lamentation,
Till all the great and learned munis arrived.

> Then Muni Vasishtha related many legends
> In keeping with the occasion,
> Thus removing everyone's sorrow
> With the light of his wisdom. (156)

He had the king's body placed in a boat filled with oil,
And summoning messengers, instructed them thus:
'Run as fast as you can to Bharat,
But of the king's death, tell no one, anywhere.
When you are with Bharat, say only this,
"Your guru has sent us to summon both you brothers."'
Upon receiving the muni's order, they rushed away
At a speed that would shame the fastest horses.
From the time that these misfortunes began in Avadh,
Bharat had been visited by bad omens.
He had terrifying nightmares at night,
And waking, imagined countless disasters.
Daily, he feasted Brahmans and gave them alms,
And offered worship to Shiv in many ways.
Propitiating the great god in his heart, he begged of him
The well-being of his mother, father, kinsfolk and brothers.

> In this way was Bharat worrying
> When the messengers arrived,
> And as soon as he heard his guru's command,
> He set forth, invoking Ganesh. (157)

He went, urging on his horses, as fleet as the wind,
Crossing treacherous rivers, mountains and dense forests,
But in his heart was great anxiety and nothing gave him comfort,
And he wished that he could fly.
An instant seemed like a year to him.
In this manner, Bharat drew near the city,
And as he entered, evil omens began to appear—
Crows, perched in inauspicious places, cawed ominously,
Donkeys and jackals called harshly, presaging misfortune—
Listening to these sounds was like a spear in Bharat's heart.
Lakes, rivers, forests and gardens were without lustre,
And the city appeared dismal and desolate.
The birds, deer, elephants and horses were impossible to look upon,
So wasted were they by the evil disease of separation from Ram.
The men and women of the city were utterly miserable,
As though they had all lost all that they possessed.

> The townsfolk he met said nothing,
> But made obeisance and went away.
> They could not ask after Bharat's well-being,
> For their hearts were full of fear and grief.   (158)

The marketplaces and streets were as deserted and desolate,
As though a great fire had swept through the city in all
     ten directions.
When the princess of Kaikeya heard of her son's approach,
She, who was the moon to the lotuses of the solar line, rejoiced.
She made ready the arti, and springing up, happily ran to greet him.
Meeting him at the gate, she brought him into the palace.
Bharat saw his family distressed and sad,
Like a cluster of lotuses stricken by frost.
Only Kaikeyi was happy, and as joyfully jubilant
As a Kirat woman who has set the forest on fire.
Seeing her son fearful and anxious,

She asked, 'Is all well at my father's home?'
Bharat assured her that all was well,
And asked after the well-being of his own family.
'Tell me, where is Father, where all my mothers?
Where is Sita, and where my dear brothers, Ram and Lakshman?'

> Hearing her son's words full of love,
> She filled her eyes with false tears,
> Then, uttering words that pierced Bharat's ears and heart
>   like a spear,
> The sinful woman spoke.   (159)

'Son, I had arranged everything so well
With poor Manthara's help.
But then fate spoilt some of my plans halfway,
And the lord of this earth left for Indra's realm.'
Hearing this, Bharat was overcome with grief,
Like an elephant petrified by a lion's roar.
Crying 'Father! Father! Hai, my father!'
He fell to the ground, utterly distraught.
'I could not see you when you left me,
Nor did you entrust me to Ram, dear Father.'
Then, taking courage and composing himself, he stood up.
'Tell me the cause of my father's death, mother.'
Hearing her son's question, Kaikeyi replied
As though cutting open his vital organs and pouring poison into
     the incision.
She related with a joyous heart, from the very beginning,
All her cruel and deceitful doings.

> Bharat forgot even his father's death
> When he heard of Ram's departure for the forest,
> And realizing that he himself was the cause,
> Stood still, speechless with shock.   (160)

Seeing him distraught, she began to comfort her son—
But it was as though she was rubbing salt into a burn.
'Dear son, the king is not worthy of grief—
He gathered merit and fame, and experienced life's pleasures to
    the full.
Living, he obtained all the fruits of his birth,
And at the end, he left for Indra's abode.
Consider this, and give up grief,
And with your court, reign over this city.'
Listening to her, the prince was filled with dismay and
    great trepidation—
Her words were like burning sparks upon a festering wound.
Pulling himself together, he drew a deep breath and said,
'Wretched woman, you are in every way the ruin of our line!
If such indeed was your wicked desire,
Why did you not kill me as soon as I was born?
You cut down a great tree to water a shoot,
And drained the pond of water to keep a fish alive!

> Though I belong to the solar dynasty, with Dasharath as
>   my father
> And brothers like Ram and Lakshman,
> You, Mother, became my mother!
> Truly, nothing prevails against fate!   (161)

Depraved woman, when you conceived of this vile plan in
    your mind,
Why did your heart not shatter into pieces?
Demanding the boon, was there no pain in your heart?
Did your tongue not rot, or your mouth fester with maggots?
And how did the king trust you?
At the hour of death, Vidhi robbed him of his good sense!
But even the Creator does not know the ways of a woman's heart—
Repository of all deceit, crime and wrongdoing.

Straightforward, good-natured and virtuous was the king—
How could he understand a woman's nature?
What living creature is there in this world,
To whom Raghunath is not dear as life?
That same Ram seemed to you an enemy!
Tell me the truth, who are you?
But you are what you are—so blacken your face with ink,
And get up and go sit somewhere out of my sight!

> From one whose heart was hostile to Ram
> Did Vidhi bring me forth,
> So who is as sinful as I?
> In vain do I say anything to you.'   (162)

When Shatrughna heard of their mother's cruelty,
He burned with anger, but was helpless.
At that very moment the hunchback appeared,
Made up in fine clothes and jewels of many kinds.
Seeing her, Lakshman's twin was filled with rage,
Like a burning fire upon which has been poured a libation of ghee.
He sprang forward and taking aim, kicked her on the hump
And she fell flat on her face upon the ground, bawling and yelling.
Her hump was shattered, her skull split,
Her teeth broken, and her mouth streamed with blood.
'Oh God, what harm did I do,
To receive this unjust reward for the good I did?'
Hearing this, and seeing that she was deceitful from head to toe,
Ripuhan[ix] grabbed her by her topknot and began dragging
     her about,
Till the merciful Bharat made him release her.
The two brothers then went to Kaushalya.

[ix] Shatrughna

In shabby garments, distraught with grief, her face pale
And her body wasted with the heavy burden of sorrow,
She was like a lovely golden vine from Indra's garden
Destroyed by frost in the forest.   (163)

Seeing Bharat, she sprang up and ran to meet him,
But swooned and fell in a faint to the ground.
Seeing this, Bharat was deeply distressed,
And fell at her feet, forgetting his own state.
'Mother, where is my father? Show him to me.
Where is Sita, and where my two brothers, Ram and Lakshman?
Why was Kaikeyi born into this world,
Or if born, why couldn't she have been barren,
She who gave birth to me, I, a blot upon our lineage,
A receptacle of disgrace and the enemy of those I love?
In all the three worlds, who is more unfortunate than I,
Because of whom, Mother, you have been reduced to this state?
My father is in the abode of the gods, and Raghubar is in
        the forest—
I, like inauspicious Ketu, am the cause of all these injustices.
Fie on me, for I have become the forest fire in the bamboo grove,
And an accomplice in causing intolerable anguish,
        suffering and disgrace.'

The mother, hearing Bharat's sweet and gentle words,
Rose again, collecting herself.
Raising him up, she clasped him to her bosom
As tears flowed freely from her eyes.   (164)

That kind and gentle mother held him to her heart
With deep love, as though Ram himself had returned to her.
She then embraced Lakshman's younger brother—
Her grief and love could not be contained in her heart.
All those who saw her forgiving nature said,

'She is Ram's mother, so how else could she behave but so?'
That mother took Bharat upon her lap,
And wiping away his tears, spoke sweet and tender words.
'Even now, my beloved child, take courage,
And recognizing this to be an unpropitious time, abandon sorrow.
Do not dwell any more on loss and grief in your heart,
For you know that the course of time and fate is unalterable.
Do not blame anyone, my beloved son,
For fate has turned against me in every way,
That it keeps me alive in such grief.
Who knows what may be its pleasure next?

> It was at his father's command, dear son,
> That Raghubir gave up his jewels and fine clothes,
> And with neither dismay nor joy in his heart
> Donned his garments of bark.   (165)

With a cheerful countenance, neither attachment nor anger
    in his heart,
He comforted us all in every way.
Sita, hearing that he was leaving for the forest, clung to him—
She refused to remain behind, for she is devoted to Ram's feet.
The instant he heard this, Lakshman jumped up to
    accompany them,
And would not stay, though Raghunath made many efforts to
    dissuade him.
Then, bowing his head to all, Raghupati
Left with Sita and his younger brother.
Ram, Lakshman and Sita departed for the forest,
But I did not go with them, nor did I send my life's breath
    after them.
All this took place in front of these very eyes,
Even then my unfortunate spirit did not leave my body,
And yet I feel no shame at seeing my love—

I, the mother of a son like Ram!
The king knew when to live and when to die,
But my heart is a hundred times harder than adamant.'

> Hearing Kaushalya's words,
> Bharat and all the royal women
> Grew distraught, and broke into such cries of anguish
> That the king's palace seemed the abode of sorrow.   (166)

As Bharat and Shatrughna wailed in grief,
Kaushalya clasped them to her bosom.
She comforted Bharat in many ways
With wise and discerning words.
Bharat, too, comforted all the mothers,
With legends and tales from the Vedas and Puranas.
Then, without deceit, and in gentle words that were simple
    and pure,
Bharat spoke, folding his hands—
'The sins of killing one's mother, father, or son,
Of burning a cowshed or a Brahman village,
The sins of killing a woman or a child,
Or of poisoning a friend or a king—
All sins, great or small,
Of word, thought or deed, that are enumerated by the poets—
May God let all these sins be mine, Mother,
If this happened with my permission.

> Those who abandon the feet of Hari and Har
> And worship terrifying ghouls and demons instead—
> May God give me their fate, Mother,
> If I complied with these doings!   (167)

Those who sell the Vedas and milk dharma for their ends,
The traitors and informers, who proclaim the sins of others,

The deceitful, the dishonest, the quarrelsome or the bad-tempered,
Those who ridicule the Vedas, or are the enemies of the world,
The greedy, the dissolute, the lustful and lecherous,
Who look covetously at the wealth and wives of others—
May I share their dreadful fate, Mother,
If I agreed to any of this.
Those who have no regard for the company of the good,
Unfortunates who turn from the path of highest truth,
Who, gaining a human form, do not worship Hari,
And are not pleased by the glory of Hari and Har,
Who abandon the path of the Vedas to walk instead a
     contrary road,
Scoundrels who disguise themselves and cheat and swindle
     the world—
May Shankar give me their fate, Mother,
If I even knew of this plot.'

When his mother, Kaushalya, heard Bharat's words,
So honest and sincere,
She said, 'You are always beloved of Ram,
Dear son, in speech, mind, and body.   (168)

Ram is dearer to you than your own life's breath,
And dearer to Raghupati than his own life are you.
The moon might drip poison or snow emit fire,
Water-creatures turn away from water,
Or wisdom dawn without delusion dying—
But you could never be hostile to Ram.
Those in this world who say that you agreed to this,
Will never, even in their dreams, find happiness or salvation.'
So saying, his mother clasped Bharat to her bosom,
As her breasts flowed with milk and her eyes filled with tears.
Grieving and lamenting thus,
They sat, and, in this manner, the whole night passed.

Then the munis Vamdev and Vasishtha came,
And summoned all the ministers and prominent citizens.
Muni Vasishtha then gave Bharat much advice,
Discoursing on the highest truth in words appropriate to the occasion.

> 'Son, take courage and remaining steadfast in your heart,
> Do what the occasion demands today.'
> Hearing his guru's words, Bharat rose
> And ordered that all be made ready.   (169)

The king's body was bathed in accordance with the Vedas
And a magnificent bier prepared.
Clasping their feet, Bharat kept back all his mothers[31]
And the queens lived on in the hope of seeing Ram again.
Many loads of sandalwood and agarwood arrived
And countless kinds of other fragrant substances.
A funeral pyre was built on the banks of the Sarju,
Like a glorious stairway to the abode of the gods.
Thus all the cremation rites were performed,
And after the ritual bath, the offering of sesame seeds was made.[32]
After due study of the sacred texts and all the Vedas and Puranas,
Bharat made the final offering to the dead king's soul.[33]
Whatever orders the great muni gave,
Bharat carried out fully and a thousand times over.
After he had been ritually purified, he gave gifts and alms
Of cows, horses, elephants and chariots of many kinds,

> Thrones, ornaments, fine raiment,
> Grain, land, money and houses—
> All this Bharat gave the Brahmans, and they, gods upon earth,
> Receiving it, had their every wish fulfilled.   (170)

The manner in which Bharat performed all the last rites for his father
Cannot be told even by a thousand tongues.

Then, determining an auspicious day, the great
    Muni Vasishtha came
And summoned all the ministers and important citizens.
They all took their seats in the royal council chamber.
The muni then sent for Bharat and Shatrughna.
Vasishtha seated Bharat by his side,
And discoursed on duty and right conduct.
First, the great sage recounted the full story
Of Kaikeyi's devious doings,
And praised the king's devotion to dharma and truth,
Who gave up his body to fulfil his love.
As he described Ram's virtues and gentle nature,
The great muni's eyes filled with tears and he trembled
    with emotion,
Then, as he spoke of Lakshman and Sita's love for Ram,
That wise and learned muni was lost in grief and love.

    'Listen, Bharat, destiny is powerful,'
    Said the lord of munis, lamenting.
    'Loss and gain, life and death,
    Fame and disgrace—all lie in the hands of providence.   (171)

Considering this, whom can we blame
And with whom, without reason, can we be angry?
Dear son, reflect upon this in your heart:
King Dasharath does not require your grief.
Grieve for the Brahman who is ignorant of the Vedas,
And who, abandoning his dharma, remains immersed in
    sensual pleasures.
Grieve for the king who knows not prudence nor statecraft,
And whose subjects are not dear to him as life.
Grieve for the merchant who is a miser despite being wealthy,
And who knows not his duty towards a guest nor the worship
    of Shiv.[34]

Grieve for the Shudra who insults a Brahman,
And who is foul-mouthed, arrogant and vain about his knowledge.
Grieve too for the woman who deceives her husband,
And who is perverse, quarrelsome and self-willed.
Grieve for the student who abandons his own vows,
And who does not follow the commands of his guru.

> Grieve for the householder who, in the grip of delusion,
> Abandons the path of duty.
> Grieve for the ascetic who is addicted to this world of illusion
> And lacks both discernment and detachment.   (172)

Worthy of your grief is that hermit who
Has abandoned penance and prefers the pleasures of this world.
Grieve for the traitor, for the one angry without reason,
And the one against his mother, father, guru, or brother.
Grieve in every way for the one who injures others,
Who cherishes his own body but is utterly merciless.
In every way deserving of grief is the one
Who does not abandon deceit to become a follower of Hari.
But the king of Koshal does not deserve grief,
For his might and power are manifest in all the fourteen spheres.
There never was, or is, or will ever be,
A protector of the earth, Bharat, like your father.
Vidhi, Hari, and Har, Indra and the lords of the eight quarters,
All sing the praises of Dasharath.

> Tell me, dear son, in what manner
> Can one praise him enough
> Who has such pure and virtuous sons
> Like Ram, Lakshman, you and Shatrughna?   (173)

The lord of the earth was fortunate in every way,
And there is no point in lamenting over him.

Hear this and consider, and abandoning grief,
Honour and carry out the king's royal command.
The king has given you the office of king,
And you should fulfil your father's word,
Who gave up Ram for the sake of his promise,
And then sacrificed his body in the fire of his anguish at separation
    from Ram.
His word was dear to the king of men, he did not care about his life,
Make true then, son, your father's promise.
With reverence obey the king's royal command,
For in this lies all manner of good for you.
Parashuram, honouring his father's command,
Killed his mother, as all the spheres of the world are witness,[35]
And Yayati's son gave him his own youth.[36]
For obeying a father's command, they incurred neither sin nor infamy.

> Those who, without thought of right or wrong,
> Uphold their father's word,
> Become receptacles of bliss and glory
> And later dwell in the abode of Indra, lord of
>   the immortal gods.   (174)

You must certainly fulfil the king's word
And look after your subjects, abandoning your grief.
The king will be pleased in the abode of the gods,
While you will earn merit and glory and no blame.
It is prescribed in the Vedas, and is agreed upon by all
That he to whom a father gives it, gets the crown.
So rule the kingdom, abandoning remorse.
Listen to my advice, knowing it is to your benefit.
Hearing of it, Ram and Vaidehi will be happy,
And no wise man will call it inappropriate.
Kaushalya and all your other mothers,
Will be happy in the happiness of your subjects.

Knowing your great bond with Ram,
They will in every way regard your action as good.
Hand over the kingdom to Ram on his return,
And serve him with flawless affection.'

    The ministers, with folded hands, entreated,
    'Please do as your guru commands,
    And when Raghupati returns, do at that time
    Whatever seems right and fitting.'   (175)

Kaushalya composed herself and said,
'Son, your guru's command is for your benefit,
So understanding this, respect and obey him.
Grieve no more, knowing the ways of fate.
Raghupati is in the forest, the lord of men in the abode of the gods,
Yet you, dear son, are hesitating in this fashion.
You, son, are now the sole support
Of your kinsfolk, subjects, ministers and all your mothers.
Seeing that providence is against us and times are harsh,
Take courage. I, your devoted mother, declare
That you should honour your guru's commands and do as he says,
Look after your subjects and ease our family's sorrow.'
Bharat heard the words of his guru and the approval of
    the ministers
And they were as soothing as sandalwood paste to his heart.
He then listened to his mother's sweet words,
Steeped in kindness, love and sincerity.

Hearing his mother's guileless words,
Bharat grew distraught.
His lotus eyes streamed with tears,
And watered fresh shoots of anguish in his heart.
Seeing his state at that moment,
All there forgot about themselves

Says Tulsi, and with reverence praised
That epitome of innate love.

> Bharat, most resolute of the resolute,
> Composed himself, and folding his lotus hands,
> In words that seemed dipped in amrit
> Made fitting reply to all.   (176)

'My guru has given me sound advice,
With which subjects and ministers all agree.
Considering it right and fitting, my mother, too, has given me
    her command,
And I certainly wish to honour her wishes and do as she says.
The word of guru, father, mother, master, or friend
Should be joyfully heard and obeyed, knowing it is for our
    own good.
To ponder whether it is right or wrong
Destroys dharma and piles a heavy burden of sin upon our heads.
You are giving me sincere advice,
Which if I follow, will be to my benefit.
Though I understand this very well,
My heart is still not content.
Now, please listen to my humble request,
And then give advice suitable for me.
Forgive my offence that I answer you back,
For the good do not tally the faults and virtues of the distressed.

> My father is in heaven, Sita and Ram in the forest,
> And you tell me to rule this kingdom?
> Do you see some benefit to me in this,
> Or will it fulfil some great purpose of your own?   (177)

My good lies in serving Sita's lord—
This my mother's treachery took away from me,

But I have searched my heart and come to the conclusion
That no other solution is good for me.
Of what account is this kingdom, filled with sorrow,
If I cannot see the feet of Lakshman, Ram and Sita?
A load of jewels is useless if one has no clothes,
Reflection upon the Absolute is pointless without detachment.
Sensual pleasures are useless for a body that is ill or in pain,
Prayer and penance are in vain without devotion to Hari,
A beautiful body is worthless without life,
And everything is worthless to me without Raghurai.
Give me your permission that I may go to Ram,
For in this alone lies my good.
In making me king, you seek your own good,
But you say so in the grip of delusion caused by love.

> Kaikeyi's son, of bent and crooked mind,
> Hostile to Ram, and without shame or honour—
> And you, in your delusion, hope for happiness
> Under the rule of a vile wretch like me!   (178)

I speak the truth, so hear me, all, and believe what I say—
A ruler of men must be upright and virtuous.
If you, insisting, give me the kingdom,
Earth will sink into hell that very instant.
Who is such an abode of sin as I,
Because of whom Sita and Ram were exiled to live in the forest?
The king banished Ram to the forest,
And the instant he was parted from him, left for the abode of the gods.
And I, the wretch who is the reason for all this injustice,
Sit and listen to it all with my reason intact.
I see this palace without Raghubir,
And endure the world's ridicule, yet my life's breath remains,
For it is indifferent towards the pure nectar that is love for Ram
And has an insatiable hunger for land and worldly pleasures.

How do I describe my hard heart,
Which has achieved notoriety by shaming adamant?

> But the effect is always harsher than its cause—
> That is no fault of mine.
> The thunderbolt is more formidable than the bones from
>   which it was fashioned,[37]
> And iron harder than the rock from which it is mined.   (179)

Enamoured of its body born of Kaikeyi,
My wretched spirit is exceedingly unlucky.
Since separated from the one I love, life is still dear to me,
I will have to see and hear much worse ahead.
She exiled Lakshman, Ram and Sita to the forest,
And did her husband a service by sending him to heaven.
She brought widowhood and infamy upon herself,
Gave grief and sorrow to our subjects,
And to me, joy, renown and a noble kingdom—
Kaikeyi has certainly taken care of everyone!
And now, what greater benefit than this can I have?
And on top of all this, you would give me the crown!
But since I was born into this world from Kaikeyi's womb,
None of this is wrong or unseemly for me.
Providence has accomplished all for me,
So why, then, do our subjects and this assembly need to help me?

> If a man possessed by the malign planets is also afflicted by a
>   disorder of the humours,
> And if he is then stung by a scorpion—
> If such a man is made to drink hard liquor,
> Tell me, what kind of remedy is that?   (180)

Whatever was fitting in this world for Kaikeyi's son,
The wise and discerning Creator has already given me.

But that I am also Dasharath's son and Ram's younger brother,
These honours Vidhi has bestowed upon me in vain.
All of you tell me to let myself be crowned,
For the king's command is good for all.
What answer can I give, and to whom?
Tell me freely what pleases you.
Leaving aside me and my wretched mother,
Who will say that all this was well done?
In this animate and inanimate creation, who is there, except me,
To whom Sita and Ram are not dear as life itself?
That this supreme loss seems a great gain to you all,
Is my misfortune and no one's fault.
You are overwhelmed by doubt, goodness and love,
So whatever any of you say is all fitting and right.

       Ram's mother is most gentle and kind-hearted
       And has special affection for me.
       Seeing my miserable state,
       She speaks out of innate love.   (181)

The world knows that my guru is an ocean of discernment,
For whom the universe is like a ber fruit on the palm of his hand.
Yet he, too, is ready with preparations for my coronation,
For when fate turns its face away, so does everyone else.
Except Ram and Sita, there is no one in this world
Who will not say that I did not agree to all this.
And I must listen and bear it gladly,
For where there is water, there will be mud.
I do not fear being called vile in this world,
Nor am I concerned about my fate in the next.
Only one intolerable anguish burns my heart—
That Sita and Ram are suffering because of me.
Lakshman has received life's best reward—
Giving up everything, he has fixed his mind on Ram's feet.

But I was born to exile Raghubar to the forest.
Unlucky me—of what account is my false remorse?

> I proclaim my terrible wretchedness
> Before you all with bowed head—
> Unless I see Raghunath's feet,
> The burning in my heart will not be soothed.   (182)

I can think of no other remedy—
For who but Raghubar can understand my heart?
Stamped upon my mind there is only this one resolve—
At dawn, I must go to my lord.
Even though I am a wicked sinner,
And all these troubles arose because of me,
Yet, seeing me before him, seeking refuge,
He will forgive it all in his extraordinary compassion.
Good-natured, gentle, with an utterly guileless disposition,
Raghurai is the abode of love and compassion.
Ram has never hurt even an enemy,
And I, though contrary, am his child and slave.
So, all of you assembled here, knowing it to be for my good,
Give me your permission and your blessing,
So that, hearing my prayer and knowing me to be his servant,
Ram will return to the capital.

> Though I was born of an evil mother,
> And am a rogue and forever to blame,
> I have faith that, knowing me to be his own,
> Raghubir will not abandon me.'   (183)

Bharat's words pleased everyone,
Steeped as they were in the nectar of his love for Ram.
The people, scorched by the deadly poison of separation,
Heard them like a potent healing mantra and revived.

Mothers, ministers, guru, and the men and women of the city,
All grew distraught with love.
They praised Bharat again and again, saying,
'Ram's love is embodied in your form!
But Bharat, dear son, you would not say otherwise,
For you are as dear to Ram as his own life's breath.
The vile wretch who, in his own stupidity,
Would ascribe to you your mother's wickedness,
That rogue, with millions of his ancestors,
Will dwell in hell for a hundred kalpas!
A serpent's crest-jewel does not take within itself the snake's sins
        and evil doings,
But removes poison, and destroys poverty and pain.

        Most definitely let us go, Bharat, to the forest where Ram is—
        Your plan is good,
        And to all of us drowning in this ocean of grief,
        You have given support.'   (184)

There was great happiness in everyone's heart,
They rejoiced like peacocks and chataks hearing the rumble
        of rainclouds.
Seeing his firm resolve to depart at dawn,
Bharat became as dear as life to them all.
Saluting the muni and bowing their heads to Bharat,
They all took their leave and returned home.
'Blessed is Bharat's life in this world!' they cried,
Praising his goodness and love as they went.
Declaring to each other, 'A great decision has been taken!'
They all began to make preparations for departure.
Those who had to stay behind to guard the houses,
Felt as if their throats had been cut.
Some said, 'Don't ask anyone to stay behind,
For who in this world does not want life's reward?

Let them burn, those riches, houses, luxuries,
Friends, mothers, fathers, brothers
Who do not gladly help
To bring you to Ram's feet.'   (185)

In every home, vehicles of many kinds were prepared,
Every heart was full of joy at the thought of the departure at dawn.
Bharat returned home, reflecting,
'This city, with its horses, elephants, mansions, treasuries—
All this wealth belongs to Raghupati.
If I leave without making any effort to safeguard it,
The result will not be good for me,
For injury to a master is the crowning sin.
A servant is one who acts for his master's good,
Even though others accuse him of a million faults.'
Reflecting thus, he summoned trusty servants
Who would not, even in dream, stray from their duty.
Confiding his concerns to them, he courteously explained what he
      required of them,
And assigned to each tasks suited to his ability.
Making all arrangements and appointing the guards,
Bharat went to Ram's mother, Kaushalya.

Bharat, who understood the nature of love,
Knew that all his mothers were in distress,
And so he ordered palanquins to be prepared
And carriages with comfortable seats.   (186)

Like chakwas and chakwis, the men and women of the city
Longed for dawn with anguished hearts.
The night passed in wakefulness—till it was dawn,
And Bharat summoned his wise ministers,
Saying, 'Take with you all that is necessary for the coronation,
For Muni Vasishtha will crown Ram king in the forest itself.

Go at once!' Hearing this, the ministers bowed
And quickly readied horses, chariots and elephants.
With his wife, Arundhati, and all that was needed for a
    fire-sacrifice,
The sage Vasishtha was the first to mount a chariot.
Then a host of other Brahmans, storehouses of asceticism and
    spiritual radiance,
Mounted various vehicles and followed.
All the townsfolk, in their fully equipped and decorated carriages,
Departed too, for Chitrakut.
All the queens climbed into palanquins
Too beautiful to describe, and went forth.

> Leaving the city in the care of trusted servants,
> And after respectfully seeing everyone off,
> The two brothers, Bharat and Shatrughna, set forth,
> Meditating on Ram and Sita's feet.   (187)

Seized with the longing to see Ram, all the men and women
Rushed forward as eagerly as thirsty elephants spying water.
Reflecting in their hearts that Sita and Ram were in exile in
    the forest,
Bharat and his younger brother went on foot.
Seeing their love, the people were enraptured,
And dismounting, continued on foot, forsaking elephants, horses
    and chariots.
Then, going up to Bharat, stopping her palanquin by his side,
Ram's mother gently said,
'I, your mother, entreat you with love—mount your chariot,
    dear son,
Otherwise all our dear kinsfolk will suffer.
Since you are walking, everyone else is walking too,
But, weak with sorrow, they are not fit for the road.'
Honouring her words, and bowing their heads at her feet,

The two brothers mounted a chariot and continued on their way.
That first day, they made camp by the Tamasa,
And the second day, they rested by the banks of the Gomati.

> Some drank only water and ate only fruit,
> Some ate only one meal at nightfall.
> For Ram's sake, they observed these vows and fasts,
> Giving up all pleasure and adornment.   (188)

After resting by the banks of the Sai, they set forth at daybreak,
And soon drew near Shringberpur.
The Nishad chief, Guha, heard the news of their approach,
And reflected sadly to himself,
'For what reason does Bharat go to the forest?
He definitely has some treacherous plan in mind.
If he had no deceit in his heart,
Why would he bring an army with him?
He thinks, "I will kill Ram and his young brother, Lakshman,
And then happily reign, unopposed."
Bharat has given no thought to the principles of sound statecraft—
First he brought disgrace upon himself, and now he is bent on
     losing his life,
For even if all the gods and demons unite to fight,
They cannot conquer Ram in battle.
But what wonder that Bharat is acting thus—
After all, poisonous vines never bear life-giving fruit.'

> Thinking thus, Guha said to his kinsmen,
> 'Be watchful and vigilant, all.
> Gather the oars and boats and sink them,
> And guard all the ghats.   (189)

Arm yourselves fully and block the ghats,
Stand firm all of you, and be ready to die.

I will confront Bharat in single combat,
And as long as I live, I will not let him cross the sacred Ganga.
To die in battle, and that too on the banks of the holy river,
While serving Ram's purpose with this transient body,
At Bharat's hands, his brother and a king—and I
    a lowborn servant!
What great good fortune to receive such a death!
I will do battle to serve my master's purpose,
And my fame will make bright the fourteen spheres,
As I give up my life for Raghunath's sake.
I hold the sweets of bliss in both hands.[38]
One who is not numbered amongst the good,
Or counted amongst Ram's devotees,
Lives in vain in this world, a burden on the earth,
And an axe to the tree of his mother's youth.'

    His grief departing, the Nishad chief
    Roused all his men,
    And, meditating upon Ram, called at once
    For his quiver, bow and armour.   (190)

'Quickly, brothers, make ready your weapons,
And on hearing my command, let no one hold back.'
'Very well, lord,' said all with joy,
And began to encourage and spur each other on.
Bowing to their chief one by one, the Nishads set forth,
Valiant warriors, all eager for battle.
Meditating upon the sandals of Ram's lotus feet,
They tied on their small quivers, and strung their short bows.
They put on their armour, donned their helmets of iron,
And made ready their axes, bamboo cudgels and spears.
Some who were especially adept with shield and sword,
Leaped in the air so lightly, it was as though they had left
    the earth.

Preparing their battle gear and forming their own companies,
They went and bowed before Guha, their chief.
Looking upon his valiant warriors and knowing them to able in
    every way,
He respectfully greeted them all, addressing each one by name.

    'Do not let me down, brothers—
    Today, my greatest task lies ahead of me.'
    His brave warriors thundered in reply,
    'Stay firm, mighty hero!   (191)

By Ram's great majesty and your strength, lord,
We will render Bharat's army without soldiers, without horses.
As long as we live, we will not set a foot in retreat,
But will strew the earth with trunks and heads!'
Looking at his brave band of warriors, the Nishad chief
Called out, 'Sound the battle drums!'
Just as he said this, someone on his left sneezed,
And soothsayers declared, 'The battlefield is favourable,
    we will win.'
But one old man, reflecting upon the omen, said,
'Meet Bharat. There will be no fight.
He goes to persuade Ram to return—
The omen says there will be no battle.'
Hearing this, Guha replied, 'The old man speaks well;
Fools act in haste and later repent.
Without ascertaining the goodness of Bharat's nature
And understanding his true disposition, to fight may do
    great harm.

    Hold the ghats and stay in your companies, warriors all,
    While I go to meet him and find out what's in his heart.
    Determining if he is friend or foe or neutral,
    I will return and take action accordingly.   (192)

I will know his love from his good behaviour,
For enmity and affection cannot be hidden.'
So saying, he began to put together a gift,
And called for tubers, roots, fruits, fowl and venison.
Bearers also brought load after heavy load
Of fat and full-grown pathin fish.
He prepared his offering, and departed to meet Bharat—
Auspicious omens of happiness and good fortune
    accompanied him.
Sighting Bharat's party, he declared his name, and from afar
Prostrated himself before the lord of sages.[x]
Knowing he was dear to Ram, the great muni gave him
    his blessing,
And then told Bharat about him.
Just hearing that he was Ram's friend, Bharat abandoned
    his chariot—
Dismounting, he ran to meet him, full of love.
Guha told him his name, caste and village,
And made obeisance, his forehead to the ground.

    Seeing him lying prostrate in homage before him,
    Bharat raised him and clasped him to his bosom.
    It was as though he had met Lakshman,
    And his heart could not contain his love.   (193)

Bharat embraced Guha with deep affection.
And the people enviously praised love's ways.
With bliss-conferring cries of 'Blessings, blessings!'
The gods rained down flowers and lauded them.
'He who is considered base and lowborn in every way by worldly
    custom and the Vedas,
The touch of whose shadow requires a purificatory bath,

---

[x]   Vasishtha, who was leading the procession from Avadh

That same man does Ram's younger brother embrace,
His whole body trembling with joy at meeting him.
Those who say "Ram, Ram" even while yawning,
Are never approached by the multitude of sins.
And here is one whom Ram has taken into his heart,
Bestowing upon him and his people the power to purify the world.
If Karamnasa's water falls into the sacred Ganga,
Who, tell us, will not pour it on his head?
As the world knows, merely by repeating the name of
        Ram backwards,
Valmiki became equal to Brahma!

> Even the ignorant, the baseborn, the savage, the outcast,
> Kols, Kirats, Shvapachas, Shabaras, Khasiyas and Jamanas,[39]
> By merely uttering the name of Ram become supremely pure
> And renowned in all the worlds.   (194)

This is no wonder, it has been so age after age,
For whom has Raghubir not exalted?'
The gods thus declared the glory of Ram's name,
And, hearing their praise, the people of Avadh rejoiced.
Bharat met Ram's friend with great affection
And asked after his well-being, health and happiness.
The instant he saw Bharat's goodness and love,
The Nishad chief was so enraptured that he lost all awareness
        of his own body.
The awe, love and joy in his heart grew so great,
That he just stood still and stared at Bharat.
Then, composing himself, and bowing again at Bharat's feet,
He folded his hands, and lovingly spoke these humble words:
'Now that I have seen your lotus feet, the source of all well-being,
I know my welfare to be assured in all three times, past, present
        and future.
And now, lord, by your supreme grace,

I am supremely blessed, with countless generations of my
 forefathers and descendants.

 Considering my past deeds and base descent,
 And then seeing the Lord's greatness in his heart,
 He who still does not worship Raghubir's feet,
 Has been cheated by the Creator of this world. (195)

I am deceitful, cowardly, dull-witted and baseborn,
And outside the laws of society and scripture.
Yet, from the moment that Ram made me his own,
I have become the ornament of the worlds.'
Seeing his love and hearing his courteous and modest words,
Bharat's younger brother, Shatrughna, then embraced him.
And the Nishad chief, courteously giving his name,
Made reverent obeisance to all the queens.
Considering him the same as Lakshman, they gave him their blessing,
'May you live happily for ten million years!'
Seeing the Nishad, the men and women of the city
Were as glad as though they had seen Lakshman,
And declared, 'He has received his life's reward,
For gracious Ram has embraced him, enfolding him in his arms!'
The Nishad, hearing this praise of his good fortune,
Led them with a rejoicing heart.

 At a sign from him, all his attendants,
 Understanding their master's wish, went ahead
 And made ready resting-places in homes, beneath trees,
 Beside ponds, in gardens and in groves. (196)

When Bharat saw Shringberpur,
He was overcome with love and grew weak in every limb.
As he walked leaning upon the Nishad for support, they looked
 so glorious,

It seemed as though Humility and Love had assumed bodily form.
Thus Bharat, accompanied by his entire army,
Went and looked upon the Ganga, which purifies the world.
He made obeisance at the ghat where Ram had bathed,
And became as lost in joy as though meeting Ram himself.
The men and women of the city also made obeisance,
And gazed rejoicing at the water infused with the divine.
After taking a dip in the river, they prayed with folded hands,
'May our love for Ramchandra's feet never diminish.'
Bharat declared, 'River of the gods, your sand
Bestows happiness upon all, and to your servants it is the divine
     cow that grants all desires.
With folded hands, I ask this boon of you:
Simple, innate, spontaneous love for Sita and Ram's feet.'

> In this manner, after bathing in the river,
> And receiving his guru's permission,
> Having made sure that all the mothers had bathed in
>   the sacred river too,
> He went to the encampment, taking them with him.   (197)

The people had pitched their tents here and there,
And Bharat inquired after them all.
Then, having worshipped the gods, and received their
     guru's permission,
The two brothers went to Ram's mother.
Pressing their feet, and speaking sweet words,
Bharat honoured all the mothers.
Then, entrusting their care to his brother,
He himself summoned the Nishad chief.
He walked hand-in-hand with his friend,
His body weak, for his love was great.
He asked his friend, 'Show me that place,
To soothe the burning in my eyes and heart,

Where Sita, Ram and Lakshman slept at night.'
As he spoke, the corners of his eyes filled with tears.
Hearing Bharat's words, the Nishad was filled with grief,
And immediately took him there,

> Where, under the sacred sinsupa tree,
> Raghubar had rested.
> Prostrating, Bharat made obeisance,
> With profound love and reverence.   (198)

Seeing the lovely mat of kush grass,
He offered homage, reverently pacing around it from left
    to right,[40]
And took the dust of their footprints upon his eyes.
It is impossible to describe the magnitude of his love.
He saw a few gold sequins,
And placed them upon his head, regarding them the same as Sita.
Then, with his eyes full of tears, and a heart full of remorse,
He said to his friend in gentle tones,
'Separated from Sita, these have lost their beauty and brilliance,
Just like the men and women of Avadh dulled with sorrow.
Her father is Janak—to whom shall I compare him,
Who holds both worldly pleasure and spiritual practice in the palm
    of his hand?
Her father-in-law, Dasharath, was the lord of the earth, the sun of
    the solar dynasty,
Envied even by Indra, lord of Amaravati.
And the lord of her life is Ram, lord of the Raghu line,
From whose glory derives all greatness.

> I see the mat of grass upon which lay Sita,
> That jewel amongst virtuous and devoted wives,
> And still my heart does not burst with horror!
> O Har! It must be harsher than Indra's thunderbolt!   (199)

My younger brother, Lakshman, so handsome and worthy
    of affection—
There never was a brother such as he, or is, or ever will be,
Beloved by the people, the darling of his father and mother,
As dear as their own lives to Sita and Raghubir,
Of delicate frame and youthful nature,
Whose body has never been touched by the hot winds
    of summer—
He is bearing all kinds of hardships in the forest!
Oh, this heart of mine puts to shame a million thunderbolts!
Ram, by taking birth, has filled the world with light,
For he is an ocean of beauty, goodness, joy and all virtue.
Subjects, kinsfolk, guru, father, mother—
Ram's good nature gives delight to all.
Even his enemies praise Ram,
For his speech, affability and humility steal all hearts.
A million Sharadas or a billion Sheshnags
Cannot enumerate the Lord's multitude of virtues.

    That he, bliss personified, jewel of the Raghu line,
    And abode of good fortune and joy,
    Should sleep upon the ground on a bed of grass—
    The ways of fate are truly mighty!   (200)

Ram's ears had never heard of sorrow,
For the king protected him like a tree of life,
And as eyelids guard the eyes and cobras their crest jewels,
Our mothers protected him day and night.
He now roams the forest on foot,
Living on tubers, roots, fruits and flowers.
A curse on Kaikeyi, root of misfortune,
Who turned against her husband, more beloved than her life.
Twice cursed am I, an unfortunate ocean of sin,
Because of whom this whole calamity happened.

The Creator made me the disgrace of my family,
And an evil mother made me my lord's enemy.'
Hearing his words, the Nishad chief lovingly consoled him,
'Master, why do you make these needless laments?
Ram is dear to you and you are dear to Ram,
And this much is certain—the fault lies with contrary fate alone.

Cruel are the doings of contrary fate,
Who drove your mother mad.
But that night, again and again,
The Lord with reverence praised you.
No one is as utterly dear to Ram as you—
I declare this on my oath.
Know that there will be joy at the end,
And take courage in your heart.

Ram knows the inner hearts of all,
He is the abode of humility, love and compassion.
Reflecting on this, steady your heart
And come now and rest.'   (201)

Hearing his friend's words, Bharat took courage
And went to his place of rest, meditating upon Raghubir.
The men and women of the city, learning where Ram had spent
    the night,
Went, full of grief, to see the place.
They paid homage, pacing reverently around the spot, and made
    obeisance,
Cursing Kaikeyi to their heart's content.
Their eyes filling with tears again and again,
They blamed contrary fate.
Some of them praised Bharat's love,
While others declared the king had fulfilled his own till the end.
They reproached themselves and praised the Nishad—

Who can describe their love and grief?
In this way, the people stayed awake all night,
And when dawn broke, the river crossing began.
The guru was helped into a sturdy, handsome boat,
And all the mothers into another newly built.
Within two hours, the whole party had crossed,
And Bharat, disembarking, made sure that all were safe.

After performing his morning rites, he saluted his mothers' feet
And bowed his head before his guru.
Then, sending the Nishad troop ahead,
He ordered his army to move.   (202)

He placed the Nishad chief at the head as their guide,
And sent all the palanquins of the queen mothers behind,
Summoning his younger brother, Shatrughna, to go with them,
While the guru set out with the Brahmans.
Then, saluting the divine river, Ganga,
And remembering Lakshman and Sita and Ram,
Bharat himself set forth on foot,
A spare horse being led by its reins beside him.
His devoted servants begged again and again,
'Master, please ride your horse.'
But Bharat replied, 'Ram went on foot—
And for me, chariots, elephants and horses have been prepared!
It would be more fitting that I go there on my head,
For a servant's dharma is the harshest of all.'
Seeing Bharat's state and hearing his gentle words,
All his servants melted with remorse.

During the third watch of the day,
Bharat entered Prayag,
Calling, 'Ram, Sita! Ram, Sita!'
With overflowing love.   (203)

Blisters glistened on his feet,
Like drops of dew on lotus buds.
Hearing that Bharat had made that day's journey on foot,
The whole company grew sorrowful.
Ascertaining that everyone else had bathed,
Bharat came to the triveni and saluted the confluence of the
    sacred streams.
He bathed as prescribed in the light and dark waters,[41]
And honoured the Brahmans, gods on earth, with gifts.
Gazing upon the light and dark waves,
His body trembling with elation, Bharat folded his hands,
'You fulfil every wish, king of sacred places,
And your power is praised in the Vedas and manifest in the world.
Abandoning my own dharma, I beg your favour,[42]
For to which low deed will a distressed man not stoop?
And knowing this in their hearts, the wise and generous
Fulfil the prayers of suppliants in this world.

> I have no wish for wealth or religious merit, or sensual pleasures,
> Nor do I seek liberation from rebirth.
> Love for Ram's feet, in birth after birth—
> I beg this boon and no other.   (204)

Even if Ram himself should consider me deceitful,
Or people say I am the enemy of my guru and my master,
May my love for the feet of Sita and Ram
Grow stronger each day, by your grace.
Though the raincloud forgets the chatak all her life,
Or when she pleads for raindrops, may throw down thunderbolts
    and hailstones,
If the chatak stops calling to the cloud, she is diminished,
But if her love increases, she is honoured in every way.
Just as gold is made more lustrous by fire,
Those who fulfil the vow of devotion to their beloved's feet are
    made bright.'

Hearing Bharat's words, there came from waters of
    the triveni,
A sweet voice bestowing blessings.
'Bharat, dear son, you are in every way honourable and good.
And your love for Ram's feet is fathomless.
You needlessly hold grief and remorse in your heart,
For no one is as dear to Ram as you.'

    His body trembled and his heart rejoiced
    Upon hearing those gracious words from the
        sacred confluence.
    'Bharat is blessed, blessed!' called the gods,
    Joyfully raining down flowers.   (205)

All those residing at that king of pilgrimage sites—
Hermits, students, householders, ascetics—were overjoyed.
Gathering in small groups, they said to each other,
'Bharat's love and goodness are pure and true.'
Heeding only the charming enumeration of Ram's virtues,
Bharat came to the great sage, Bharadvaj.
The muni, seeing him prostrate himself in homage,
Felt that his own good fortune had taken bodily form.
He ran and raised Bharat up and clasped him to his bosom,
And by giving him the blessing he desired, fulfilled his wish.
He gave him a seat, and Bharat sat down with bowed head
As though longing to run away to hide in shame's abode,
Very worried that the muni would ask him a question.
Seeing his goodness and humility, the rishi said,
'Listen Bharat, I have already heard everything—
We have no control over the way fate works!

    So do not hold guilt and remorse in your heart
    Thinking about what your mother has done.
    Son, it is not Kaikeyi's fault either,
    For Gira deprived her of her good sense.   (206)

Even if I said this, many would not approve of it,
For the wise acknowledge the authority of both the Vedas and the world.
But, son, singing of your clear and untarnished fame,
Both the world and the Vedas will be exalted.
Worldly custom and the Vedas agree, and all declare
That he gets the kingdom upon whom a father bestows it.
The king, true to his promise, would have summoned you
And given you the crown, encouraging happiness, righteousness
    and fame.
But the root of the calamity was Ram's exile to the forest,
Hearing of which caused anguish to the whole world.
That was subject to what had been decreed, and the unwise queen
Did wrong, but in the end has regretted her misdeeds.
But anyone who ascribes even the slightest blame to you for it,
Is contemptible, ignorant and vile.
Had you ruled, you would not have been at fault,
And even Ram, hearing of it, would have been content.

> But now, Bharat, you have done very well,
> And this sentiment is what truly befits you,
> For the root of all well-being in this world
> Is love for Raghubar's feet.   (207)

That is your wealth, your life and your very breath—
Who, then, is as fortunate as you?
But, dear son, all this is little wonder for you—
Dasharath's son and Ram's beloved brother.
Listen Bharat, in Raghubar's heart,
No one receives as much love as you.
Lakshman, Ram and Sita love you dearly,
And spent all that night here praising you.
I came to know their inmost feelings when they bathed at Prayag,
For they were immersed in love for you!
Raghubar's love for you

Is like that of a fool's for a life of worldly pleasure.
But this is no excessive praise of Raghubir,
For the lord of the Raghus protects a suppliant's whole family.
And you, Bharat—and this is my belief—
Are the very embodiment of Ram's love.

> What you call disgrace, Bharat,
> The rest of us call instruction,
> And for the attainment of devotion to Ram,
> This time has been propitious, like Ganesh.   (208)

Your renown, son, is a new and different moon, unblemished,
For the lilies and chakors that are Raghubar's servants.
Forever rising, it does not set,
Nor does it wane, but grows twofold every day in the sky that is
    this world.
The kok that is the three spheres loves it dearly,
And the sun of Ram's glory does not steal its brilliance.
Forever giving happiness, night and day, to all,
It is not eclipsed even by the Rahu of Kaikeyi's actions.
It is full of the nectar of Ram's love,
And unblemished by the stain of insulting its guru.[43]
Now Ram's devotees may drink of this nectar to their satisfaction,
For you have brought it within reach of the earth!
King Bhagirath brought down the divine river, Ganga,
Remembering which is the storehouse of all blessings.
And the multitude of Dasharath's virtues is beyond description—
How can there be one greater when there is none to even equal him
    in this world?

> He, compelled by whose love and humility,
> Ram became manifest in this world—
> Ram, whom even Har, with his heart's eyes,
> Never tires of beholding.   (209)

You have created an incomparable moon of glory
Upon which is stamped Ram's love in the shape of a deer.
Son, you hold sorrow in your heart to no purpose—
Though you have found the philosopher's stone, you are still afraid
        of poverty.
Listen Bharat, I utter no untruths—
I am an ascetic, living in the forest, disinterested and detached
        from the world
And I have already received the best fruit for all spiritual practices
When I beheld Ram, Sita and Lakshman.
But the fruit of that fruit is the sight of you,
And I, with Prayag, am most fortunate.
Blessed are you, Bharat, for you have conquered the world with
        your renown.'
Saying this, the muni was overcome with love.
Hearing the muni's words, the whole assembly rejoiced,
And the gods, praising Bharat's goodness, rained down flowers.
Cries of 'Blessed, blessed!' resounded in the sky and Prayag,
And Bharat, listening, was lost in love.

> His body trembling, Ram and Sita in his heart,
> And his lotus eyes filled with tears,
> He made obeisance to the assembly of munis
> And spoke in a voice choked with emotion.   (210)

'In this assembly of sages, in the most holy of sacred places,
To swear even a true oath is the utmost impropriety,
And if, in this sacred place, I were to utter a lie,
There would be no sin or vileness equal to that.
I speak truly—for you are all-knowing
And Raghurai pervades the inmost recesses of one's heart—
I do not grieve over what my mother has done,
Nor hold any sorrow in my heart if the world thinks I am base
        and worthless.
I do not fear the ruin of my prospects in the next life,

Nor do I grieve over my father's death.
His virtue and renown fill the world with splendour—
That he had sons like Lakshman and Ram,
And that, when separated from Ram, he gave up his transient body.
What occasion, then, to mourn the king?
But that Ram, Lakshman and Sita, without shoes on their feet
And clad as ascetics, wander from forest to forest,

> Wear garments of deerskin, eat only wild fruits,
> Sleep on the ground spread with grass and leaves,
> Live beneath trees and daily endure
> Cold, heat, rain and wind—   (211)

It is the fire of this sorrow that constantly burns my heart,
And I have no appetite by day nor sleep by night.
There is no medicine for this awful disease—
I have searched the whole world with my heart.
My mother's wickedness, the root of all sins, was the carpenter,
Who used my welfare as his adze
To fashion, out of the vile wood of discord, the evil charm of
    his exile
Which he buried while chanting the cruel mantra of fourteen years.
It is for me that she devised this evil scheme
And flung the whole world into ruin and confusion.
This calamity will cease only when Ram returns.
Only then will Avadh flourish again—there is no other way.'
The sages were pleased to hear Bharat's words,
And all praised him in many ways. Muni Bharadvaj said,
'Son, do not grieve and worry so much—
All sorrow will disappear when you see Ram's feet.'

> Thus consoling him, the great muni said,
> 'Now be my beloved guest,
> And grant me your grace by accepting
> The tubers, roots, fruits and flowers I offer.'   (212)

Hearing the muni's words, Bharat grew worried,
'This is a difficult predicament at an unhappy time!'
Then, reflecting on the importance of a guru's words,
Bharat touched his feet and said, with folded hands,
'To humbly respect and obey your command,
Is my supreme duty, master.'
Bharat's words pleased the great muni's heart,
And summoning his trusted servants and pupils, he said,
'We must show our hospitality to Bharat,
So go and bring tubers, roots and fruits.'
'Very well, master,' they replied, bowing their heads,
And cheerfully left to carry out their respective tasks.
But the muni worried, 'I have invited an exalted guest,
And a god's worship must befit the god.'
At this, the Riddhis, Anima and the other Siddhis appeared, saying,[44]
'Give us your commands, master, we will fulfil them all.'

> Pleased, the great sage replied,
> 'Bharat is distraught with grief at separation from Ram,
> And so is his young brother, Shatrughna, and all their
>   companions.
> Look after them and ease their weariness.'   (213)

The Riddhis and Siddhis bowed their heads to the great muni's
    command,
And considered themselves most fortunate.
The gathered magic powers said to each other,
'Ram's younger brother is a guest beyond compare.
So bowing at the muni's feet, let us now do
Whatever will please all the royal party.'
Saying this, they fashioned bright and pleasing abodes of
    many kinds
At the sight of which even the flying chariots of the gods were put
    to shame.

They filled them with splendour and luxuries,
Upon which even the immortal gods gazed with longing.
Serving men and women stood by with all that was needed,
Their full attention on the needs of the guests.
The Siddhis organized in an instant
Comforts undreamt of even in the abode of the gods.
First, they gave everyone their quarters,
Beautiful, comfortable, and to each one's taste.

> Then they attended to Bharat and his family,
> For such had been the rishi's orders.
> By the strength of his penance, the great muni,
> Had produced such magnificence as astonished even
>   the Creator.   (214)

When Bharat beheld the muni's power,
The dominions of the celestial guardians all appeared small and
    mean to him.
The luxuries assembled surpassed description—
Upon seeing them, even the wise would forget detachment.
There were couches, beds, curtains and canopies,
Groves, gardens, and deer and birds of many kinds,
Fragrant flowers and fruits like nectar,
Lakes, ponds, streams and many sorts of reservoirs of clear water,
And food and drink, pure and sweeter than amrit,
Seeing which the people were overawed, and hesitated to accept,
    like ascetics.
The divine cow and tree of plenty belonged to all,
And seeing them, even Indra and Shachi grew envious.
The season was spring, cool, soft and fragrant breezes blew,
And the four rewards of life were available to all.
Seeing the garlands, sandal-paste, women and other
    sensual delights,
The people were overcome with joy and dismay.[45]

The grandeur was the chakwi, Bharat the chakwa,
And the muni's order the facetious fowler
Who held them imprisoned that night
In the cage of the ashram, until it was dawn.   (215)

After bathing in the sacred confluence at that king of sacred sites,
Bharat, with all his company, bowed his head to Muni Bharadvaj,
Reverently received his blessing and permission to depart,
And prostrating himself, paid him homage in many humble words.
Accompanied by skilled guides well-acquainted with the way, and
    taking everyone with him,
Bharat set out, single-mindedly focused on Chitrakut.
Holding the hand of Ram's friend, Guha,
He walked like love incarnate,
With no shoes on his feet, no royal umbrella held over his head,
And unfeigned love, self-restraint, austerity and virtue,
Asking his companion for the story of Lakshman, Ram and
    Sita's journey,
Which Guha related in gentle tones.
Seeing the places where Ram had rested and the trees under which
    he had sheltered,
He could not contain his love within his heart.
Seeing his state, the gods rained down flowers,
And the ground grew soft, and the path easy and pleasant.

The clouds followed him, providing shade
And a soft and pleasing breeze blew.
Not even for Ram had that path become
As pleasant as it now became for Bharat as he went.   (216)

Innumerable inanimate and animate beings along the way,
Who had seen the Lord, or whom the Lord had seen,
Had all become worthy of the highest state—
Now, the sight of Bharat cured them of the disease of rebirth.

Yet this was not a great feat for Bharat,
Upon whom Ram himself meditates in his heart.
Those in this world who say 'Ram' even once,
Cross over the sea of rebirth, and can take others across as well.
And then Bharat is dear to Ram, his own younger brother,
So how could his path not bring him every blessing?
So said the Siddhas, the sadhus and the great sages,
And, gazing at Bharat, rejoiced in their hearts.
Seeing his effect on everyone, the king of the gods grew worried,
For the world appears good to the good, and vile to the vile.
He said to his guru, Brihaspati, 'Lord, employ some ruse
So that Ram and Bharat do not meet.

> Ram is gentle and won over by love,
> And Bharat is an ocean of love.
> What has already been accomplished may be undone,
> So devise some stratagem to prevent it!'   (217)

Hearing his words, the guru of the gods smiled
To see the thousand-eyed one without eyes,
And said, 'Give up your needless anxiety and tricks,
Any deception here will cause disaster.
If you practise any maya upon the servant of maya's master,
It will recoil upon you, king of the gods!
You interfered before, knowing you had Ram's approval,[46]
But any misbehaviour now will only do you harm.
Listen, king of the gods, it is Raghunath's nature—
He is never angered by an offence against himself,
But one who commits an offence against his devotee,
Burns in the fire of Ram's wrath.
The story is well-known in the world and the Vedas,
Of how Durvasa came to know this glorious trait.[47]
And who loves Ram like Bharat,
Whose name Ram repeats while the world repeats 'Ram'?

Do not allow in your mind, lord of immortals,
  even the thought
Of harming a devotee of Raghubar.
It will bring you infamy in this world, grief in the next,
And an ever-increasing burden of distress.   (218)

Listen, king of gods, to my advice—
His devotee is supremely dear to Ram.
He is pleased by any service rendered to his servants,
But bears great enmity to those who are hostile to them.
Though he is the same to all, with neither love nor anger,
And receives into himself neither sin nor virtue, merit nor flaw,
Though he has set karma as supreme in this world,
So that one's deeds determine the fruit that one tastes,
Even so, he acts impartial or hostile
Depending on whether one has the heart of a devotee or a sceptic.
Without attributes, unblemished, free from pride, unchanging,
Ram takes on form, yielding to the love of his devotees,
For Ram always honours the wish of his servants,
As the Vedas, the Puranas, the sadhus and gods bear witness.
Understanding this, abandon guile and deception,
And cherish perfect love for Bharat's feet.

Ram's devotees are constantly engaged in the good
  of others—
They are compassionate, and sad in the sadness of others,
And Bharat is the crest jewel of his devotees.
So do not be afraid of him, protector of the gods. (219)

The Lord is true to his word and a benefactor of the gods,
And Bharat is obedient to Ram's orders.
In the grip of self-interest, you are troubled—
This is not Bharat's fault, but your own delusion.'
When the chief of gods heard the wise words of the divine guru,

Joy arose in his heart and his worry vanished.
Rejoicing, the king of gods rained down flowers
And began to praise Bharat's noble nature.
In this manner, Bharat continued on his way,
And seeing his state, munis and Siddhas grew envious.
Whenever he sighed and said 'Ram',
It seemed as if love overflowed on every side.
Adamant and stones melted hearing his words,
And the love of the people of Ayodhya defied description.
Making camp along the way, he reached the Jamuna,
And, seeing its waters, his eyes filled with tears.

> Gazing at that beautiful river, its waters
> The same hue as Raghubar, Bharat and his retinue,
> Drowning in an ocean of grief at their separation from him,
> Climbed into the boat of discernment.   (220)

That day, they made camp by the banks of the Jamuna,
And appropriate arrangements were made for everyone.
During the night, came boats from every ghat
In numbers greater than could be counted or described,
And at dawn, all crossed the river in a single trip,
Well pleased by this service rendered by Ram's friend, Guha.
After bathing in the river and bowing their heads to it,
The two brothers set forth again, the Nishad chief with them.
Ahead, in their magnificent carriages, went the great munis,
While all the royal company followed behind.
Behind them went the two brothers on foot,
Their adornments, clothes and appearance exceedingly simple
    and plain.
Accompanied by their servants, friends and the ministers' sons
They went, remembering Lakshman, Sita and Ram.
Wherever Ram had stopped or rested,
They lovingly paid homage.

Hearing of their approach, men and women who lived along
    the way
Left their homes, abandoning chores, and came running.
Beholding their beauty and love,
They all rejoiced, for they had received their
    birth's reward.   (221)

Lovingly, the women asked one another,
'Friend, are these Ram and Lakshman, or not?
In age, form, complexion and beauty they are the same, my dear,
In courtesy and affection too, they are like them, and their gait is
    also the same.
But their garb is different, dear friend, Sita is not with them,
And ahead of them marches a great army with infantry, cavalry,
    elephants and chariots.
Their faces are not happy, there is sadness in their hearts—
These differences, my dear, make me doubtful.'
Her reasoning appealed to the other women,
And all declared, 'No one is as clever as you.'
Praising her and agreeing to the truth of her words,
Another woman spoke in sweet tones,
And lovingly repeated the full story
Of how the joy of Ram's coronation had been destroyed.
The fortunate woman then began to praise Bharat,
His goodness, love and disposition.

'He walks on foot, eating only wild fruits,
Giving up the kingdom his father gave him,
To persuade Raghubar to return.
Who today can equal Bharat?   (222)

Bharat's affection for his brother, his devotion and conduct—
To tell or hear of them destroys sin and sorrow.
But whatever I may say, my dears, is too little,

For he is Ram's brother, so how can he be otherwise?
All of us, having seen Bharat and his younger brother,
May now be counted among blessed women.'
Hearing his virtues and seeing his state, they lamented,
'This son does not deserve a mother like Kaikeyi.'
But some women said, 'This is not really the queen's fault—
Providence favoured us and arranged all this.
For of what account are we—excluded from worldly and
     Vedic rites,
Lowly women, impure by birth and doings,
Living in a miserable village in a wild and uncivilized land,
     despised even amongst women—
To see this vision that is the reward of great religious merit?'
Such was the joy and wonder in every village,
As though the wish-yielding Kalpataru had sprung up in a desert.

     Looking upon Bharat, the people living along the way
     Were favoured by great good fortune,
     As though the inhabitants of Singhal[xi] had,
     By the will of Fate, gained easy access to Prayag.   (223)

Hearing these praises of his own virtues and Ram's,
Bharat continued his journey, meditating upon Raghunath.
At the sight of holy places, a muni's ashram, or a temple,
He bathed and made obeisance,
Asking in his heart this one boon only—
Love for the lotus feet of Sita and Ram.
Whomsoever he met—Kirats, Kols, other forest-dwelling tribes,
Hermits, students, ascetics, mendicants—
He would reverently salute and ask
In which forest were Lakshman, Ram and Vaidehi.
They all gave him news of the Lord,

[xi] Ravan's kingdom of Lanka

And, seeing Bharat, obtained their birth's reward.
Those who said, 'He is well, we have seen him,'
He considered as dear as Ram and Lakshman.
In this way, he inquired of everyone in soft and courteous tones,
And listened to the story of Ram's forest life.

> He halted there that day, and at dawn
> Set forth again, meditating upon Raghunath.
> All those who were with Bharat
> Yearned as he did to look upon Ram.   (224)

Good omens occurred for everyone,
Their eyes fluttered and their limbs quivered auspiciously.
Bharat and the whole company grew elated at the thought
That they would soon meet Ram and the fire of their grief would
    be extinguished.
Each held a wish according to his heart,
And all walked on, drunk on the wine of love,
Their limbs languid, their feet unsteady on the path,
Their speech incoherent with love.
Just then, Ram's friend, Guha, pointed out
The jewel of all mountains,[48] in all its natural splendour,
Near which, on the banks of the Payasvini,
The two mighty heroes dwelt with Sita.
Seeing it, all fell prostrate in homage
Crying, 'Glory to Ram, life of Janaki!'
The royal company was as immersed in love,
As if Raghuraj had turned back towards Avadh.

> Bharat's love at that moment was such
> That it could not be described even by Shesh,
> And is as far beyond the poet as is the bliss of union with
>   the Absolute
> For a man stained by covetousness and pride.   (225)

All were so weakened by their love for Raghubar,
That they had travelled only two kos by the time the sun set.
Finding a safe place with water close by, they halted there, and
    when the night had passed,
Bharat, beloved of Raghunath, continued his journey.
Meanwhile, Ram awoke while the night still remained,
And Sita told him what she had seen in a dream:
'It seemed Bharat came with a great number of people,
His body burning with the fever of separation from his lord.
All were sad at heart, miserable and wretched,
And I saw my mothers-in-law, quite changed in appearance.'
On hearing Sita's dream, Ram's eyes filled with tears,
And the liberator from sorrow became overpowered by sorrow.
'Lakshman, this dream does not bode well,
Somebody will bring us some very bad news.'
So saying, Ram bathed along with his brother,
Worshipped Purari, and paid homage to the saints.

After worshipping the gods and paying homage to the munis,
Ram sat down and turned his gaze to the north,
For the sky was full of dust, and many birds and deer
Were running, panic-stricken, towards the Lord's ashram.
Tulsi says that Ram, seeing this, stood up, astonished—
'What can be the reason for this?' he wondered,
And at that very moment the Kols and Kirats arrived
And told him all the news.

As soon as he heard their happy and auspicious words,
His heart rejoiced, his body trembled with joy,
And his eyes, bright as the autumn lotus,
Filled with tears of love, says Tulsi.   (226)

Then Sita's lord became anxious again—
'What can be the reason for Bharat's coming?' he mused.

Then came one and said,
'There comes with him a vast army, complete with infantry,
        cavalry, elephants and chariots.'
Hearing this, Ram grew greatly troubled—
On one side were his father's words, on the other his respect for
        his brother.
Musing upon Bharat's nature in his mind,
The Lord could find no satisfactory explanation.
But his mind was set at rest when he reflected,
'Bharat listens to me, and is good and wise.'
Lakshman saw that the Lord's heart was troubled,
And said what he considered would be prudent behaviour on
        the occasion.
'I will make bold, master, to say something without your asking,
For sometimes a servant's boldness is not impudence.
You, Lord, are the crest-jewel of the all-knowing,
But I, your devotee, will speak only according to my understanding.

        Master, you are exceedingly kind-hearted, sincere and
                without guile,
        A treasury of goodness and affection.
        You love and trust everyone,
        And believe they are all like you.   (227)

But when one given to worldly pleasure attains power,
The fool reveals himself to be in delusion's grip.
Bharat is resolved upon righteousness, good and wise,
And devoted to your feet, Lord—as the whole world knows.
But today, that same Bharat, having taken your place as king
        of Avadh,
Sets forth to destroy the bounds of duty and righteousness.
That deceitful, evil brother, seeing it to be a difficult time,
And knowing you, Ram, to be in exile in the forest alone,
Has made his vile plans, gathered an army,
And come here to make his reign free from thorns.

Plotting countless kinds of crookedness,
The two brothers have assembled an army and come.
If there was no deceit or treachery in their hearts,
Why would they want to bring chariots, horses and elephants?
But why should anyone needlessly blame Bharat?
The whole world goes mad on gaining kingly status.

> The Moon seduced his guru's wife,
> Nahush rode on a palanquin borne by Brahmans,
> And in turning his face away from both worldly custom
>   and the Veda,
> No one was as contemptible as King Vena.[49]   (228)

Sahasrabahu, Indra and Trishanku—[50]
Who has not been tainted by the madness of kingly power?
Bharat has adopted the right strategy,
For no one leaves the smallest trace of an enemy or a debt.
But in one matter Bharat has not done well—
He has insulted you, Ram, in believing you helpless.
He will understand this fully today,
When he sees your wrathful face, Ram, in battle.'
Saying this, Lakshman forgot his measured, prudent tones,
And, like a tree bursts into flower, his body thrilled with the spirit
    of battle.
Falling at his Lord's feet, placing their dust upon his head,
He spoke honestly, with his natural vehemence.
'Master, do not think it unbecoming of me if I say
That Bharat has done us enough service.
How long must I suffer this, holding myself in check,
When you are with me, master, and my bow in my hand?

> I am a warrior, born into the Raghu line,
> And known in the world as Ram's faithful servant.
> Is there anything lower than dust?
> But even that, if kicked, rises up to fall upon one's head.'   (229)

He rose, and folding his hands, awaited permission,
Like valour itself aroused from slumber.
Binding his matted hair, he fastened his quiver to his waist,
Made ready his bow, and, with his arrows in his hand, said,
'Today I will attain fame as Ram's servant,
And, in battle, teach Bharat a lesson.
Receiving the fruit of their disrespect to Ram,
Those two brothers will sleep upon battle's couch.
It is good that the whole army has gathered together,
For I can manifest my accumulated rage today.
Just as the king of the beasts tears into pieces a herd of elephants,
Or a hawk pounces upon and carries off a quail,
So will I contemptuously destroy Bharat with his army
And his younger brother upon the battlefield.
Even if Shankar comes to help him,
I swear by you, Ram, that I will kill him in battle.'

When they saw Lakshman flash with such fury
And heard his solemn oath,
The spheres grew fearful, and their terrified guardians
All wanted to run away.   (230)

The universe was immersed in fear and a voice was heard in
      the sky
Praising Lakshman's great strength of arm.
'Son, who can tell or comprehend
Your might and majesty?
But before doing anything, it is well to deliberate carefully
If the deed is right or wrong, say all.
One who acts without thought and later repents
Is unwise, as the Vedas and the learned declare.'
Hearing these words of the gods, Lakshman was abashed,
But Ram and Sita respectfully said to him,
'Dear brother, you gave us prudent advice—

The wine of royal power is the most intoxicating of all,
And those kings who do not serve the holy and the good
Become maddened by a single sip.
But listen, Lakshman—goodness like Bharat's,
Has not been seen or heard of in Vidhi's creation.

> Bharat would never be intoxicated by royal power,
> Even if he were given the thrones of Vidhi, Hari and Har,
> For can a few drops of sour kanji ever
> Curdle the celestial ocean of milk? (231)

Darkness might swallow the noonday sun,
The sky merge and become one with the clouds,
Or Ghatjoni might drown in the puddle made by a cow's hoof,
The earth abandon her natural forbearance,
Or a mosquito's breath blow Mount Meru away—
But, dear brother, Bharat can never be intoxicated by the wine of
    kingly power.
Lakshman, I swear by you and our father,
There is no brother as true and good as Bharat.
By mixing the milk of virtue with the water of sin,
    little brother,
Did the Creator fashion this world.
But Bharat is the swan born on the lake of the solar line,
Who has separated good from evil.
Choosing the milk of virtue and discarding the water of sin,
He has illuminated the world with his renown.'
Speaking of Bharat's virtues and his good and gentle nature,
Raghurao was immersed in a sea of love.

> The gods, hearing Raghubar's words
> And seeing his love for Bharat,
> All began to praise him, saying,
> 'What Lord is as compassionate as Ram?' (232)

Had Bharat not taken birth in this world,
Who would have been the upholder of all dharma on earth?
The enumeration of Bharat's virtues is beyond all poets,
For who but you can comprehend them, Raghunath?'
Lakshman, Ram and Sita, upon hearing these words of the gods,
Felt such joy as cannot be described.
Meanwhile, Bharat and all his retinue,
Bathed in the pure and sacred Mandakini.
Then, leaving everyone by the river,
And with the permission of his mother, his guru and his minister,
Bharat went to where Sita and Ram were,
Taking with him the Nishad chief and his young brother.
Thinking of his mother's doings, Bharat cringed with shame,
And formed countless worries in his mind—
'May Ram, Lakshman and Sita, hearing my name,
Not get up and go somewhere else, abandoning this place.

> If he takes me to be my mother's accomplice,
> Nothing he might do would be too harsh.
> But considering me on his side, he will forgive
> My sins and faults and receive me with kindness.   (233)

But whether he spurns me as a black-hearted wretch,
Or honours me as his faithful servant,
My only refuge is Ram's sandals,
For Ram is a good master, and the fault all lies in his servant.
Only the chatak and the fish are deserving of glory in this world,
For their vows of fidelity and love, which they are adept in keeping
    ever new.'51
Thinking such thoughts, Bharat walked on,
His limbs made weak with diffidence and love.
His mother's vile deed would have dragged him back,
But the strength of his fortitude and devotion, like a sturdy bullock,
    pulled him forward,

And whenever he thought of Raghunath's loving nature,
His feet moved swiftly on the path.
Bharat's state at that time
Was like that of a water-insect upon the current of a stream.
Beholding Bharat's anxiety and love,
The Nishad chief lost all awareness of his own self at that moment.

> Auspicious omens began to occur,
> And the Nishad, hearing and reflecting upon them, said,
> 'Sorrow will disappear and joy emerge,
> Though there will be sorrow again in the end.'   (234)

Knowing his servant's words to be all true,
Bharat drew near the ashram.
Gazing upon its forests and mountains,
He was as delighted as a starving man finding a good meal.
Like people terrified of calamities,
Tormented by the triple afflictions, or troubled by planets or pestilence,
Who run away to a well-governed and prosperous land and find bliss—
Bharat's state was exactly like theirs.
The riches of the forest where Ram lived shone bright,
Like happy subjects who had found a good king.
Detachment was the minister, discernment their king,
The beautiful forest their pure and sacred country,
Self-restraint and moral discipline the warriors, the mountain the
     capital city,
And peace and good sense the virtuous and lovely queens—
That good king's kingdom was complete in all parts,
His heart filled with bliss, for he had taken refuge at Ram's feet.

> Having conquered the king that is delusion and his army,
> The monarch of discernment
> Reigned without impediment,
> And there was joy, prosperity and plenty in his city.   (235)

In this forest realm, the numerous dwellings of munis and
    holy men
Were like groups of cities, towns, villages and hamlets,
And the many rare and wonderful birds and animals
Were his subjects beyond count.
Rhinoceros, elephant, lion, tiger, boar,
Buffalo and bull—the king's magnificent entourage was a sight to
    praise and admire.
Forgetting their natural enmity, they grazed together,
Roaming everywhere like the king's fourfold army,[52]
Waterfalls thundered and mast elephants trumpeted,
Like the sounding of drums of many kinds.
Flocks of chakwas, chakors, chataks, parrots, koels
And graceful swans sweetly called with happy hearts.
Swarms of bees hummed and peacocks danced,
In celebration everywhere across that happy kingdom.
Vines, trees and grasses bore flowers and fruit,
And the whole land was a source of happiness and bliss.

    Seeing the splendour of Ram's mountain,
    Bharat's heart was filled with profound love,
    And he was as blissful as an ascetic who,
    Completing his vows of austerity, finally receives
        their fruit.   (236)

The boatman, Guha, then ran and climbed up high
And raising his arm, called out to Bharat,
'Master, look at those great trees—
Pakar, jambu, mango and tamal,
And in the midst of those noble trees, a magnificent banyan,
Beautiful and vast, its sight captivates the heart.
Its leaves are dense and dark, its fruit red,
And its deep shade is pleasing in all seasons,

As though Vidhi had gathered together darkness and the red light
   of dawn
And from them, fashioned this tree of beauty.
That tree, master, is close to the river
Where stands Raghubar's hut of leaves.
Many graceful tulsi shrubs grow there,
Some planted by Sita, some by Lakshman.
And in the shade of this very banyan tree is a fire-altar
Built by Sita with her own lovely lotus hands,

    Where, in the company of munis and sages,
    Daily sit wise Sita and Ram,
    And listen to all the tales and legends
    From the Vedas, the Shastras and Puranas.'   (237)

Hearing his friend's words and seeing those trees,
Bharat's eyes overflowed with tears.
The two brothers paid reverent homage as they went,
And even Sharada herself was hesitant to describe their love.
On seeing Ram's footprints, they rejoiced
Like paupers finding the philosopher's stone.
Placing their dust upon their heads, hearts and eyelids,
They felt the bliss of meeting Raghubar himself.
Seeing Bharat's utterly indescribable state,
Birds, beasts and all created beings, animate or inanimate,
   were lost in love.
Their guide, Guha, was so overwhelmed with love that he lost the way,
But the gods revealed the right path and rained down flowers.
Looking upon them, Siddhas and sages were filled with love
And began to praise Bharat's simple and sincere affection.
'Had Bharat not been born upon this earth,
Who would have made the inanimate animate, and the animate
   inanimate?

For the benefit of the gods and the sages, the compassionate
    Lord, Raghubar,
Churned the deep and fathomless ocean that is Bharat
With the Mount Mandar of his anguish at separation
    from Ram,
And brought forth the amrit that is love.   (238)

The two handsome brothers and their companion Guha
Were hidden by the dense forest, so Lakshman did not see them.
But Bharat saw the Lord's pure and sacred ashram,
The lovely abode of all blessings.
As he entered the ashram, the fire of his grief was extinguished,
As though a yogi had attained salvation.
He saw Lakshman standing in front of the Lord,
Lovingly replying to some question,
With matted hair upon his head, a hermit's bark cloth tied round
    his waist,
His quiver fastened, arrows in hand, and his bow at his shoulder.
Around the fire-altar was gathered a company of munis and sages
And amidst them, with Sita, was Raghuraj resplendent
In his garments of bark, with matted hair, and his dark form—
It seemed as though Rati and Kamdev had taken on the guise
    of munis.
His lotus hands played with his bow and arrows,
And his smiling glance removed the heart's burning anguish.

In the midst of that noble company of saints,
    Sita and the moon of the Raghus shone bright
    As though, in wisdom's assembly,
    Bhakti and the brahm had taken bodily form.   (239)

With his brother and his friend, Bharat was so immersed in love
    for Ram,
That he forgot all joy and sorrow, pleasure and pain.

Crying, 'Protect me, Lord! Protect me, my master!'
He fell prostrate upon the ground.
Lakshman recognized his loving voice
And knew at once that it was Bharat making obeisance—
On one side was his great love for his brother,
And on the other the powerful demand of service to his master.
He could not embrace him, nor could he shun him—
Only a great poet could describe the state of Lakshman's heart.
Giving greater weight to Ram's service, Lakshman stayed where
    he was,
Like a soaring kite tugged back by its flier.
Bowing his head to the ground, he lovingly said,
'It is Bharat who salutes you, Raghunath.'
Hearing this, Ram sprang up, impatient in his love,
Shoulder-cloth falling, quiver, bow and arrows dropping from
    his hands.

    Firmly raising him up,
    The compassionate Lord clasped Bharat to his heart.
    All those who saw the meeting of Bharat and Ram,
    Lost all awareness of themselves.   (240)

How can the love of their meeting be described?
It is beyond poets, in thought, deed and word.
Both brothers, Bharat and Ram, were filled with supreme love,
Mind, reason, intellect and pride forgotten.
Tell me, who could reveal such great love?
What shadow of it should the poet's mind follow?
A poet's true strength lies only in word and meaning,
As a dancer moves only according to the beat.
Bharat and Raghubar's love is beyond conception
Even for the hearts of Vidhi, Hari and Har.
So how can I, with my dull mind, describe it?
Can melodious music be played on strings of coarse grass?

Seeing the meeting of Bharat and Raghubar,
The gods grew afraid and their hearts beat faster.
It was only when their guru explained that those blockheads awoke
And began raining down flowers, praising and applauding.

> After lovingly greeting Ripusudan,
> Ram embraced the Nishad chief,
> While Bharat embraced Lakshman with great love
> As he, with reverence, greeted him.   (241)

Lakshman embraced his younger twin, Shatrughna, with a shout,
And then clasped the Nishad to his breast.
Then the two brothers, Bharat and Shatrughna, paid homage to
     the gathering of munis,
And upon receiving from them the desired blessing, rejoiced.
Their hearts overflowing with love, Bharat and his younger
     brother
Placed the dust of Sita's lotus feet upon their heads
And saluted her again and again. She raised them up,
Stroking their heads with her lotus hands, and seated them.
Sita blessed them in her heart,
And, immersed in love, she had no awareness of her own body.
Perceiving Sita well-disposed to them in every way,
They became free of worry and their fears disappeared.
No one said a word or asked anything,
Their hearts were filled with love and empty of their usual
     restive ways.
Then the Nishad chief composed himself,
And saluting with folded hands, humbly said,

> 'Lord, together with the lord of munis,
> Distressed by separation from you, have come
> The mothers, all the people of the city,
> Your servants, military commanders and ministers.'   (242)

When Ram, the ocean of propriety and courtesy, heard that his
    guru had come,
He left Ripudaman[xii] there with Sita,
And quickly went, that very instant,
He, the steadfast upholder of dharma, and the all-merciful Lord.
Seeing his guru, he and Lakshman were overcome with
    affection,
But as the Lord began to prostrate himself,
The great muni ran and clasped him to his heart.
And embraced both brothers with overflowing love.
Guha, trembling with love, gave his name,
And from a distance, made obeisance, prostrating reverently.
But the rishi firmly raised up and embraced Ram's friend,
As though gathering up love that had fallen upon the ground.
'Devotion to Raghupati is the root of all blessing!'
Cried the gods in the sky as they sang his praises and
    rained down flowers.
There is no one more lowly than the Nishad,
And no one more exalted than Vasishtha in the world.

    Yet the king of sages, seeing him,
    Meets him with greater delight than he did Lakshman,
    And so makes manifest the glorious power
    Of devotion to Sita's Lord!'   (243)

Ram knew how distressed the people were,
For he is the compassionate and all-wise God,
Therefore, whatever was the wish of each person,
He satisfied according to his longing.
He and his brother embraced them all in an instant,
And put out the terrible fire of their anguish.
This was no great feat for Ram—

---

xii Shatrughna

It was like the single sun reflected in millions of water-pots.
Embracing their Nishad guide with joyous affection,
The citizens of Ayodhya all praised his good fortune.
Ram saw that his mothers were sorrowful,
Like a row of graceful vines blighted by frost.
Ram embraced Kaikeyi first,
Melting her heart with his innate and simple devotion.
Then falling at her feet, he consoled her,
Attributing all blame to time, karma and fate.

> Raghubar embraced all his mothers,
> And consoled and comforted them all, saying,
> 'Mother, the world is subservient to God,
> So no one should be blamed.'   (244)

The two brothers, Ram and Lakshman, touched the feet of their
        guru's wife, Arundhati,
And those of the Brahman wives who had come with her,
Honouring them all as they would Ganga and Gauri,
And the delighted women blessed them in sweet voices.
After touching her feet, they hugged Sumitra
Like destitutes clutching treasure.
Then the two brothers fell at Kaushalya's feet,
Their limbs trembling with love.
Their mother clasped them to her heart with profound affection,
And bathed them in tears of love.
But the joy and sorrow of that moment—
How can a poet describe them? Can a mute describe taste?
After greeting their mothers, Raghurao and his brother
        Lakshman
Invited their guru to come with them to their ashram.
The townspeople, receiving the muni's command,
Began searching for water and suitable spots close by and setting
        up camp.

Taking with them Brahmans, the minister, their mothers,
    the guru
And some selected people,
Bharat, Lakshman and Raghunath
Proceeded to the sacred ashram.					(245)

Sita came and embraced the great muni's feet,
And received the appropriate blessing her heart desired.
The guru's wife and the wives of the other munis
Met her with love that is beyond description.
One by one, Sita touched their feet
And received their words of blessing so dear to her heart.
But when the young and gentle Sita saw all her mothers-in-law,
She grew afraid and shut her eyes,
For they looked like swans fallen into the clutches of a fowler.
'What has cruel providence done!' she wondered.
Looking at Sita, they too were deeply distressed, but reflected,
'We must endure what fate gives us to suffer!'
Then Janak's daughter took courage in her heart,
And with her blue-lotus eyes full of tears,
Went and met all her mothers-in-law—
At that moment, tenderness and compassion spread over the earth.

Falling at the feet of each of her mothers-in-law,
Sita met them with deep affection.
Overcome by love, they blessed her from their hearts,
'May you always remain a happy wife, beloved of
    your husband.'					(246)

Sita and the queens were distracted with love,
But the wise guru bade them all sit down.
The lord of munis then spoke of the illusory nature of the world,
And discoursed a little on salvation and spiritual truth.
He then told of the king's departure for the abode of the gods—

Hearing this, Raghunath was overcome by profound grief,
And realizing that the king had died out of love for him,
He, the most composed and forbearing of all, grew deeply
      troubled.
Hearing these bitter words, cruel as a thunderbolt,
Lakshman, Sita and the queens began to weep and wail,
And the whole company was so distraught with grief,
It was as though the king had just died that very day.
Then the noble muni comforted Ram,
And he and all the assembly bathed in the sacred Mandakini.
That day, the Lord fasted, abstaining even from water,
And despite the muni's urging, no one else took any water either.

> At dawn the next day, Raghunandan
> Followed the orders given by the muni—
> With faith and devotion, the Lord
> Reverently performed all the ceremonies.   (247)

Performing his father's last rites as prescribed in the Vedas,
He, the sun to the darkness of impurity, became pure again.
He, whose name is the fire to the cotton wick of suffering and sin,
And remembering whom is the root of all good fortune,
Became pure. The sages and sadhus agree that it was as if
The divine stream of the Ganga had been sanctified by invoking
      other sacred streams.
When two days had passed after his purification,
Ram said affectionately to his guru,
'Master, our people are all so miserable here,
Living on tubers, roots, wild fruits and water.
When I look at Bharat and Shatrughna, at the ministers, and all
      my mothers,
A moment seems to me like an aeon.
Return with all of them to the city,
For you are here, and the king in Amaravati, Indra's abode.

But I have said too much and been too bold—
Do whatever is fitting and proper, lord.'

> 'You are dharma's bulwark and compassion's abode,
> So how could you have spoken otherwise, Ram?
> Our people are distressed; so let them, for a few days more,
> Look at you and rest from sorrow.'   (248)

On hearing Ram's words, the assembly had grown as fearful
As a tossing ship upon the ocean,
But upon hearing the guru's auspicious speech,
It was though the winds had turned in their favour.
They bathed three times every day in the pure and holy Mandakini,
The sight of which destroys a torrent of sins,
And filled their eyes with sight of Ram, the embodiment of all blessings,
Joyfully prostrating before him again and again.
They went to see Ram's hill and forest,
Where there is every joy and no sorrow,
Where torrents flow with water as sweet as nectar,
And soft, cool and fragrant breezes blow that put out the triple
        fires of affliction,
Where grow innumerable varieties of trees, creepers and grasses,
And fruits, flowers and leaves of many kinds,
Where there are cliffs and boulders pleasing to the eye, and the
        soothing shade of trees.
Who can describe the beauty of that forest?

> The lakes were filled with lotuses,
> Waterbirds called and black bees hummed,
> While colourful birds and beasts of many kinds,
> Roamed the forest, abandoning their natural enmity.   (249)

The Kols, Kirats, Bhils and other forest residents,
Brought honey pure and clear, and as delicious as nectar,

In beautifully fashioned leaf-bowls filled to the brim,
As well as bundles of tubers, roots, wild fruits and sprouts,
And offered them to all, saluting humbly,
Naming and describing the taste, variety and virtues of each food.
The people offered them a large price, but they would not
    accept it,
And returned it in Ram's name.
In sweet tones steeped in love they said,
'The good respect love when they see it.
You are virtuous beings, and we are lowly Nishads,
Who have been granted a sight of you only by Ram's favour.
Being in your presence was otherwise as utterly unattainable for us
As the stream of the divine Ganga is for the desert lands of Maru.
Compassionate Ram has shown his grace to the Nishad chief—
As is the king, so should be his kin and people.

> Bearing this in mind, abandon your scruples.
> And seeing our love, graciously
> Fulfil our wish by accepting
> These fruits, herbs and sprouts.   (250)

You beloved guests have come to the forest,
But our fate has not made us worthy of serving you.
What can we offer you, masters?
Kirat friendship is only firewood and leaves,
And our greatest service to you
Is not to steal your clothes and cooking vessels.
We are brutish creatures, slayers of living beings,
Crooked, cruel, ignorant and base-born.
Our days and nights pass in sinful doings,
We wear no cloth around our waist, nor are our bellies ever full.
How can we even dream of knowing dharma?
All this is the effect of having seen Raghunandan—
Ever since we have seen the Lord's lotus feet,

Our unendurable sorrows and sins have disappeared.'
Hearing their words, the citizens of Avadh were overwhelmed
    with love,
And began to praise the good fortune of the forest people.

All began to praise their good fortune,
Addressing them in affectionate words,
And noting their speech, their courteous greeting,
And their devotion to the feet of Sita and Ram, rejoiced.
Men and women thought little of their own devotion,
When they heard the words of the Kols and the Bhils.
It was by the grace of the jewel of the Raghu line, says Tulsi,
That a boat laden with iron reached the shore.

> Each day, they all roamed the forest in every direction,
> Happy and delighted,
> Like frogs and peacocks made fat and joyous
> By the waters of the first rains.   (251)

The men and women of Avadh were immersed in love
So that their days passed like the blink of an eye.
Sita assumed as many forms as she had mothers-in-law,
And served them reverently, with equal attention,
Yet no one but Ram saw this mystery,
For all illusion is inherent in Sita's maya.
Sita, by her service, won over her mothers-in-law,
And they, greatly pleased, instructed and blessed her.
Seeing the two brothers and Sita so sincere and simple,
The perverse queen repented to the full.
Kaikeyi implored the earth and Jamraj,
But neither would the ground open up to swallow her, nor did fate
    give her death.
Tradition, the Vedas and poets all declare—
Even hell does not take in one hostile to Ram.

In everyone's mind was this uncertainty now—
'Oh God, will Ram return to Avadh or not?'

> With no sleep by night or appetite by day,
> Bharat was troubled by this pure thought,
> Like a fish stuck in the mud at the bottom of the pond
> Worrying about the lack of water.   (252)

'Using my mother as its excuse, fate wrought this mischief,
Like a ripening crop of rice threatened by calamities.
And now, how will Ram's coronation be accomplished?
I cannot think of a single way.
He would certainly return in obedience to our guru's command—
But the guru will order him to return only if he knows it to be
       Ram's will.
If his mother asks, then too Raghurao would return—
But will Ram's mother ever so insist?
And I, who am but his servant, I am of no account,
That too in these evil times and fate hostile to me.
Were I to insist, it would be a grievous sin—
A servant's dharma is heavier than Mount Kailash!'
Bharat could not settle his mind on a single plan,
And his whole night passed in anxious thought.
At dawn, he bathed and bowed his head to the Lord,
And had just sat down when the Rishi Vasishtha sent for him.

> Saluting his guru's lotus feet
> And receiving his permission, Bharat sat down,
> While the Brahmans, important citizens, ministers
> And all the councillors came and assembled there.   (253)

The great muni spoke in words appropriate to the occasion,
'Listen to me, councillors and you, wise Bharat.
The upholder of dharma, sun of the solar dynasty,

King Ram, is the Supreme God, dependent on none but himself,
True to his word, and preserver and guardian of the Vedas.
Ram's birth is the source of well-being to this world.
Obedient to the words of guru, father and mother,
He destroys the armies of the wicked and is the benefactor of
    the gods.
Duty, love, spiritual and material truth—
No one knows these as perfectly as Ram.
Vidhi, Hari, Har, the moon and the sun, the guardians of
    the spheres,
Maya, the soul, all karma and time,
The serpent-king, the lords of the earth and whatever other powers
    there may be,
Even the magic powers acquired through yogic practice, praised in
    the Shastras and Vedas—
Ponder well in your hearts and you will clearly see—
They are all under Ram's command.

    Therefore, it will be to our benefit
    To obey and carry out Ram's command and wish.
    Keeping this in mind, all you wise men should
    Now do what you unanimously resolve.   (254)

Ram's coronation will bring happiness to all,
And is the only path to well-being and joy.
But how can Raghurao be persuaded to return to Avadh?
Think about this and propose a plan, and on it we shall act.'
All listened reverently to the great muni's speech
Steeped in justice, truth and worldly wisdom,
But no one had an answer, for no one could think of a plan.
Then, bowing his head, Bharat said with folded hands,
'There have been many kings in the dynasty of the sun,
Each one greater than the last.
All owe their birth to their fathers and mothers,

But it is providence that dispenses the good or bad fruit of
     their actions.
But the whole world knows that it is your blessing alone
That destroys sorrow and bestows all happiness.
It is you, lord, who have altered the course of destiny,
Who, then, can change a decision you have made?

          And yet now, you ask me for a plan—
          This is all my misfortune.'
          Hearing these affectionate words,
          The guru's heart swelled with love.   (255)

'Son,' he said, 'what you say is true, but it is all Ram's grace.
He who is hostile to Ram cannot achieve success even in dream.
There is one way, my son, though I hesitate to say it,
The wise will sacrifice half when the whole is in danger of
     being lost—
Do you two brothers go into exile in the forest,
And let Lakshman, Sita and Raghurao be brought back.'
Upon hearing these pleasing words, the two brothers rejoiced,
And their entire bodies were suffused with joy.
Their hearts were as elated and their bodies as radiant with joy
As though the king was alive again and Ram had become king.
For the people, this seemed great gain and little loss,
But the queens wept, for their sorrow was equal to their joy.
Said Bharat, 'Doing as the muni proposes,
Will yield the fruit of giving to all beings in the world what they desire.
I will live in the forest all my life—
There is no greater happiness than this for me.

          Ram and Sita pervade all hearts,
          And you are all-knowing and wise.
          If you do mean what you say, lord,
          Make your words come true.'   (256)

Hearing Bharat's words and seeing his love,
The muni and the whole assembly lost all awareness of themselves.
Bharat's immense glory was the ocean,
And the muni's proposal, a woman standing on its shore,
Longing to cross, and searching for ways to do so,
But finding neither boat, nor ship, nor raft.
Who else, then, can tell of Bharat's glory?
Can the ocean be contained in a pond-mussel's shell?
Deeply pleased with Bharat in his heart, the muni
With the whole assembly, came to Ram.
The Lord made obeisance and offered him a seat of honour,
And all sat down on receiving the muni's permission.
The noble muni then spoke words he had considered well,
And which were appropriate to the place, time and circumstances.
'Listen, Ram, all-knowing and wise,
You are the abode of dharma, prudence, virtue and wisdom.

>You dwell in the hearts of all,
>And know all sentiments, good and bad.
>The citizens of Avadh, the royal mothers and Bharat—
>Give me, then, a solution that will benefit them all.   (257)

The distressed speak without thinking,
And a gambler sees only his own move.'
On hearing the muni's words, Raghurao replied,
'Master, the solution is in your own hands,
For it will be beneficial to all to follow your wishes,
And gladly obey your commands, regarding them as the truth.
First, whatever be your command to me,
I will fulfil, reverently carrying out your instruction.
And then, master, whatever command you give, to whoever,
He will carry out fully, devoting himself to your service in
    every way.'
The muni replied, 'Ram, you have spoken truly,

But Bharat's love has deprived me of my ability to think.
That is why I will say again and again,
That my mind is overwhelmed by Bharat's devotion,
And in my opinion—as Shiv is witness—whatever you do,
Honouring Bharat's wishes, will be the best.

> Listen, first, with attention to Bharat's prayer,
> And reflect upon it,
> Then, extracting the wisdom of saints, worldly
>   opinion,
> The rules of kingship, and the Vedas, do as
>   they enjoin.'   (258)

Seeing the guru's love for Bharat,
Ram's heart was especially glad.
Knowing Bharat to be a staunch upholder of dharma
And his own faithful servant in body, mind and speech,
Ram, in accordance with the guru's command,
Spoke gentle, soft and pleasing words.
'Master, I swear by you and by my father's feet—
There has never been a brother like Bharat in this world.
Those who love their guru's lotus feet,
Are considered very fortunate in this world and in the Vedas,
So who can describe Bharat's good fortune,
For whom you hold such love?
Knowing that he is my younger brother, my mind shrinks
From praising Bharat to his face.
But whatever Bharat says will be good for us to do.'
So saying, Ram became silent.

> Then the muni said to Bharat,
> 'Now abandon all hesitation, son,
> And to the ocean of compassion, your own dear brother,
> Say what you have in your heart.'   (259)

Hearing the muni's words and receiving Ram's consent,
Bharat was gratified to know that his guru and his master were on
    his side.
But knowing the whole burden to be upon his head,
He could say nothing, and remained lost in thought.
His body trembling, he stood there in the assembly,
His lotus eyes overflowing with tears of love.
'The king of sages has already spoken for me—
What more shall I say?
I know my own master's disposition,
He is never angry even with those who do wrong.
He holds especial kindness and love for me,
For even at play I never saw him angry.
From childhood, I have never left his side,
And he has never broken my heart.
I have seen in my heart the Lord's gracious ways,
Even if I were losing in a game, he would make me win.

> And I, constrained by love and diffidence,
> Have never opened my mouth in front of him.
> And my eyes, thirsting for his love,
> Have not yet been sated by his sight.   (260)

But fate could not bear to see me so loved,
And in the form of my vile mother, caused a rift between us.
To say this does not befit me even today,
For who becomes virtuous and pure by his own estimation?
That my mother is base and I am noble and good—
To even admit this into the heart is equal to a million misdeeds.
Can an ear of kodo yield good rice,
Or a black snail bring forth a pearl?
Not even in dream does the smallest particle of blame attach
    to anyone,
For it is my bad luck that is a fathomless ocean.

Without understanding the result of my own sins,
I vainly hurt my mother by harsh words.
Searching my heart in every direction, I am defeated,
And in one way only is my good assured—
With the great muni for my guru, and Sita and Ram for my masters,
I feel that all will be well in the end.

In this assembly of good men, in the presence of my guru and
    my lord,
And in this holy place, I speak what I truly feel,
And whether this is love or deceit, falsehood or truth,
The muni and Raghurao know.   (261)

To the king's death, honouring his promise of love,
And my mother's wickedness, the whole world is witness.
The royal mothers are so distraught, I cannot bear to look at them,
The men and women of Avadh burn in intolerable anguish.
It is I who am the cause of all this suffering,
And I endure the pain of hearing and knowing.
When I heard that Raghunath had left for the forest
In the robes of an ascetic, with Lakshman and Sita,
On foot and without shoes—
May Shankar be my witness—I survived this wound.
And again, when I saw the Nishad's love,
My adamant-hard heart refused to break.
Now, coming here, I have seen all with my own eyes,
But my unfeeling soul continues to live and will make me suffer it all.
Those at the sight of whom even snakes and scorpion on the road
Abandon their deadly venom and fierce anger—

Those same Raghunandan, Lakshman and Sita,
Appeared to Kaikeyi as her enemies.
Upon whom, then, but her son should fate
Inflict intolerable anguish?'   (262)

Hearing Bharat's greatly distraught but noble speech,
Steeped in anguish, love, humility and justice,
The whole assembly grew bewildered and was plunged into grief,
Like a cluster of lotuses blighted by frost.
Then, by relating many ancient tales and legends,
The wise and learned muni comforted Bharat,
And Raghunandan, moon to the lilies of the sun's dynasty,
Spoke words that were fitting and right.
'Dear brother, you distress your heart in vain,
For know that your soul is subject to the ways of God.
In my opinion, in all time, past, present and future, and in all the
    three spheres,
All the most virtuous and righteous souls are less than you.
To accuse you of treachery even in one's heart,
Would bring ruin in this world and the next.
Those who blame your mother are fools
Who have never served their guru or the good.

> All sin and delusion, and the whole burden
> Of misfortune will be destroyed,
> And glory in this world and bliss in the next attained
> By the mere recollection of your name.   (263)

By my nature, I speak the truth, and with Shiv as my witness, I say,
Bharat, this earth continues in your guardianship.
Dear brother, do not needlessly blame yourself,
For even upon trying, enmity and love cannot be concealed.
Birds and beasts venture close to munis,
But seeing fowlers and huntsmen, they flee.
Even animals and birds know friend from foe,
And man is the abode of virtue and wisdom!
Dear brother, I know you well,
But what can I do? There is great confusion in my heart.
The king, to keep his promise, abandoned me,

And to keep his vow of love, discarded his body.
To disregard his word would grieve my heart,
But even more than that, I bow to you.
Moreover, our guru has given me his command—
So, whatever you say, I want most certainly to do.

> Therefore, with a happy heart and casting away this diffidence,
> Speak out, and I will do what you wish this very day.'
> Hearing this speech of Raghubar's, who is ever truthful to his word,
> The gathering grew glad.   (264)

But Indra and the other gods grew afraid,
And worried, 'Now all our plans will be undone.'
They could think of no scheme or stratagem,
So they all turned to Ram in their hearts.
Then they reflected and said to each other,
'Raghupati is always won over by a devotee's devotion.'
Remembering Ambarish and Durvasa,
The gods and their king became utterly disheartened.
The gods had endured great distress for many ages,
Until Prahlad had caused Narhari[xiii] to become manifest.
Beating their heads, they whispered in each other's ears,
'This time, the work of the gods is in Bharat's hands—
There is no other solution in sight, divine ones.
Ram acknowledges service done to his faithful servants,
So, with hearts full of love, let us all invoke Bharat,
Who has won over Ram by his virtue and goodness.'

> Hearing the decision of the gods, their guru, Brihaspati, declared,
> 'This is well done and great is your good fortune,
> For the root of all well-being in this world
> Is devotion to Bharat's feet.   (265)

[xiii] Vishnu's fourth avatar

Service of a servant of Sita's lord
Is as good as a hundred Kamadhenus.
Now that devotion to Bharat has entered your hearts,
Abandon worry, for fate has now accomplished your purpose.
Behold, lord of the gods, Bharat's power and influence—
The lord of the Raghus is utterly subject to his sincere and
    guileless nature.
Make still your minds, gods, and do not fear,
Knowing Bharat to be Ram's shadow.'
Hearing the fears of the gods and the advice of their guru,
The Lord, who pervades all hearts, grew anxious.
Bharat, believing the whole burden to be on his head,
Pondered countless ways and means in his mind.
After much thought he came to the conclusion
That it was in obeying Ram's will that his own happiness lay.
'He will break his own vow to fulfil mine—
So great is his kindness and love.

    Great and immeasurable grace
    Has Sita's lord shown me in every way.'
    Bowing low, and folding his lotus hands,
    Bharat spoke.   (266)

'Now, what more can I say or have others say for me, Lord?
You are an ocean of compassion and pervade all hearts.
My guru is pleased, my master well-disposed towards me,
So the imagined anguish of my troubled mind has disappeared.
My fears were unfounded, my anxiety baseless—
It is not the sun's fault, Lord, if one loses one's way.
My ill-fortune, my mother's wickedness,
The tortuous ways of providence, the cruelty of fate,
All came together vowing to destroy me.
But you, protector of suppliants, upheld your vow and protected me.
This is not a new or novel way for you to act—

It is well known in the world and in the Vedas, and no secret!
If the world is hostile, and you, master, alone are favourable,
Tell me, by whose grace but yours can one's good be achieved?
Your nature, divine Lord, is like the celestial Kalpataru,
Always favourable, and never hostile to anyone.

> When one approaches that tree, recognizing it as such,
> Its shade alone destroys all sorrow,
> And everyone in this world, whether prince or pauper,
>   good or bad,
> Receives his heart's desire merely upon asking.   (267)

Seeing my guru and my master to be loving in every way,
My anxiety has vanished, my mind freed from doubt.
Now, ocean of compassion, do that by which
You have no worry in your heart, Lord, over this lowly servant.
A servant who would constrain his master,
Desiring only his own good, is mean-minded and worthless.
A servant's good lies in his master's service,
Laying aside all pleasures and wants.
Your return is in the interest of all, master,
But in doing your will, lie countless kinds of good,
For it is the essence of all truth, mundane and sublime,
The fruit of all good actions, and adorns even salvation.
Divine Lord, listen to this one prayer of mine,
And then do whatever may be right—
I have brought everything that is needed for your consecration—
Let it all be properly used, Lord, if you are agreeable.

> Send me with our younger brother, Shatrughna, to the forest,
> And returning to Avadh, give the people their king and
>   protector,
> Or send back both our brothers, master,
> And let me accompany you.   (268)

Or else, let us three brothers go to the forest,
While you, Raghurai, return home with Sita.
Whatever, Lord, may please your heart,
Ocean of compassion, do only that.
Divine Lord, you have placed the whole burden on me,
Though I have no political wisdom, or know the right course
    of conduct.
All that I say is motivated by self-interest,
For the mind of one in anguish lacks discernment.
The servant who hears his master's orders but answers him back,
Is a sight that even shame is ashamed to look upon.
Such am I, a bottomless ocean of sin,
Though my master, from his love for me, praises me as good.
Now, compassionate Lord, I am happy with the plan
That will not constrain my master's heart in any way.
By my Lord's feet I swear and sincerely declare
The only way to ensure the world's well-being—

    Whatever order our Lord, with a pleased heart
    And without hesitation, may give anyone,
    We must all fully and reverently obey,
    And all this injustice and turmoil will end.'   (269)

Hearing Bharat's pure speech, the gods rejoiced
And praising his goodness, they rained down flowers.
The residents of Avadh were overwhelmed by uncertainty,
Though the ascetics and other forest-dwellers were delighted.
Hesitant, Raghunath himself remained silent,
And seeing the Lord's state, the gathering grew anxious.
At that very moment messengers from Janak arrived,
And Muni Vasishtha, hearing of their arrival, sent for them at once.
Saluting reverently, they looked at Ram,
And seeing his attire, grew deeply sorrowful.
The noble muni asked the messengers,

'Tell me, is all well with Videha's king?'
At this they grew abashed, and bowed their heads to the ground,
Then folding their hands, the royal messengers replied,
'Your courteous inquiry, master,
Is itself a reason for well-being, sire,

> For otherwise, all our happiness left,
> Along with the king of Koshal,
> Who has left the whole world orphaned,
> Especially Mithila and Avadh.   (270)

Hearing of the king of Koshal's death, the residents of Janak's city
All became demented with overwhelming grief.
Anyone who saw Videh at that time,
Would not think his name to be true.[53]
When the lord of men heard of the queen's evil,
He could make no sense of it and was as bewildered as a serpent
    bereft of its jewel.
Bharat to be king, and Raghubar exiled to the forest!
The news plunged Mithila's king into deep distress.
The king asked his council of wise men and ministers,
"Think carefully and tell me—what is the right course of action now?"
Considering the state of turmoil in Avadh and in doubt about
    both actions,
No one could say whether he should stay or go.
The king then composed himself and after deep reflection,
Sent four clever spies to Avadh, instructing them thus:
"Find out if Bharat is well-disposed or hostile,
And come back quickly, without being recognized."

> The spies went to Avadh, ascertained
> Bharat's state and observed his actions,
> And when Bharat departed for Chitrakut,
> The four left for Terahuti.   (271)

The spies returned and gave an account of Bharat's actions,
According to their understanding, in Janak's court.
Hearing their report, our guru Shatanand, the king's household, his
    ministers, and the king himself
Grew distraught with love and worry.
Then, collecting himself and praising Bharat,
The king summoned his best warriors and army chiefs,
Appointed sentries to guard his palace, the city and the kingdom,
And had elephants, horses, chariots and vehicles of many kinds
    made ready.
Then, determining an auspicious moment within the hour, he left
    without delay—
The lord of the earth did not even rest along the way.
At dawn this very day, he bathed at Prayag,
And when the host began to cross the Jamuna,
Our lord sent us on ahead to gather information.'
Saying thus, they bowed their heads to the ground.
Giving them an escort of six or seven Kirat men,
The great muni immediately sent the messengers back.

    Hearing that Janak was coming,
    The whole party from Avadh was delighted.
    But Raghunandan himself felt greatly embarrassed,
    And Indra, lord of the gods, was overwhelmed
        with worry.   (272)

Perverse Kaikeyi was tormented by remorse,
But to whom could she speak, and whom could she blame?
Men and women rejoiced when they realized
That they could now stay a few days longer.
In this way, that day was spent.
At daybreak next morning, all began their morning ablutions,
And after bathing, the men and women performed their
    morning worship

Of Ganpati, Gauri, Tripurari and Tamari.[xiv]
They then paid homage to the feet of Ramaa's lover,
And with folded hands and outspread anchals, pleaded,
'Let Ram be our king, and Janaki our queen,
And their capital, Avadh, become the pinnacle of joy,
Thriving and prospering with its people once again.
Let Ram make Bharat his heir-apparent.
Immersing all in this nectar of joy,
God, give us all the reward of our existence in this world.

> With the help of his guru, council of ministers, and brothers,
> Let Ram rule over the city,
> And let us die in Avadh while Ram is still king!'
> Thus did everyone plead.   (273)

Hearing the love-filled words of the people of Ayodhya,
Learned munis scorned their own asceticism and detachment.
In this way, completing their daily worship, the citizens of Avadh
Paid homage to Ram, their bodies trembling with joy.
Of high, low and middle estate, men and women
All obtained a sight of him, each according to their
        own inclination.
He honoured them all with careful attention,
And all praised him as the abode of compassion.
'From childhood it has been said of Raghubar,
That recognizing love, he upholds what is right.
An ocean of goodness and restraint is Raghurao,
With his beautiful face,[54] bright eyes, and artless disposition.'
Lovingly recounting the sum of Ram's virtues,
All began to praise their own good fortune,
'Few in this world are as full of merit as we,
Whom Ram recognizes and accepts as his own!'

_____

xiv   Tamari, 'the destroyer of darkness', i.e., the sun

All were thus immersed in love,
When they heard that the king of Mithila approached.
The sun to the lotuses of the solar dynasty,
Together with that whole assembly, rose in
      confused haste.   (274)

With his brothers, his minister, his guru and the people of Ayodhya,
Raghunath went forth to receive the king.
The moment the lord of the Janak dynasty saw Kamadgiri, that
    noble hill,
He made obeisance to it and abandoned his chariot to walk.
In their longing and eagerness to see Ram,
No one felt even the slightest fatigue or distress from the journey.
Their minds were with Raghubar and Vaidehi,
And how can a body without a mind know pain or pleasure?
Janak with his entourage approached, walking
As if intoxicated with love.
Seeing them draw near, all were filled with love,
And began to reverently greet each other.
Janak made obeisance at the feet of Vasishtha and the munis
    from Ayodhya,
And Raghunandan paid homage to Shatanand and the rishis
    from Mithila.
Ram and his brothers then greeted the king,
And escorted him and his retinue to their hermitage.

Their ashram was an ocean filled
With the pure water of tranquillity,
Into which Raghunath led
Janak's host, a river of tender despair.   (275)

The river overflowed its banks of wisdom and detachment,
As words of grief that were its tributary streams and torrents
    flowed into it.

Sighs and lamentations were the wind and waves
That uprooted the great trees of fortitude along its shore.
Terrible anguish was its swift current,
And fear and delusion its countless eddies and whirlpools.
The learned were the ferrymen, and wisdom their great boat,
But even they could not row across it, for they could not gauge the
    river's depth.
The poor Kols and Kirats who roam the forest
Were like wayfarers, dazed and disheartened upon seeing it,
And when it met the ocean that was the ashram,
It was as though that great ocean surged up in turmoil.
Both royal retinues were distraught with grief,
And lost all wisdom, fortitude and restraint.
Praising the dead king's majesty, virtue and goodness,
They plunged into an ocean of sorrow, weeping.

Immersed in an ocean of sorrow, deeply distraught,
Women and men lamented in their anguish.
All angrily blamed fate, and asked,
'What has perverse providence done?'
Gods, Siddhas, ascetics, yogis
And munis beheld Videh's condition,
And, says Tulsi, not one amongst them was capable
Of crossing that river of his love.

> Everywhere, in countless ways,
> Great munis consoled the people with wise advice,
> And Vasishtha said to Videh,
> 'Take courage, lord of men!'   (276)

The sun of whose wisdom destroys the night of rebirth,
And the bright rays of whose words make the lotuses that are
    the munis, bloom—
Can delusion or attachment even come near him?

This grief was the splendour of his love for Sita and Ram!
Those engaged in worldly pursuits, those seeking spiritual truth,
    and the wise who have attained perfection—
These are the three types of living beings in this world,
    say the Vedas.
But only one whose heart is sweetened by love for Ram
Is greatly honoured in the assembly of holy men.
Learning without love for Ram does not please or adorn,
But is like a ship without a helmsman.
The muni consoled Videh in many ways,
And all the people bathed at Ram's ghat.
All the men and women were full of grief,
And that day passed without anyone taking a sip of water.
Even the cattle, birds and deer did not eat,
So what can be said of Ram's own dear family and household?

    At dawn next day, the two parties bathed
    With Nimi's royal descendant and the lord of the Raghu line,
    And then all went and sat under the banyan tree,
    Their hearts heavy, their bodies weak and thin.   (277)

The Brahmans—from Dasharath's city, Avadh,
And those from the capital of the king of Mithila,
With the guru of the solar line and Janak's family priest,
Who had explored the paths to worldly prosperity and
    spiritual truth—
Began to give numerous discourses
Filled with dharma, prudence, detachment and discernment.
Rishi Kaushik related ancient tales and legends,
Eloquently instructing the entire assembly.
Then Raghunath said to Kaushik,
'Master, yesterday, everyone remained without water.'
Said the muni, 'Raghurai speaks rightly—
Two and a half watches of this day have also passed.'

Perceiving what was in the Rishi's mind, the king of Terahuti said,
'It is not fitting, here, to partake of grain.'[55]
The king's gracious words pleased everyone,
And, receiving his royal permission, they went to bathe.

At that same time came the forest-dwellers,
Bringing with them great quantities
Of fruits, flowers, shoots and roots of many kinds
In brimming baskets slung on poles across their shoulders.   (278)

By Ram's favour, the hills became granters of all desires,
And merely to look upon them removed all sorrow.
Lakes, streams, forests, and every part of the land
Seemed to overflow with joy and love.
Creepers and young trees became laden with fruits and flowers,
And birds, beasts and bees called in harmony.
At that time, the forest was overflowing with immense joy,
And cool, soft and fragrant breezes soothed and delighted all.
Its heart-enchanting beauty was impossible to describe—
It was as though earth herself was welcoming Janak as her guest.
Then, all the people in Janak's train bathed,
And, receiving permission from Ram, Janak and Vasishtha,
The townsfolk delightedly picked out suitable trees,
Beneath which they set up camp.
Shoots and fruits, tubers and roots of various kinds,
Pure, fresh and delicious as nectar,

Were reverently sent to all by Ram's guru, Vasishtha
In laden baskets, filled to the brim.
After offering worship to ancestors, gods, guests and guru,
They began their meal of fruit and forest fare.   (279)

In this way, four days went by,
And gazing upon Ram, the men and women were blissful.

In the hearts of both companies was this feeling:
'It is not good to return without Sita and Ram.
Living in the forest with Sita and Ram
Is ten million times more delightful than living in Indra's
    immortal city.
One who would prefer home,
Leaving Lakshman, Ram and Vaidehi,
Is surely ill-fated.
For it is only when the gods are favourable to us all,
That we can we live close to Ram, in the forest.
Bathing daily all three times in the Mandakini,
Seeing Ram, the accumulation of joy and well-being,
Wandering on Ram's hill, through the forests, and amidst the
    ascetics' hermitages,
Feasting on nectar-sweet tubers, roots and fruits,
The period of twice-seven years will pass in bliss
Like a moment, and we will not even know of its passing.'

    'But we are not worthy of such happiness,
    We do not have such good fortune,' said all.
    Such was the innate and artless love
    In both parties for Ram's feet.   (280)

Thus they all yearned for their heart's desire,
And to hear their loving words stole one's heart away.
Just then, handmaidens sent by Sita's mother
Came, and determining a suitable hour for a visit, returned.
Learning that all Sita's mothers-in-law were at leisure,
The royal women of King Janak's family came there.
Kaushalya reverently welcomed them,
And offered them such seats as the situation allowed.
There was such courtesy and love on both sides
That to see it or hear of it would melt even adamant.
Their weak bodies trembling with love, their eyes full of tears,

They sat sorrowing, scratching the earth with their toenails.
All were like personifications of love for Sita and Ram,
Like pity itself sorrowing in many forms.
Sita's mother said, 'Perverse is the mind of fate,
That he uses a chisel of adamant to shatter the foam on milk!

> We hear of amrit, but can see only poison,
> And the actions of the Creator are terrible indeed.
> Crows, owls and storks are everywhere,
> But the virtuous swan, only upon the Manas lake.'   (281)

Hearing this, the lady Sumitra sorrowfully agreed,
'The ways of the Creator are contrary and strange,
Who makes and nurtures, and then destroys—
Destiny is as mindless as a child at play!
Kaushalya said, 'It is no one's fault,
For grief and joy, loss and gain, all are subject to our past deeds.
The ways of karma are inexorable and known only to the Creator,
Who dispenses all its fruits, good and bad.
God's command prevails over all,
On creation, preservation, destruction; on life-destroying poison
       and life-giving nectar.
It is no use, divine lady, to grieve thus in the grip of affection,
For such is this illusory world created by Brahma—
       unalterable, eternal.
Recalling the king's life and death,
We grieve, my dear, only considering our own loss.'
Sita's mother replied, 'Your words are true and wise,
Queen to that pinnacle of virtue, the lord of Avadh!'

> 'If Lakshman, Ram and Sita go to the forest,
> The end result of that will be good, not bad,'
> Kaushalya said, and added with a heavy heart,
> 'But I am worried about Bharat.   (282)

By God's grace and your blessing,
My sons and their wives are as pure as the water of the
    divine Ganga.
I have never yet sworn an oath on Ram,
But I do now, dear friend, and say to you truthfully,
That Bharat's gentle nature, virtue, modesty, gracious generosity,
His brotherly affection, devotion, trustworthiness and goodness—
In praising them even Sharada's eloquence falters.
After all, can the ocean be emptied out with a shell?
I have always known Bharat to be the light of our dynasty,
As the king, too, told me again and again.
Gold is tested when rubbed on a touchstone, a precious gem in the
    hands of an expert,
And a man by his behaviour in his hour of trial.
But it is not right for me to speak thus today,
For grief and love leave us with little wisdom.'
Hearing her words, as pure as the divine river,
The queens all grew distraught with love.

> Kaushalya said, composing herself,
> 'Listen, my lady, queen of Mithila—
> Who can instruct you,
> The beloved of Janak, that storehouse of discernment?   (283)

But, queen, finding a suitable opportunity, say to the king,
Explaining in your own fashion,
"Let Lakshman be kept at home and Bharat go to the forest."
If this proposal is agreeable to the king,
He should think it through carefully and try to make it happen,
For I am deeply anxious about Bharat.
In Bharat's heart is such profound love,
That if he stays home, I fear that it will not end well.'
Seeing her gentle nature, and hearing her straight and simple words,
All the queens were overcome with tender pity.

Flowers fell from the sky amidst cries of praise and blessings,
And Siddhas, yogis and munis grew weak with love.
All the royal women were astounded at the sight,
But then, collecting herself, Sumitra said,
'My lady, an hour of the night has already passed.'
Hearing this, Ram's mother rose lovingly,

> And with concern and affection said,
> 'Return quickly to your tents.
> Our only refuge now is God,
> And the help of Mithila's king.'   (284)

Seeing her love and hearing her soft and gentle words,
Janak's beloved queen clasped Kaushalya's sacred feet.
'My lady, this modesty of yours is entirely fitting,
For you are Dasharath's wife and Ram's mother.
The great honour those who are less than them,
Just as fire crowns itself with smoke and a mountain with grass.
The king of Mithila is your servant in thought, word and deed,
And Mahesh and Bhavani are your constant helpers.
Who in this world is worthy of being your assistant?
Can a lamp attain glory by helping the sun?
Having gone to the forest and accomplished the gods' purpose,
Ram will return to reign firmly in Avadh.
Gods, Nagas and men, by the might of Ram's arm,
Will live in peace and happiness, each in their own realms.
All this was foretold by Jagbalik—
And, divine lady, a muni's words are never in vain.'

> So saying she clasped Kaushalya's feet, and with
>   great love asked
> That Sita might go with her.
> Receiving Kaushalya's gracious permission,
> Sita's mother then left with Sita.   (285)

Vaidehi met her beloved kinsfolk
In a manner befitting each one.
When they saw Janaki in ascetic's attire,
They all became distraught with sorrow.
Janak, receiving permission from Ram's guru,
Left for his camp, and arriving there, saw Sita.
Taking her in his arms, Janak clasped Janaki to his heart—
She, the guest of his pure love and life's breath—
And in his bosom surged up an ocean of love for his daughter.
The king's heart became like Prayag,
For in the swelling flood he saw growing the banyan of Sita's love,
And upon it, resplendent, the infant that was love for Ram.
The immortal sage that was Janak's bewildered wisdom,
Began to drown, but reached out for the child's help and
    was saved.[56]
Videh's mind was not one to be overcome by attachment—
This was the glory of his love for Sita and Raghubar.

    Sita, overwhelmed by her father and mother's love,
    Was so distraught she could scarcely control herself,
    But understanding the circumstances and her noble duty,
    The daughter of the earth took courage.   (286)

When Janak saw Sita in ascetic garb,
He was filled with special love and deeply gratified.
'Daughter, you have sanctified both families,
And your fair renown has made bright the whole world, say all.
The river of your fame surpasses even the river of the gods
As it flows through countless universes.
The Ganga exalts only three sites[57] on earth,
But the river of your fame sanctifies innumerable congregations of
    holy men.'
Her father lovingly spoke words that were true and gracious,
But Sita, embarrassed, seemed to shrink into herself.

Her father and mother again clasped her to their hearts,
Giving her wise advice and blessing her, for her good.
Sita did not say so, but was uneasy in her heart,
'It is not proper for me to stay here for the night.'
Perceiving her hesitation, the queen told the king,
And both praised her chaste and modest disposition in their hearts.

> Again and again they embraced Sita
> And reverently bade her farewell.
> Seeing now a good opportunity, the wise queen
> Eloquently described Bharat's state to the king.   (287)

When the lord of the earth heard of Bharat's conduct,
Like gold infused with sweet perfume, or nectar that is the moon's
        radiant essence,
He closed his tear-filled eyes, his body trembling with love,
And began joyously praising Bharat's great renown.
'Listen carefully, my beautiful, bright-eyed one,
For Bharat's story breaks the bonds of worldly existence.
Of righteousness, statecraft and reflections upon the Absolute,
I have some knowledge, according to my intellect,
But this mind of mine cannot even pretend to touch
The shadow of Bharat's greatness, much less describe it.
Vidhi, Ganpati, Sheshnag, Shiv and Sharada,
Poets, scholars, learned men and those renowned for their intellect,
To all of them, Bharat's story, his fame, actions,
Righteousness, goodness, virtues and stainless glory—
When heard or contemplated, give joy,
And are purer than the sacred Ganga, and sweeter than amrit.

> Of infinite virtues, a man without compare—
> Know that Bharat alone is like Bharat.
> The minds of all poets would hesitate
> To say Mount Sumeru weighs a ser.   (288)

His greatness, my lovely one, is as impossible to describe,
As it is for a fish to walk upon dry land.
Bharat's infinite majesty, my queen,
Ram alone understands—but even he cannot describe it.'
Thus, having affectionately praised Bharat's greatness,
The king understood his wife's wish, and said,
'If Lakshman returns and Bharat goes to the forest,
It may be good for all, and it is what everyone wants.
But, my lady, Bharat and Raghubar's
Love and trust for each other is beyond conception.
Bharat is the perfection of love and devotion,
Even though Ram is the pinnacle of objective equanimity.
Salvation, self-interest, or all the worldly pleasures—
Bharat has never looked at these, not even in his dreams.
Both the means and the end are in devotion to Ram's feet—
This, it seems to me, is the single principle of Bharat's creed.

> Bharat would never think, even by mistake,
> To flout Ram's command.
> So do not, overpowered by love, give way to worry.'
> Thus spoke the king, his voice full of tears.   (289)

Thus in lovingly recounting Ram's and Bharat's virtues,
The night passed like an instant for the couple.
At daybreak, both royal parties awoke,
Bathed, and began offering worship to the gods.
After bathing, Raghurai went to his guru, Vasishtha,
Paid homage to his feet, and, receiving permission, spoke.
'Master, Bharat, the people of Avadh, and the royal mothers,
Are all distraught with grief and exhausted by living in the forest.
The king of Mithila and his entire retinue, too,
Have been enduring hardships for many days now.
Therefore do whatever is proper, lord,
For the good of all is in your hands.'

Having spoken thus, Ram was greatly embarrassed,
But the muni was delighted to see his modest nature.
'Without you, Ram, every facility for comfort
Is like hell to both the royal parties.

> Ram, you are the very life-breath of life,
> The soul of souls, the joy of bliss itself.
> Ill-fated are those, dear son, who,
> Abandoning you, prefer their homes.   (290)

Let that happiness, those actions, and that dharma be destroyed
In which there is no love for Ram's lotus feet.
That meditation is false meditation, and that wisdom, ignorance
In which love for Ram is not supreme.
Without you all are sad, and if they are happy, they are so only
     through you,
For you know whatever there is in every heart.
All honour your commands,
For you, merciful one, know well their true state.
And now, return to your ashram.'
Saying this, the lord of munis was overcome by love.
Then Ram bowed to him and departed,
And the rishi, composing himself, went to Janak.
The guru repeated Ram's words to the king—
So innately graceful, loving and beautiful.
'Great king, now do what
Is righteous and to the advantage of all.

> Protector of your people, you are a storehouse of wisdom,
> Wise and true, and the upholder of righteousness.
> Who but you is capable at this time
> Of resolving this dilemma?'   (291)

Hearing the muni's words, Janak was overcome with love
And his wisdom and detachment left him.

Weak with love, he thought to himself,
'In coming here, I have not done well.
King Dasharath told Ram to go to the forest,
And then gave the ultimate proof of his love for his dear son.
But I will now send him from this forest into another,
And return rejoicing and praising my wisdom!'
The ascetics, munis and Brahmans heard and saw all this,
And overpowered by love, grew deeply troubled.
Considering the moment, the king composed himself,
And went, with his retinue, to see Bharat.
Bharat advanced to receive him,
And offered him the best seat that circumstances allowed.
'Bharat, dear son,' said the king of Terahuti,
'You know well Raghubir's nature.

> Ram is true to his word and devoted to his duty,
> And is kind and affectionate to all.
> Constrained by consideration for others, he endures
>   all problems.
> So whatever your command, now let him be told.'   (292)

Hearing this, Bharat's whole body trembled and his eyes filled
    with tears.
Gathering all his courage, he said,
'Lord, you are as beloved and revered as our father,
And our family guru is even more a well-wisher than mother or
    father.
And gathered here are Muni Kaushik and other sages, ministers
    and councillors,
And today, you yourself, ocean of wisdom, are here.
I am your son and servant, obedient to your commands—
Know me as such and tell me what to do, master.
In this assembly and in this holy place you question me—
If I stay silent, I will be a sinner, and if I speak, a madman.
Even so, insignificant though I am, I speak of important matters—

Forgive me, sire, knowing that providence is against me.
It is renowned in the Vedas, Shastras and Puranas,
And the world knows that the dharma of service is difficult.
Serving a master conflicts with self-interest,
Enmity is blind, and love unwise.

> So, keeping in mind Ram's wish, dharma and sacred promise
> And knowing me to be his servant,
> Do as all desire and for the good of all,
> Recognizing their love.'   (293)

Hearing Bharat's words and seeing his conduct,
The king and all the assembly began to praise him.
Simple yet profound, soft and sweet, yet resolute and firm,
His speech was vast in its meaning, though his words were few.
As the reflection of one's own face in the mirror cannot be grasped,
Though the mirror be held in one's hands—such was the mystery
    of his extraordinary speech.
Then the king, with Bharat, Vasishtha and the assembly
Went to Ram who delights the gods as the moon does the lilies.
Hearing what had happened, the people all grew restless
    with worry,
Like fish made uneasy by the season's first rain.
As for the gods, first they saw Vasishtha's state,
Then Videh's extraordinary love,
And then beheld Bharat, so full of devotion to Ram—
And the self-interested gods were dismayed and lost heart.
Seeing everyone filled with love for Ram,
They were overcome by inconceivable anxiety.

> 'Ram is ruled by love and humility,'
> Cried the worried king of the gods.
> 'We must together devise some scheme,
> Or else all will be undone!'   (294)

The gods invoked Sharada and, singing her praises, said,
'Goddess, we gods seek refuge in you, protect us!
Through the use of your maya, alter Bharat's mind,
And protect the race of immortals by spreading over them the cool
    shade of deception.'
When the wise goddess heard the gods' appeal,
She realized that their selfishness had made them dull, and replied,
'You ask me to alter Bharat's mind!
Your thousand eyes cannot see Sumeru!
The maya of Vidhi, Hari and Har is exceedingly potent,
But even that cannot see into Bharat's mind—
And that is the mind you ask me to bewilder?
Can moonlight steal away the flaming sun?
Bharat's heart is the abode of Sita and Ram—
Can darkness remain there, where shines the sun's light?'
Saying this, Sharada returned to Brahma's realm,
Leaving the gods as distraught as kok birds in the night.

    The gods, self-seeking and black of heart,
    Plotted together and devised an evil plan.
    Weaving a mighty net of delusion and deceit,
    They spread fear, confusion, sadness and worry.   (295)

Having done his evil deed, the king of gods began to think,
'Our purpose, its success or failure, is all in Bharat's hands!'
As Janak and the others came up to Raghunath,
The light of the solar dynasty received them all with honour.
In keeping with the occasion, the gathering and dharma,
Vasishtha, priest of the Raghu dynasty, spoke,
Relating the conversation between Janak and Bharat,
And Bharat's beautiful speech.
'Ram, dear son, whatever order you give,
Everyone will obey—that is my opinion.'
At this Raghunath folded his hands,

And spoke words that were truthful, simple and sweet.
'In your presence and that of the king of Mithila,
For me to speak will be in every way inappropriate.
Whatever you and the king command,
I swear by you, all of us will honour.'

> Hearing Ram's vow, the muni, King Janak,
> And all the assembly were disconcerted.
> They all looked at Bharat's face,
> Unable to reply.   (296)

When Bharat saw the assembly so overcome by awe,
Ram's brother gathered all his courage,
And, knowing it to be the wrong time, controlled his love
As the jar-born sage Agastya had stopped the rising
    Vindhya mountains.[58]
Grief, like Kanakalochan, stole the earth of their intellect,
But from the womb of Bharat's spotless perfections
Sprang forth the mighty boar of discernment,
And effortlessly delivered it that instant.[59]
With folded hands, Bharat bowed to everyone,
And humbly addressed Ram, the king, the guru and the sages.
'Forgive my very unbecoming behaviour today,
As with tender lips I speak harsh words.'
He invoked gracious Sharada in his heart,
And she came from the Manas lake of his heart to grace his
    lotus mouth.
Shining with pure wisdom, piety and righteousness,
Bharat's speech was a beautiful swan.

> Seeing with the eyes of wisdom
> An assembly made feeble with love,
> Bharat bowed to them all and spoke,
> Invoking Sita and Raghuraj.   (297)

'Lord, you are father, mother, friend, guru and master,
The one I revere, my greatest benefactor, knower of my heart.
Simple and sincere, a gracious master, the abode of goodness,
Protector of the weak, all-knowing and wise,
All-powerful benefactor of those who seek refuge,
You appreciate virtue and destroy vice and sin.
Lord, amongst all masters, you are like you alone,
And in my hostility to my master, I am like myself alone.
In delusion's grip, pushing aside your command and our father's,
I came here bringing with me a crowd of men and women.
In this world there is good and bad, high and low,
Amrit and immortality, poison and death,
But I have never heard and nowhere seen
One who goes against Ram's command, even in thought.
Yet, though that is what I have done in every way,
You, Lord, have taken my effrontery as love and service.

        In your grace and goodness, master,
        You have favoured me
        So that my faults have become like ornaments
        And my bright fame has spread in all directions.   (298)

Your ways, your gracious speech and your greatness
Are known throughout the world and sung in the Vedas and Shastras.
The cruel, the crooked, the vile, the evil-minded, the disgraced,
The base, the ill-natured, the godless and the unscrupulous—
If you hear that they have come to you for refuge
And have made but one obeisance, you take them as your own.
You see their faults but never take them to heart,
And hearing of their virtues, you praise them in the assembly of
    holy men.
What other master is so gracious to his servant
That he himself provides him with every necessity
And does not, even in a dream, reflect upon his own gracious actions,

But is always concerned in his heart about embarrassment to
    his servant?
There is no other lord like you—
So I solemnly declare with arms upraised.
Beasts may dance and parrots cleverly repeat a lesson,
But their skills depend upon their dancing-master and teacher.

    By thus ever reforming your servants and treating them
        with honour,
    You make them the crowning jewels of holy men.
    Who else but you, compassionate one,
    So persistently maintains his own great reputation?　　(299)

Out of grief, love, or mere childishness
I came here, in defiance of your royal command.
Yet, compassionate Lord, looking within yourself,
You think only well of me in every way.
I behold your feet, root of all well-being,
And know you, master, as innately benevolent to me.
In this vast gathering, I see my good fortune—
That despite my great error, my master loves me.
You have filled every part of me with kindness and mercy,
Compassionate Lord, more than I ever deserved,
And you have loved and cherished me, master,
In your natural benevolence and goodness.
Lord, I have been utterly presumptuous,
Discarding all deference to my master and this assembly,
Speaking as I have pleased, rudely or humbly.
Forgive me, divine Lord, knowing my deep distress.

    But it is a great fault to say too much
    To a loving, wise and gracious master.
    So now, Lord, give me your command,
    For you have fulfilled all my wishes.　　(300)

I swear by the dust of my Lord's lotus feet,
The glorious pinnacle of truth, good deeds and happiness,
And by that oath declare my heart's desire,
Whether awake, asleep, or dreaming—
Service to my master with love that is pure and true,
Relinquishing self-interest, deceit and life's four rewards.
There is no service like obedience to a gracious master,
And so, Lord, let your servant receive this favour.'
Saying this, Bharat was utterly overcome by love.
His body trembled and his eyes filled with tears,
And deeply agitated, he clasped the Lord's lotus feet—
That moment and that love cannot be described.
The ocean of mercy honoured him with gracious words,
And, taking his hand, seated him at his side.
Hearing Bharat's humble entreaty and seeing his noble nature,
The gathering and Raghurao grew weak with love.

Raghurao grew weak with love, as did the gathering of holy men,
Muni Vasishtha, and the king of Mithila,
And in their hearts, all praised the glorious greatness
Of Bharat's devotion and love for his brother.
Even the gods praised Bharat, though their hearts were anxious,
And rained down flowers.
Hearing Bharat's words, says Tulsi, all the people were
*   deeply troubled—*
And shrank into themselves like lotuses upon the coming of night.

Seeing every man and woman in both royal parties
Miserable and wretched,
Black-hearted Maghvan[xv] still sought his own well-being
By slaying those already dead.   (301)

[xv] Indra

The king of the gods is the very extreme of deceit and villainy,
To him is dear another's loss and his own gain.
Pakripu's[xvi] ways are like those of a crow—
Crafty, malicious, trusting no one.
First he made a vicious plot, then gathering together deceit,
Heaped worry and apprehension on everyone's head.
His divine maya deluded all the people,
But they never wavered in their love for Ram.
In the grip of fear and anxiety, their minds were unsteady—
One moment they yearned for the forest, one moment for
     their homes.
The people were distressed by this dilemma, their state of mind
     as turbulent
As the water where a river meets the sea.
In two minds, they could not find peace or comfort anywhere,
Nor did they tell each other their secret thoughts.
Seeing their state, the abode of compassion smiled to himself
     and said,
'A dog, Maghvan, and a youth are all the same!'

    Except for Bharat, Janak, the munis,
    The ministers and the enlightened sadhus,
    Everyone, according to their predisposition,
    Was affected by Indra's divine maya.   (302)

The ocean of compassion saw his people in distress
Due to their love for him and Indra's powerful trickery.
The assembly, king, guru, Brahmans, ministers—
The minds of all were spellbound by Bharat's devotion.
Still as painted figures, they gazed upon Ram,
Diffidently uttering words they seemed to have learnt by rote.
Bharat's love, courtesy, humility and greatness

[xvi] Indra

Are pleasing to hear, but difficult to describe.
Observing the smallest particle of his devotion,
The sages and Mithila's king became immersed in love,
So how, then, can Tulsi describe his majesty?
His devotion and nobility cause sublime thoughts to spring up in
    the poet's heart.
But realizing the smallness of its own thoughts, and the immensity
    of Bharat's glory,
The poet's mind hesitates, mindful of the dignity of all poets.
Enraptured by his perfections, yet unable to describe them,
The state of the poet's mind is like a child's inarticulate speech.

       Bharat's spotless fame is the unblemished moon,
       And the poet's mind, a young chakori,
       Gazing unblinking upon it as it rises
       In the clear sky of a devotee's heart.   (303)

Even the Vedas do not understand Bharat's noble nature,
So poets, forgive the faltering of my meagre intellect.
Telling and hearing of Bharat's true and faithful nature,
Who does not become enamoured of the feet of Sita and Ram?
If love for Ram is still not easily attained
Even by remembering Bharat, one is most unfortunate!
Seeing everyone's state, and the condition of his servant's heart,
Compassionate and all-wise Ram,
Steadfast upholder of dharma, resolute, adept in statecraft,
Ocean of truth, love, goodness and bliss—
Having considered place, time, circumstance and those
    gathered there,
Raghuraj, protector of love and righteousness,
Spoke words that arose from the depths of his heart,
Beneficial in their result and like the moon's nectar to hear.
'Dear brother, Bharat, you are the upholder of duty and righteousness,
Learned in custom and the Vedas, and wise in love.

In your purity of action, word and thought,
You, brother, are like you alone.
Yet, in this assembly of our elders, and in these
        adverse times,
How may a younger brother's virtues be told?   (304)

You know, dear brother, the customs of the solar line,
The renown and love of our father, who was ever true to his word,
The gravity of this occasion, the dignity of this assembly and of our
        revered elders,
And the hearts of our friends, our enemies and those who
        are neutral.
You alone know the imperative duty of all,
And the dharma that is best for you and me.
I have complete faith in you,
Yet, given these circumstances, I speak.
Dear brother, in the absence of our father, our interests
Are protected by the grace of our family guru.
Otherwise, with our subjects, household and family,
We would all have been ruined.
If the sun, lord of day, should set before it is time,
Tell me, who in this world would not suffer?
Providence has caused just such a calamity, dearest brother,
But the muni and Mithila's king have saved us all.

All the affairs of state, our honour, name, virtue,
Land, wealth and houses,
All will be protected by our guru's authority,
And all will be well in the end.   (305)

Your protector and mine, as well as our people's—
At home or in the forest—is the grace of our guru.
Obedience to the command of a mother, father, guru, or master
Is the celestial Sheshnag, bearing the earth of all dharma.

So act accordingly, and enable me to do the same.
Dear brother, be the protector of the solar line!
To an aspirant, this sole practice gives all spiritual accomplishments—
It is the triple stream of renown, power and salvation.
Reflecting upon this, though the grief you must endure will be heavy,
Make our subjects and our kinsfolk happy.
My misfortune has been shared by all, brother,
But upon you will be the greatest hardship for the entire duration
     of my exile.
Though I know that you are gentle and sweet, I speak harsh words,
But given these contrary times, it is not unjustified on my part.
In calamitous times, a good brother alone is one's helper,
Just as even a thunderbolt's strike is deflected by the shield of
     one's hand.'

          A servant should be like hands, feet and eyes,
          And the master, the mouth.
          Hearing of this way of love, says Tulsi,
          Good poets praise it.   (306)

When the whole assembly heard Raghubar's speech,
Steeped in nectar churned from the ocean of love,
All were overcome and entranced by love—
Seeing their state, Sharada herself was silent.
Bharat became supremely content—
His Lord was before him, and sorrow and guilt had left him.
His face joyous, his heart free of anguish,
Like a mute favoured by Gira with the gift of speech,
He again made loving obeisance
And folding his lotus hands, said,
'Lord, I have obtained the joy of having accompanied you
And received the reward of birth into this world.
Now, compassionate one, I will reverently and humbly do
Whatever you command.

But, divine Lord, give me some tangible support,
By the help of which I may pass the period of your exile.

> Divine Lord, for your coronation,
> And following our guru's instruction,
> I have brought with me water from all the holy places.
> What is your command regarding this?   (307)

And I have one more great longing in my heart,
But out of fear and awe, I cannot say it.'
'Tell me, dear brother,' said Ram, and thus receiving the Lord's
    permission,
Bharat replied in soft and loving tones.
'Chitrakut, its holy places and sacred forests,
Its birds and deer, its lakes, streams, waterfalls, its range of hills,
And especially its earth, marked with the imprint of your feet, Lord—
If you give me permission, I would like to go and see them all.'
'Of course, dear brother! Honour the sage Atri's commands,
And roam without fear through these woods and groves.
It is the muni's favour that makes this forest so benevolent,
So pure and supremely beautiful, my brother.
And wherever the lord of the rishis commands,
There deposit the water from the holy sites.'
Bharat was delighted to hear the Lord's words,
And joyfully went and bowed his head at the muni's lotus feet.

> Upon hearing Bharat and Ram's conversation—
> The root of all well-being—
> The selfish gods praised the Raghu dynasty,
> And rained down flowers from the divine Kalpataru.   (308)

'Praised be Bharat! Glory to Lord Ram!'
Cried the gods with great delight.
Vasishtha, Mithila's king and all the assembly

Rejoiced to hear Bharat's words.
The king of Videha, trembling with joy, praised
The virtues of Bharat and Ram and their mutual love,
The charming dispositions of servant and master,
And their loyalty and love, that made even the purest pure.
The ministers and councillors were enraptured,
And all began to praise the brothers, each according to
　　his understanding.
Hearing and listening to Ram and Bharat's conversation,
The hearts of both parties were filled with joy and sorrow.
Ram's mother, knowing joy and sorrow to be the same,
Comforted the other queens, relating Ram's virtues.
Some spoke of Raghubir's greatness,
While others praised Bharat's goodness.

　　　Then Atri said to Bharat,
　　　'Close by this mountain is a beautiful well.
　　　Pour into it the water from the holy sites,
　　　Pure, sweet as nectar, and without compare.'　　　(309)

Bharat, receiving Atri's permission,
Despatched all the water vessels,
And with his brother Shatrughna, the sage Atri, and other holy men,
Himself went to that deep and fathomless well,
And deposited the pure water in that sacred place.
Delighted, Atri lovingly said,
'Son, this place has brought success to the aspirant from eternity,
But hidden by time, it was known to no one.
Then my disciples, perceiving this spot to be endowed with
　　subterranean springs,
Dug a deep well here for this good water.
Now, by Fate's decree, the whole world has been benefitted—
That religious merit which was considered most difficult, has now
　　become easily attainable.

From now on, people will call this "Bharat's well",
Made most pure by having mixed into it water from the holy sites.
All those who bathe in it with love and according to ritual,
Will become pure in deed, thought and speech.'

> Relating the well's glory,
> Everyone returned to Raghurao,
> And Atri related to Raghubir,
> The sacred effect of that holy place.   (310)

In lovingly narrating sacred legends,
The night pleasantly passed and soon it was dawn.
After performing their daily rituals, and having received
Permission from Ram, Atri and their guru, Bharat and Shatrughna
Set off with their retinue, all simply clad,
To wander Ram's forest on foot.
As they walked without shoes upon their tender feet,
Earth grew embarrassed and made her surface soft and smooth.
Spiky blades of kush grass, thorns, pebbles, cracks and crevices,
And all such sharp, hard and unpleasant things she hid.
Earth made their path pleasant and easy,
While cool, soft and fragrant breezes blew, giving delight.
The gods rained down flowers, the clouds spread their shade,
The trees burst into flower and bore fruit, the grass grew soft,
And the deer with their glances, the birds with their sweet calls,
All served Bharat knowing him to be Ram's beloved brother.

> When an ordinary man can easily attain all accomplishments
> Merely by saying 'Ram' while yawning,
> For Bharat, as dear as life to Ram,
> This was no great wonder.   (311)

In this manner, Bharat roamed the forest,
And seeing his devotion and love, even the munis were overawed.

The sacred ponds and lakes, the tracts of land,
The birds, deer, trees, grass, hills, groves and gardens
Were all extraordinarily beautiful and especially pure and holy.
Seeing their divine beauty, Bharat asked about them.
Atri, king of rishis, heard his question and with a joyous heart
    told him
Their origin, name, attributes and spiritual efficacy.
In some places Bharat bathed, in others he paid homage,
Or simply gazed at their heart-enchanting beauty,
And in others, with the muni's permission, he sat
Meditating upon Sita and his two brothers.
Seeing his noble nature, his love and devoted service,
The forest gods were delighted and gave him their blessings.
So he would wander for two and a half watches of each day,
Before returning to gaze upon the lotus feet of his Lord.

> In five days, Bharat
> Saw all the sacred spots and holy places,
> And in relating and listening to the radiant glory of
>   Hari and Har,
> The fifth day also passed, and it was dusk.   (312)

Next morning at dawn, after bathing, all assembled,
With Bharat, the Brahmans and Terahuti's king.
Though knowing in his heart that it was an auspicious day for
    them to leave,
Ram, in his compassion, did not say so.
Seeing his guru, the king, Bharat and the gathering,
Ram hesitated and lowered his gaze to the ground.
The whole assembly praised his gentle goodness, thinking,
'Nowhere is there a master as courteous as Ram!'
But wise Bharat understood Ram's wish,
And lovingly rose, gathering all his courage.
Prostrating himself before Ram, he said with folded hands,

'Lord, you have honoured all my wishes.
For my sake, everyone has endured hardship,
And you, too, have suffered in many ways.
Now, Lord, give me your permission
To go back and serve Avadh for the duration of your exile.

> By whatever means, this servant may see
> Your feet again, merciful Lord—
> Instruct me in those means, compassionate king of Koshal,
> For the duration of your exile.   (313)

The people of Avadh, your kinsfolk and your subjects, Lord,
Are all made pure steeped in joy because of their bond of love
    with you.
The fiery anguish of birth and rebirth is worth it for your sake;
Without you, even salvation is worthless.
Lord, you are all-wise, and know the hearts of all,
And the wishes, longings and devotion of your servant's heart.
Protector of suppliants, you protect us all,
And sustain both this world and the next, divine Lord, till the
    very end.
Such is my total and complete faith,
And even when I reflect upon it, I have not the slightest doubt,
But my own misery, combined with my Lord's love,
Made me too bold.
Removing this great fault of mine, master,
And abandoning hesitation, instruct your devoted servant.'
All those who heard Bharat's entreaty, praised it,
For it was like the swan that separates milk from water.

> The befriender of the humble heard
> His own brother's humble and guileless words,
> And then, in accordance with place, time and circumstance,
> Ram, the all-wise, spoke.   (314)

'Dear brother, your care and mine and of our kinsfolk,
At home or in the forest, rests with our guru and the king.
As long our guru and the king of Mithila are our guardians,
You and I will suffer no distress even in our dreams.
Our supreme purpose, yours and mine,
Our self-interest, renown, duty and salvation,
All lie in this, that we two brothers follow our father's command—
By thus honouring the king's vow, the dignity of the world and the
    Vedas will be maintained.
Following the instruction of guru, father, mother and master,
Our feet will not stumble into a ditch even if we must travel a
    difficult road.
Reflecting upon this, put aside all worry,
And go back to nurture and protect Avadh for the duration
    of my exile.
The realm, the treasury, our family and household—
Their burden rests upon the dust of our guru's feet,
While you will protect our lands, subjects and capital city
In obedience to the instructions of the muni, our mothers and
    the ministers.'

        A ruler must be like the mouth,
        Which alone eats and drinks,
        But nourishes and protects all the parts of the body,
        Says Tulsi, with wisdom and discretion.   (315)

Herein lies the whole of a king's dharma,
Like desires lie hidden within the heart.'
Ram consoled his brother in many ways,
But without some tangible support, Bharat's mind found neither
    comfort nor peace.
Before Bharat's goodness, and their guru, ministers and people,
Raghuraj was overpowered by modesty and love,
And so, the Lord graciously gave him his sandals,

Which Bharat reverently accepted and placed upon his head.
The wooden sandals of the abode of compassion
Were like twin guardians of his people's lives,
A casket for the jewel that was Bharat's love,
The two syllables of Ram's name that bring salvation to people,
The two doors to guard the house of Raghu, two hands for good
    and noble work,
And the clear eyes of service and righteousness.
Receiving this support, Bharat was as delighted
As if Sita and Ram had agreed to remain in Avadh.

    Bowing reverently, he asked permission to depart,
    And Ram clasped him to his heart.
    But malevolent Indra, lord of the immortals,
    Seized this evil chance to make the people sad
        and weary.   (316)

But his villainous act proved good for all—
Like the hope of the end of Ram's exile, it became the life-giving
    Sanjivani of their lives,
Otherwise, all would have died, distraught, of the fatal disease
That was the grief of separation from Lakshman, Sita and Ram.
By Ram's grace, this difficulty was resolved,
And the hostile army of immortals became a benevolent protector.
Ram gathered Bharat in his arms and hugged him—
The bliss that is derived from his love cannot be described.
Ram's body, mind and speech overflowed with love,
So that that epitome of self-restraint abandoned composure,
And tears flowed from his lotus eyes.
Seeing his state, the assembled gods grew sorrowful,
And even those as steadfast as the munis, the guru and Janak—
The gold of whose minds had been refined in the fire of wisdom,
And whom Viranchi had created free from attachment,
Like lotus leaves born in the water that is this world—

Even they, seeing Raghubar and Bharat's
Incomparable and infinite love,
Were drowned in it—mind, body and speech,
Together with their detachment and discernment.   (317)

When the minds of Janak and the guru were overcome,
To call it common or ordinary would be a great mistake,
And to hear the description of the parting of Raghubar and Bharat
Would make the people think the poet cruel.
The tenderness of that moment is inexpressible, and the poet's
    sweet voice,
Remembering that loving moment, hesitates.
Raghubar embraced Bharat and comforted him,
And then gladly drew Ripudavan[xvii] to his heart.
Servants and ministers, with Bharat's approval,
Left and set about their tasks.
Both parties were profoundly sad to hear this,
And began to make preparations to leave.
After making obeisance at the Lord's lotus feet, the two brothers
Set out, in reverent obedience to Ram's command,
Paying homage to munis, ascetics and forest gods
And honouring them again and again.

They embraced Lakshman and paid him homage,
Placed the dust of Sita's feet upon their heads,
And hearing her blessing, root of all well-being,
They lovingly set forth.   (318)

Ram and his younger brother bowed their heads to the king,
With many expressions of humility and respect.
'Lord, moved by pity, you have suffered great anguish,
In coming to the forest with your retinue.

---

xvii Shatrughna

Now give us your blessing and set out for your city.'
Composing himself, the lord of the earth departed.
Ram honoured the munis, Brahmans and ascetics,
And took leave of them considering them to be the same as Hari
    and Har.
The two brothers then went to their mother-in-law,
Paid homage to her feet, and receiving her blessing, returned.
Then the sages Kaushik, Vamdev, Jabali,
The people of the city, his kinsfolk and faithful ministers—
In the proper manner, with humble salutation,
Ram, with his brother, took his leave of them all.
Men and women, of low, middling, or high station,
Were honoured and sent back by the treasure-house of mercy.

> The Lord saluted the feet of Bharat's mother
> And embraced her with purest love.
> Removing all her shame and grief,
> He placed her in a palanquin, and took his leave of her.   (319)

Sita met her kinsfolk, mother and father,
And returned, pure in her love for her husband beloved as life.
She made obeisance to all her mothers-in-law and
    embraced them—
The poet's heart hesitates to describe that love.
Listening to their instruction, and receiving the desired blessing,
Sita remained immersed in both loves.[60]
Raghupati called for elegant palanquins,
And, with consoling words, helped all his mothers into them.
Again and again the two brothers embraced them,
And, with equal love, bid all their mothers farewell.
Making ready their horses, elephants and many kinds of carriages,
The parties of Bharat and the king departed.
With Ram, Sita and Lakshman in their hearts,
The people all proceeded as though dazed.

Bullocks, horses, elephants and other animals had lost heart,
And had to be coaxed along against their will, sad and dejected.

> The Lord, with Sita and Lakshman,
> Paid homage to his guru and his guru's wife,
> And returned, with mingled joy and sorrow,
> To his abode of leaves.   (320)

Respectfully, he took his leave of the Nishad,
Who left, carrying the intense grief of separation in his heart.
He then sent away the Kols, Kirats, Bhils and other
    forest-dwellers—
They too left, bowing again and again.
The Lord, Sita and Lakshman sat in the banyan's shade,
And wept at parting from their beloved family.
Ram praised Bharat's love, noble nature and gentle words,
To his beloved and his younger brother, at length.
Bharat's love and devotion in words, thought and deed,
Ram described with his lovely mouth, overcome with love.
At that time, even the birds, the deer, the fish in ponds and streams—
All beings, animate or inanimate—of Chitrakut, were sad
    and sorrowful.
The gods, seeing Raghubar's condition,
Rained down flowers and told him of the state of their realms.[61]
The Lord saluted and reassured them,
And they departed, with rejoicing hearts and free of all fear.

> With his younger brother and Sita,
> The Lord shone in his hut of leaves,
> Like devotion, wisdom and detachment
> Resplendent in bodily form.   (321)

The munis, Brahmans, the guru, Bharat and the king
Were all distraught with the grief of parting from Ram.

Enumerating the Lord's perfections to themselves,
They all proceeded in silence along the path.
They reached the Jamuna and all crossed to the other bank—
That first day passed without any food.
They crossed the Ganga and made their second halt—
There, Ram's friend, Guha, made all arrangements for
    their comfort.
They crossed the Sai, and bathed in the Gomati,
And on the fourth day, they reached the city of Avadh.
Janak remained in the city for four days,
Organizing the administration and affairs of the realm.
He then entrusted the kingdom to the minister, the guru
    and Bharat,
And, after making all preparations for the journey, left for
    Terahuti.
The men and women of the city, obeying the instructions of
    the guru,
Settled down to live in peace in Ram's capital.

    In their longing to see Ram again,
    The people practised austerities and kept fasts,
    And renouncing ornaments, luxuries and comforts,
    Lived only in the hope of the end of his exile.   (322)

Bharat instructed his ministers and faithful servants,
Who, receiving his orders, set about their duties as appointed.
Then, calling his younger brother to him, he instructed him,
And entrusted to him the care of all their mothers.
He summoned the Brahmans with folded hands,
And making obeisance, with humble entreaty said,
'Whether the matter be high or low, great or small,
Give me your command, and do not hesitate.'
He summoned his household, the people of the city,
    and other subjects,

He reassured them and made sure they were comfortably settled.
Then, with his brother, he went to their guru's abode,
And prostrating himself, he said with folded hands,
'With your permission, I will now live a life of austerity.'
Overwhelmed with love, the muni replied,
'Whatever you will think, say, or do,
Will be the essence of dharma for the world.'

> Hearing this, receiving his instruction and his great blessing,
> Bharat sent for the astrologers and determining an
>   auspicious day,
> Installed upon the throne, without hindrance,
> The wooden sandals of the Lord.   (323)

Bowing his head at the feet of Ram's mother and their guru,
And taking permission from the Lord's sandals,
He built a hut of leaves in Nandigram,[xviii]
And there that steadfast upholder of dharma took up his abode.
A crown of matted hair upon his head, and clad in hermit's robes,
He dug a hollow in the earth and there spread his bed of
      kush grass.
In matters of food, dress, vessels, fasting and sacred vows,
He lovingly observed the austere rules of ascetic life.
Ornaments, fine clothes and luxuries and comforts of every kind
He gave up completely, in mind, body and speech.
The kingdom of Avadh was the envy of Indra,
And merely hearing of Dasharath's wealth put Kuber to shame.
Yet, in that same city lived Bharat without attachment,
Like a bee in a garden of champak flowers,[62]
For the fortunate one who loves Ram
Discards, like vomit, Ramaa's luxuries.

[xviii] A village on the outskirts of Avadh

Bharat was the receptacle of Ram's love,
But this is not what made him great—
The chatak is praised for its constancy,
And the swan for its power of discernment.   (324)

Day by day, his body grew thinner,
And though he grew leaner, his strength and the beauty of his
          face remained.
Each day his vow of devotion to Ram grew stronger,
His dharma increased, and his heart never grew dark with despair,
Just as the waters recede in the bright light of autumn,
But reeds rejoice and lotuses blossom.
Tranquillity, austerity, self-restraint, sacred vows, and fasting
Shone like stars in the clear sky of Bharat's heart.
Faith was its North Star, the prospect of the end of Ram's exile the
          full moon night,
While his remembrance of his master sparkled like the Milky Way.
His love for Ram was the moon, unwavering, unblemished,
Shining ever clear and pure amidst its retinue of stars.
All good poets hesitate to describe
Bharat's way of life, his wisdom and actions,
His devotion, detachment and the untarnished splendour of
          his perfections—
Even Shesh, Ganesh and Gira cannot recount these.

Ever worshipping the Lord's sandals,
His heart barely able to contain his love,
He constantly sought their direction,
And then carried out the many tasks of running
          the kingdom,   (325)

His body trembling with love, Sita and Raghubir in his heart,
His tongue constantly repeating Ram's name, and his eyes
          full of tears.

Lakshman, Ram and Sita lived in the forest,
But Bharat, living at home, purified his body with penance.
Considering both sides, all declare
Bharat to be worthy of praise in every way.
Hearing of his fasts and vows, even the ascetics are overawed,
And seeing his condition, great sages are put to shame.
Bharat's conduct is supremely pure,
Sweet and charming, the cause of joy and felicity,
It removes the cruel sins and harsh distress of this age of Kali.
A sun that rips to shreds the night of great delusion,
And the lion that vanquishes the elephant herd of sin,
It is the destroyer of all burning anguish.
The joy of the faithful, it destroys the burden of birth and rebirth.
And is the nectar of the moon of love for Ram.

If Bharat, who is filled with the nectar of love for Sita and Ram,
Had never been born,
Who would have practised such self-control, penance and restraint,
And observed such rigorous vows as are unattainable even for munis?
Who, with his glory would have banished our grief,
Burning anguish, poverty, arrogance and sins?
And who, in this age of Kali, would have forced
Blockheads like Tulsi to turn towards Ram?

    Those who regularly and with reverence listen,
    Says Tulsi, to the story of Bharat's acts,
    Will assuredly become devoted to the feet of Sita and Ram,
    And indifferent to worldly delights.   (326)

Thus ends the second descent into the Manas lake of Ram's acts
that destroys all the impurities of the age of Kali.

Book III

ARANYAKAND
(THE FOREST)

Mangalacharan

He who is the root of the tree of dharma,
The full moon that delights the ocean of discernment,
And the sun to the lotus of detachment,
Who dispels the deep darkness of sin, and removes every sorrow
*   and distress,*
Who is the heaven-born wind that scatters the thick clouds of delusion,
Shankar, Brahma's offspring, who destroys all flaws
And is the beloved of King Ram—
I pay him homage.   (1)

He whose graceful form is as dark as a rain cloud and is
*   the embodiment of joy,*
Who is clad in the beautiful yellow robes of an ascetic,
Who carries in his hand a bow and arrows,
And at whose waist gleams a well-equipped quiver—
He, with large lotus-eyes, and head adorned with matted locks,
The most glorious,
Travelling with Sita and Lakshman, Ram the most beautiful—
I worship him.   (2)

O Uma, Ram's perfections are mysterious and profound—
Wise men and munis who understand them, attain
    detachment,
But fools who are hostile to Hari and have no love for dharma,
Find only delusion.   (0)

I have sung according to my understanding of the charming
And unparalleled love of the citizens of Ayodhya and of Bharat.
Now listen to the Lord's supremely pure and holy acts
Pleasing to gods, men and munis, which he performs in the forest.
Once, picking some pretty flowers,
Ram fashioned them into ornaments with his own hands.
The Lord then reverently adorned Sita with these
As they sat together upon a beautiful crystal rock.
Just then Jayant, son of Indra, assumed the form of a crow—
The blockhead wanted to test Raghupati's might,
Like a supremely stupid ant wanting
To measure the ocean's depth.
That dolt, becoming a crow for the most dim-witted reason,
Pecked Sita's foot with his beak and fled.
Her foot began to bleed; Raghunayak saw it
And fitted a reed arrow to his bow.

    The most compassionate Raghunayak
    Ever loves the lowly—
    And it was on him the fool, that abode of mischief,
    Played this trick!   (1)

Impelled by a mantra, that arrow blessed by Brahma flew—
The crow fled, terrified.
Assuming his own proper form, he went to his father,
Who refused to protect him since he was Ram's enemy.
Losing all hope of shelter, he grew as afraid
As the Rishi Durvasa is of the Lord's chakra.

Through Brahma's realm, through Shiv's city, and all the worlds
He wandered, weary and distracted with fear and remorse.
No one even asked him to sit awhile,
For who can shelter an enemy of Ram?
Listen, Garud, steed of Hari—for such a one, his own mother
    becomes as terrible as death,
His father like Shaman,[xix] nectar turns into poison,
A friend does the deeds of a hundred enemies,
And Ganga, river of the gods, becomes the infernal Baitarni.
Listen, brother, the whole world becomes hotter than fire
For one who is hostile to Raghubir.
Narad saw the desperate Jayant
And was moved to pity, for saints are tender-hearted.
He sent him at once to Ram,
And he cried out, 'O benefactor of the suppliant, save me!'
Frantic and terrified, he went and clasped his feet,
'Mercy, mercy, O compassionate Raghurai!
I, dim-witted fool that I am, could not perceive
Your immeasurable might and matchless glory.
I have received the fruit of my own actions,
Now, Lord, save me, for I have come seeking refuge in you.'
When the merciful one heard his exceedingly distressed words,
He dismissed him, Bhavani, merely blinding him in one eye.

Although, in the grip of delusion, he had acted so maliciously
That to kill him would have been appropriate,
The Lord, taking pity on him, let him go!
Who is as compassionate as Raghubir? (2)

Whilst living in Chitrakut, Raghupati performed
Many holy acts, sweet as nectar to hear.
Then Ram considered in his heart,

---

xix 'The Destroyer'; here, Yama, the god of death

'Crowds will come thronging here, now that everyone knows
     who I am.'
So, taking leave of all the munis,
The two brothers left with Sita.
When the Lord drew close to Atri's ashram,
The great muni, hearing of his approach, rejoiced.
Overcome with joy, Atri sprang up and ran to meet him.
Seeing him, Ram, too, hurried towards him.
He began to prostrate himself in reverence, but the muni clasped
     him to his heart,
And bathed the two brothers in tears of love.
Then, his eyes soothed and gratified by looking upon Ram's
     radiant beauty,
The muni led them with reverence to his hermitage.
Paying them homage and addressing them in gracious words,
He offered them roots and fruits, which the Lord relished.

     As the Lord took his seat,
     The great muni, supremely wise,
     Gazing upon his beauty, filled his eyes with his radiance,
     And folding his hands, began to praise him.   (3)

You who love the devout, are compassionate,
Good-natured and tender-hearted—I salute you.
I worship your lotus feet, which bestow
Upon the dispassionate a place in your own abode.

Dark and exceedingly beautiful,
You are the mountain Mandar to churn the ocean of this existence;
With eyes like the lotus in full bloom,
You are the liberator from pride and all vices.

The strength of your long arms
And your glory, Lord, is without end.

Bearing quiver, bow and arrows,
You are the lord of the three worlds.

The ornament of the Sun's dynasty,
The breaker of Mahesh's bow,
You are the delight of the greatest saints and sages,
And the destroyer of the demon hosts.

Adored by Kam's enemy,[xx]
Waited upon by Brahma and the other gods,
The embodiment of pure consciousness,
You are the destroyer of all sin.

The receptacle of bliss, the salvation of the saints,
I salute you, Indira's lord.[xxi]
With Sita, your Shakti, and Lakshman, your younger brother,
I worship you, the beloved brother of Shachi's lord.[1]

Men who worship the soles
Of your feet without envy,
Do not fall into the ocean of worldly existence,
Turbulent with the waves of doubt and apprehension.

Those who live in solitude and constantly
And joyously worship you in the hope of salvation
Discarding all the pleasures of the senses,
Attain their own eternal form.[2]

He, who is the one, the mysterious, the all-powerful,
The passionless, all-pervading master of all,
The guru of the world, constant and eternal,
Transcending the three gunas, absolute and self-existent —

[xx]   Shiv
[xxi]   Vishnu – who is the consort of Indira (the goddess Lakshmi)

I adore him, he who holds devotion dear,
Who is not easily accessible to those attached to the pleasures of the senses,
But is the wish-yielding Kalpataru to his devotees,
Who is impartial and ever worthy of being gladly worshipped.

Of incomparable beauty, master of the earth,
Lord of the earth-born Sita—I bow to you.
I reverently salute you—be gracious to me
And grant me devotion to your lotus feet.

Those who recite this song of praise
With reverence, will undoubtedly
Attain to your abode
Together with devotion to your feet.

> Having thus paid homage to the Lord, the muni bowed
>   his head
> And once more folding his hands, cried,
> 'May my mind never abandon
> Your lotus feet, Lord!'   (4)

Sita, gentle and modest, clasped
Anusuya's feet, embracing them again and again.
The rishi's wife was greatly pleased,
And blessing her, seated her by her side.
She adorned her in celestial robes and ornaments
Which remained ever new, fresh and beautiful.
The rishi's wife spoke in tones that were simple and sweet,
And began to explain, for Sita's benefit, some of the duties of
      a woman.
'Listen, princess—a mother, father and brother
Are well-wishers, all to a limited degree.
But a husband, Vaidehi, is a giver of unbounded bliss
And contemptible is the woman who does not serve him.

Fortitude, piety, a friend and a wife—
All four are tested in times of adversity.
A woman who disrespects her husband—
Even if he be old, ill, foolish, poor,
Blind, deaf, choleric, or utterly wretched—
Suffers innumerable torments in Jam's abode.
She has but one dharma, one duty and one vow:
Devotion to her husband's feet in body, word and mind.
In this world, there are four kinds of faithful wives,
The Vedas, Puranas and the saints all say.
The best is firmly convinced in her mind
That even in dream, there exists no other man in this world.
The next regards another's husband
As her own brother, father or son.
She who holds back thinking of duty or family honour,
Is, say the scriptures, a woman base and vile.
But the one who is restrained only by fear or lack of opportunity,
Know her to be the very lowest, most vile woman in the world.
The woman who deceives her husband and loves the husband
    of another,
Languishes for a hundred kalpas in the most terrible hell.
Who is so contemptible as the woman who, for the sake of a
    moment's pleasure,
Does not consider the agony of a thousand million lifetimes?
The woman who, without deceit, takes the vow of fidelity
Attains the supreme state without effort,
But one disloyal to her husband becomes a widow in the bloom of
    her youth,
No matter where she takes birth.

A woman is inherently impure,
    But by serving her husband she attains ultimate happiness.
    It is for this that the world and the four Vedas sing
    Tulsi's glory to this day and she is beloved of Hari.[3]   (5A)

Listen, Sita, just by invoking your name,
Women will keep their vow of fidelity,
For Ram is as dear to you as life—
I merely speak these words for the benefit of the world.'   (5B)

Hearing these words, Janaki knew supreme happiness,
And reverently bowed her head at Anasuya's feet.
Then the abode of compassion said to the muni,
'With your leave, I will now go to another forest.
Continue to favour me with your grace,
And knowing me to be your servant, do not cease loving me.'
Hearing these words of the Lord, the mighty upholder of dharma,
The learned muni lovingly replied,
'The one who's favour Aj,[xxii] Shiv, Sanak and the other mind-born
    sons of Brahma[xxiii]
Seek, and all the preachers of the highest truth—
You are that same Ram—beloved of those who are free from
    desire,
And friend of the lowly—who speaks these gentle words.
Now I understand Shri's wisdom
Who abandoned all other gods and chose to worship only you.
The one whose equal there is none,
How can his courteous nature be other than it is?
How can I say, "You may go now, master?"
Tell me, Lord, for you pervade the hearts of all.'
So saying, the devoted muni gazed at the Lord,
His eyes flowing with tears, his body trembling with emotion.

His body trembling, he turned his eyes
Full of ardent love upon his lotus face,
'What prayers did I utter, what penance perform that I behold the Lord

---

xxii Brahma
xxiii The four Kumars, Sanak, Sanandan, Sanatan and Sanatkumar

Who transcends mind, knowledge and the three gunas, and cannot be
  perceived by the senses?'
It is through prayer, contemplation and religious observances
That man achieves devotion incomparable,
And therefore, night and day, his servant, Tulsi, sings
Of the holy exploits of Raghubir.

Ram's glorious fame destroys the impurities of the Kali age,
It tames the passions and the mind, and is the root of
  all bliss,
And Ram remains ever gracious
To those who with reverence hear it.   (6A)

This difficult age is a receptacle of vice,
With no piety, no wisdom, no penance or prayer.
They alone are wise who, abandoning trust in all else,
Worship only Ram.   (6B)

Bowing his head at the muni's lotus feet,
The Supreme Lord of gods, men and munis set out for the forest.
Ram walked ahead, his younger brother followed behind him,
Resplendent in the beautiful garb of ascetics.
Between them both shone Shri
Like maya between the Absolute and the soul.
The rivers, the forests, the mountains and inaccessible valleys,
Recognizing their Lord, made the road easy for him.
The clouds cast their cooling shade from the sky
Wherever the divine Raghurai passed.
As they went along the road, the Asur Viradh met them—
As he approached, Raghubir killed him,
And he at once attained celestial form.
Ram, seeing him sad, sent him at once to his own realm.
Then, together with his handsome young brother and Janaki,
He arrived where lived the muni Sarabhang.

Upon seeing the lotus of Ram's face,
The bees that were the noble muni's eyes
Reverently drank in its beauty.
Blessed was the birth of Sarabhang!   (7)

Said the muni, 'Listen, merciful Raghubir,
King of the swans upon the Manas lake of Shankar's heart—
I was about to leave for Viranchi's realm,
When I heard that Ram was coming to the forest.
I have been watching the road day and night,
And now, seeing you, Lord, my heart is at peace.
Lord, I am devoid of all accomplishment,
Yet you have shown me your grace knowing me to be your
        lowly servant.
But, Lord, you have done me no special kindness—
You have only kept your promise, you who steal the hearts of
        your devotees.
Now, for the sake of this humble servant, remain here
Until I give up this body and meet you in your own realm.'
The sage surrendered to the Lord all his practise of meditation,
Ritual sacrifice, prayer, penance and fasting, and received the boon
        of devotion.
In this way the muni Sarabhang built a funeral pyre,
And, freeing his heart from all attachment, sat upon it.

'Graceful Ram, incarnate, embodied,
Your form as dark as a dark raincloud—
With Sita and your brother, Lakshman, O Lord,
Abide eternally in my heart.'   (8)

When he had said these words, his body was consumed in
        yogic fire,
And, by Ram's grace, he departed for Vishnu's realm, Vaikunth.
There the muni did not become one with Hari,

For he had earlier received the boon of separation and devotion.[4]
When the crowd of rishis gathered there saw the great muni's
    liberation,
They were especially joyful in their hearts.
All the assembled multitude of munis broke into songs of praise,
'Glory to the friend of the suppliant and the source of
    all compassion!'
Then Raghunath continued into the forest,
A great crowd of noble sages with him.
Seeing a heap of bones, Raghurai
Felt great pity, and asked the sages about them.
'You are omniscient and pervade the hearts of all,
So though knowing everything, how is it that you ask us, master?
This pile is the bones of all the munis eaten by night-wandering
    demons.'
Hearing this, Raghubir's eyes filled with tears.

    'I will rid the earth of night-wanderers!'
    Raising his arms he vowed.
    Then, visiting all the munis in their ashrams,
    He bestowed joy and bliss upon them.   (9)

Muni Agastya had a learned disciple—
His name was Sutikshna and he was a great lover of the Lord.
In mind, action and speech he was a devotee of Ram's feet,
And did not, even in dream, have faith in any other god.
When he heard of the Lord's approach,
He rushed to meet him, eagerly wishing and wondering,
'O God, will Raghurai, the friend of the lowly,
Show mercy even on a fool like me?
Will Ram, my master, and his younger brother
Receive me as their own servant?
I have no immovable faith in my heart,
And no devotion, detachment, or wisdom in my mind.

I have not sought the company of saints, nor practised meditation,
     prayer, or ritual sacrifice,
Nor claim steadfast love for the Lord's lotus feet.
I depend on one quality of the all-merciful Lord—
That dear to him are those who take refuge in no other.
May my eyes receive their reward today
And look upon the lotus face of the Lord who sets one free from
     this existence.'
The learned muni was so utterly immersed in love,
That his condition cannot be described, Bhavani.
He could not see his way, nor tell this direction from that,
Or remember who he was or where he was going.
Sometimes he would turn back, then again move ahead,
And sometimes break into dance and sing of Ram's virtues.
The muni attained intense loving devotion,
While the Lord watched, hidden behind a tree.
Seeing his extreme love, Raghubir, who removes the fear of
     this existence,
Revealed himself in his heart.
The muni sat unmoving in the middle of the road,
Every hair on end, his body bristling like the fruit of the jak tree.
Then Raghunath drew near, pleased
To see the state of his devotee.
Ram tried to rouse the muni in many ways,
But he did not wake for he was immersed in the bliss
     of contemplation.
Then Ram hid his kingly form,
And in the muni's mind, revealed his four-armed form.
The muni then started up in alarm, bewildered
And as distracted as a noble serpent without its crest-jewel,
And saw before him the dark-bodied Ram,
The abode of bliss, with Sita and his younger brother.
Immersed in love, that great and most fortunate muni,
Fell prostrate like a stick before him and embraced his feet.

The Lord held and raised him with his mighty arms
And clasped him to his heart with supreme love.
As he embraced the muni, the compassionate one shone
Like a tamal tree embracing a tree of gold.
The muni, gazing at Ram's face, stood as still
As a figure painted in a picture.

> Then the muni, collecting himself,
> Clasped the Lord's feet again and again,
> And leading him to his ashram,
> Worshipped him in many ways.   (10)

Said the muni, 'Lord, listen to my prayer—
Though how do I sing your praise?
Your majesty is immeasurable, and my understanding meagre,
Like the glow of a firefly in the presence of the sun.
His body dark as a string of golden lotuses,
His matted hair a crown, a muni's robes his raiment,
A bow and arrows in his hands, and a quiver at his waist—
I worship ceaselessly the beautiful Raghuvir!
The fire that destroys the dense forest of delusion,
The sun to delight the cluster of lotuses that are the saints,
The king of beasts against the elephant herd of night-wandering
    demons,
The hawk that scatters the birds of this existence—may he ever
    protect us.
With eyes as bright as the red lotus, attired in glory,
The full moon to the chakor of Sita's eyes,
The young swan upon the Manas lake of Har's heart,
The broad-chested, long-armed Ram—him I adore.
An Uragad[xxiv] to devour the serpent of doubt,
The one who allays the despair of rough and quarrelsome controversy,

---

The destroyer of the cycle of rebirth, the delight of all the gods,
Within whom resides all compassion—may he ever protect us.
The Absolute and Incarnate, formless and with form,
    incomprehensible and simple,
The incomparable, transcending knowledge, speech and perception,
Pure, complete, without flaw, illimitable,
Ram, the destroyer of earth's burden—him I adore.
A grove of wish-yielding trees for his devotees,
He keeps away passion, greed, pride and lust.
Exceedingly wise, the bridge across the ocean of this existence,
The banner of the Sun's dynasty—may he ever protect us.
Unparalleled in the might of his arms, the abode of strength,
Whose name destroys the great impurities of the age of Kali,
The refuge of righteousness, in whom is gathered every
    pleasing virtue—
May that Ram ever increase our well-being.
Though you be free of desire, all-pervading, imperishable,
And reside eternally in the hearts of all,
Yet, O slayer of the Asur Khar, reside in my heart
With Shri and Lakshman, in this guise of forest-wanderer.
Those who understand, Lord, let them understand you
As sagun or nirgun, with form or without, the one who pervades
    the inmost hearts of all,
But let that Ram, who is the lotus-eyed lord of Koshal,
Make in my heart his abode.
May I never lose pride, even by mistake, in knowing that
I am his servant, and Raghupati is my Lord.'
Ram was pleased to hear the muni's words—
Delighted, he once again clasped the noble muni to his heart.
'Know me to be supremely pleased, muni.
Ask any boon, and I will grant it to you.'
The muni replied, 'I have never asked for a boon,
And cannot tell what is false and what true.
Bestow upon me, Raghurai, whatever seems best to you,

For you are a giver of bliss to your servants.'
'May you become the repository of uninterrupted devotion,
    freedom from worldly attachment,
Wisdom, knowledge, and every virtue!'
'The boon that the Lord has given me, I have received—
Now grant me that which pleases me, Lord.

With Janaki and your brother, Lakshman,
    May that Ram who bears a bow and arrows,
    Reside in my heart for ever,
    As steadfast as the moon in the sky.' (11)

'So be it,' said he who dwells in Ramaa's heart,
And joyfully set off to visit Rishi Kumbhaj.
'It has been a long time since I saw my guru,
And came to live in this ashram,' said Sutikshna.
'Now, Lord, I will go with you to visit my guru.
In this, master, there is no obligation upon you.'
The abode of compassion saw through the muni's clever ploy,
And laughing, the two brothers took him with them.
Discoursing along the way on the various forms of devotion
    to himself,
The lord of the gods reached Muni Agastya's ashram.
Sutikshna at once went to the guru,
And prostrating himself in reverence, addressed him thus:
'Lord, the son of Koshal's king,
The support of the universe, has come to meet you—
Ram, with his brother Lakshman, and Vaidehi,
Whose names you repeat, lord, night and day.'
The moment he heard this, Agastya sprang up and rushed out—
Upon seeing Hari, his eyes filled with tears.
The two brothers fell at the muni's lotus feet—
The rishi raised them up and clasped them to his heart with
    deep love.

Reverently, the learned muni asked after their well-being,
And led them to a seat of honour.
He then worshipped the Lord in many ways, saying,
'There is no other as blessed as I!'
The crowds of other munis there,
All rejoiced to see the root of all bliss.

> In the midst of the gathering of munis
> Sat Ram, his face turned towards them all,
> While they, like a flock of chakors,
> Gazed at the autumn moon of his radiant form.   (12)

Then Raghubir said to Muni Agastya,
'Lord, nothing is hidden from you,
You know the reason I have come
And therefore, sire, I did not explicitly say it.
Now, lord, give me that mantra
By which I may kill the enemies of the munis.'
The sage smiled when he heard the Lord's words.
'Lord, what makes you ask me for my advice?
It is only because of worshipping you,
O destroyer of sin, that I understand a little of your glory.
Your maya is a vast fig tree,
Its clusters of fruit the countless multitudes of universes.
All beings, animate and inanimate, are like the tiny insects
That dwell within each fruit, and know no other world.
The devourer of these fruits is harsh and cruel Time,
But even he remains ever afraid of you.
That same you, the master of the lords of the eight quarters,
Is asking me for advice like a mere mortal!
Abode of compassion, I ask this boon—
Reside in my heart with Shri and Lakshman.
Grant me unceasing devotion, freedom from desire, the company
    of holy men,

And unbroken love for your lotus feet.
Though you are brahm, indivisible, eternal,
Attainable only through experience, and whom the saints
     adore,
And though I know and praise that form of yours,
I turn again and again to love and worship you in this your form,
     brahm incarnate.
You ever praise and exalt your own servants,
And that is why you ask me for advice, Raghurai!
There is, O Lord, a supremely beautiful
And sacred spot called Panchavati.
Render pure the Dandak forest, Lord, in which it lies,
And liberate it from the great muni's curse.[5]
Reside there, O Lord of the Raghu clan,
And show all the munis your favour.'
Receiving the muni's permission, Ram set forth
And very soon came to Panchavati.

> There he met Jatayu, king of the vultures.
> And renewed their friendship in many ways.[6]
> The Lord then took up his abode by the Godavari,
> Building there a hut of leaves.   (13)

From the time that Ram began to live there,
The munis became happy and their fear disappeared.
The mountains, forests, rivers and ponds became infused
     with beauty,
And grew exceedingly lovelier day by day.
The birds and animals were full of happiness,
And the bees, humming sweetly, looked beautiful.
Even Shesh, king of the serpents, cannot describe that forest
Where shone Raghubir, resplendent in his manifest form.
Once, as the Lord was sitting at ease,
Lakshman spoke words free of deceit.

'Master of gods, men and munis, and of all creation animate
      and inanimate,
I ask you as my own Lord
To explain and tell me, divine one,
How I may serve the dust of your feet abandoning all else.
Speak to me of knowledge, detachment and maya,
Tell me of that bhakti to which you extend your compassion.

      Explain to me all the differences
      Between God and the individual soul,
      So that I may be devoted to your feet
      And my sorrow, attachment and delusion disappear.'   (14)

'I will explain it all in brief,
So listen, brother, with your mind, soul and heart.
Me and mine, you and yours—this is maya,
Which holds in its grip all the multitude of beings.
The senses and all that they perceive, and as far as the mind
      can reach—
Know it all to be maya, brother.
Now listen to its divisions, of which
There are two: ignorance and knowledge.
One is vile, full of faults and affliction personified,
And the individual soul in its grip falls into the pit of birth and
      rebirth.
The other, which fashions the world and holds sway over the
      three gunas,
Is directed by God and has no power of its own.
Spiritual wisdom has no trace of pride and other flaws,
And sees the Absolute equally in all.
Brother, he alone may be called the supreme ascetic, free from all
      desire,
Who abandons accomplishment and the three gunas like blades
      of grass.

That which knows not maya, nor God, nor its own self,
   Is called the individual soul.
He who dispenses bondage or liberation, transcends all,
   And is the impeller of maya—he is God.   (15)

From dharma comes freedom from desire, from ascetic meditation
   comes spiritual wisdom,
And spiritual wisdom bestows salvation—so declare the Vedas.
But, brother, that which moves and pleases me more quickly
Is bhakti, which bestows bliss upon my devotees.
Bhakti stands on its own, it needs no other support,
While knowledge, both of the Absolute and of the world, is
   subservient to it.
Bhakti, dear brother, is incomparable and the source of bliss,
It is attained only when the virtuous are well-disposed towards one.
I will now explain at length the means of acquiring bhakti,
The easy path by which men may find me.
First, have exceeding love for the feet of Brahmans,
And adhere, each one, to one's own duty in the manner prescribed
   by the Vedas.
The fruit of this will be freedom from worldly desires,
And then will spring up love for my dharma of bhakti.
This will strengthen the nine forms of devotion—such as listening
   to the praises of the Lord—
And bring great love in the heart for my divine play.[7]
One who has great love for the lotus feet of holy men,
Who strictly observes the practice of prayer in thought,
   action and speech,
Who recognizes me alone as his guru, father, mother, friend,
   master, god and all,
And is steadfast in my service,
Whose body thrills with delight as he sings my virtues
In a voice trembling with joy, and eyes streaming with tears
   of love,

Who is without lust, or pride, or deceit—
I am ever, dear brother, subject to the will of such a one.

> Those who, in word, deed and thought, have only me as
>   their refuge,
> And worship me selflessly, free from all desire—
> In the lotus of their hearts,
> I reside eternally.'   (16)

Upon hearing the principles of bhakti thus expounded, Lakshman
Was exceedingly glad and bowed his head at the Lord's feet.
In this manner, some days passed,
In discussions on detachment, spiritual wisdom, virtue
      and morality.
Supnakha, Ravan's sister,
Vile-hearted and venomous as a snake,
Came one day to Panchavati,
And seeing the two princes, grew distracted with desire.
When a woman sees a handsome man—
Be it her brother, father, or son, Uragari—[xxv]
She becomes mad with lust and cannot control her heart,
Just as the sun-stone melts at the sight of the sun.
Assuming a beautiful and pleasing form, she approached the Lord
And with many charming smiles, said to him,
'There is no man like you nor another woman like me—
Vidhi has made this couple with great care.
There is no man equal to me in this universe—
I have searched the three spheres for him.
That is why I have till now remained unmarried—
It is only upon seeing you that my heart is a little content.'
The Lord looked at Sita and said,
'My younger brother is unmarried.'

_____

[xxv] Garud

She approached Lakshman, who, knowing her to be their
    enemy's sister,
Glanced at the Lord and said in gentle tones,
'Beautiful one, listen—I am his servant
And dependent upon him. You will not find happiness or any
    comfort with me.
My lord is all-powerful, and the king of Ayodhya—
Whatever he does, it befits and adorns him.
A servant who wants happiness, a beggar who wants respect,
A spendthrift who desires wealth, a profligate who hopes for salvation,
A greedy man who wants glory, or an arrogant one who wants the
    four rewards of life—
These people expect milk by milking the air!'
She turned and again came up to Ram,
And the Lord again sent her to Lakshman,
And Lakshman declared, 'He alone will wed you
Who has thrown away shame completely!'
Humiliated and fuming with rage, she then went up to Ram
And revealed her own dreadful shape.
Seeing that Sita was frightened, Raghurai
Made a sign to his brother.

Lakshman, with great dexterity, at once
Cut off her nose and ears.
It was as though, through her, he had
Thrown Ravan a challenge.   (17)

Without her nose and ears she became hideous,
Like a mountain flowing with streams of red ochre.
She went weeping to Khar and Dushan, and cried,
'Shame on your manhood and your might, brothers!'
They asked her, and she told them all.
Hearing what she had to say, her Rakshasa brothers gathered an army,
And horde upon horde of night-wandering demons rushed forth,

Like multitudes of winged mountains of darkness.
Riding upon diverse vehicles, of diverse shapes and forms,
And armed with weapons of many kinds, they were terrible and
    infinite in number.
Supnakha they placed at their head,
A hideous, inauspicious form, without ears or nose.
Innumerable dreadful omens of evil occurred,
But, in the grip of death, the Rakshasa hordes paid them no heed.
Roaring, threatening, they flew through the sky,
And seeing their army, the warriors rejoiced.
Said one, 'Capture the two brothers alive,
Then kill them, and carry off their woman!'
The dome of the sky filled with dust,
And Ram called his brother to him and said,
'Take Janaki and go into a mountain cave,
A terrible army of demons is approaching—
Stay vigilant.' Obedient to the Lord's words,
Lakshman left with Shri, his bow and arrows in his hand.
Ram, seeing the enemy horde advancing,
Laughed and strung his great bow.

As he strung his great bow and bound
His matted hair upon his head, he shone
Like an emerald mountain upon which two snakes
Battled countless streaks of lightning.
As the Lord tightened his quiver at his waist, clasped his bow
In his mighty arms and made ready his arrows,
He gazed at the approaching Rakshasa hordes
Like a lion at a herd of elephants.

  The mighty warriors came rushing
  Shouting, 'Seize him, seize him!'
  Surrounding him as demons close
  Upon the rising sun, knowing it to be alone.[8]   (18)

But at the sight of the Lord, they could not loose their arrows
    upon him,
And the whole demon army stood still, astonished.
Khar and Dushan summoned their ministers and said,
'This king's son, whoever he may be, is an ornament of the human race!
We have seen innumerable Nagas, Asurs, gods, men and munis,
And killed and conquered many,
But, listen, brothers all, we have never,
In all our life, seen such beauty!
Though he has turned our sister into an ugly creature,
This incomparable man does not deserve to be killed.
"Give us at once your woman, whom you have hidden,
And return home alive, both you brothers!"
Declare to him these words of mine,
And quickly return with his answer.'
The messengers delivered this message to Ram,
And hearing it, Ram smiled and replied,
'We are Kshatriyas, warriors by birth, in the habit of hunting
    in the forest—
We search for vile animals like you.
We are not afraid at the sight of an enemy's strength,
But can fight Death himself.
Though men, we are the destroyers of the demon race,
And though young, we are the protectors of munis, and the
    torment of the vile.
If you do not have the strength, turn around and go home,
I never kill one who has turned his back on battle.
But when you have come to do battle, deceit and cunning
And mercy for your enemy is supreme cowardice.'
The messengers returned at once and repeated all that he had said,
Hearing which, the hearts of Khar and Dushan were on fire.

Their hearts on fire, they cried, 'Seize him!'
Formidable Rakshasa warriors rushed to obey,

Armed with arrows, bows, iron clubs, and spears,
Lances, swords, maces and battle-axes.
The Lord first twanged his bow—
A sound harsh, deep and terrifying
That deafened the demons, disoriented them,
And deprived them of all sense.

They now ran on more cautiously,
Realizing they faced a redoubtable foe,
And began to shower upon Ram
Arrows and missiles of many kinds.   (19A)

Raghubir cut down their weapons
Into pieces small as sesame seeds,
And then drawing his bowstring to his ear,
He let loose his arrows.   (19B)

Then flew his terrible arrows
Hissing like great serpents.
Lord Ram grew wrathful in battle,
So that his arrows flew, exceedingly sharp.
When they saw his arrows, so sharp and keen,
The Rakshasa warriors turned and fled.
The three demon brothers[xxvi] *flew into a rage—*
'We will kill with our own hands,' they declared,
Anyone who runs from the battle.'
The fleeing warriors turned back, resolved in their hearts to die,
And with weapons of many kinds
Attacked from the front.
Perceiving that the enemy was now exceedingly enraged,
The Lord fitted arrows to his bow,
And let loose the huge iron bolts.

[xxvi] Khar, Dushan and Trishira

The terrible demons were cut to pieces—
Torsos, heads, arms, hands and feet
Began to fall everywhere about the ground.
The demons screamed as the arrows struck,
And their bodies fell like mountains.
The bodies of the warriors were cut into a hundred pieces,
Yet they stood up again through the power of maya.
Countless arms and heads flew through the air,
And headless trunks ran here and there,
While birds, kites, crows and jackals,
Gnawed at them with harsh and cruel sounds.

Jackals gnashed their teeth and gnawed,
Ghosts, spirits, goblins collected skulls,
Ghouls drummed upon the heads of slain warriors
As witches danced to the beat.
Raghubir's wrathful arrows cut into pieces
The warriors' torsos, arms and heads.
They fell all around, but rose up again
With terrible cries of 'Seize him! Seize him!'
Vultures flew off, entrails clutched in their claws,
While ghouls ran after them, and grabbed the trailing ends in
*   their hands,*
So that it seemed that in the town that was the battlefield,
A crowd of children flew their kites.
Many mighty warriors were killed or overcome,
Many lay groaning, their breasts ripped open.
Seeing their army shattered, the commanders,
Trishira, Khar, Dushan and others, turned towards Ram.

Countless Rakshasa warriors, full of rage,
Hurled arrows, spears, iron clubs,
Battle-axes, javelins, swords,
At noble Raghubir, all at once.

In the blink of an eye, the Lord warded off
The enemy's arrows, and with a shout of defiance, let fly his own,
Shooting ten arrows each into the hearts
Of all the Rakshasa captains.

The Rakshasa warriors fell to the ground, but rising up again, rejoined
    the battle—
They would not die, but spread dense delusion everywhere.
The gods were afraid to see the fiends fourteen thousand strong,
And the Lord of Avadh alone.
Seeing the gods and munis afraid, the Lord,
Master of maya, played a great prank—
The enemy warriors saw each other as Ram, and
Fighting amongst themselves, perished.

    Calling 'Ram! Ram!', they gave up their bodies
    And thus attained nirvana.
    With this trick, the abode of compassion
    Slew all his enemies in an instant.   (20A)

    Rejoicing, the gods rained down flowers
    While drums of victory sounded in the sky.
    Singing his praises, they all left,
    Resplendent in vehicles of many kinds.   (20B)

When Raghunath had vanquished his enemies in battle,
Gods, men and munis, all became free of fear.
Then Lakshman brought Sita back,
And as he fell at his feet, the Lord raised him and clasped him to
    his heart.
Sita gazed at Ram's dark-hued, tender form
With utmost love, but her eyes could not be satisfied.
Thus did the divine Raghunayak dwell in Panchavati,
Doing deeds that brought bliss to gods and munis.

Meanwhile, seeing the destruction of Khar and Dushan,
Supnakha went to Ravan to incite him to take action,
And in a voice full of fury, she said,
'You have lost all thought of realm and treasury!
You drink and sleep day and night,
And do not understand that the enemy is upon your head!
Government without political insight, wealth without dharma,
Good works without consecration to Hari,
Knowledge that does not produce discernment—
All these, whether recited, practised, or acquired, bring toil as
    their only fruit.
An ascetic is quickly destroyed by attachment, a king by
    wrong counsel,
Knowledge by pride, modesty by drinking,
Love without humility, and virtue by arrogance—
So I have heard.

        An enemy, illness, fire, sin,
        A master, and a serpent must never be counted as small.'
        So saying, and with much lamenting,
        She began to weep.   (21A)

        Distraught, she lay prostrate in Ravan's court,
        And with much wailing and weeping said,
        'Should I be reduced to such a state,
        Dashkandhar,[xxvii] while you still live?'   (21B)

Hearing her words, the courtiers stood up, bewildered,
And taking her by the arm, they raised her up, consoling her.
Said the king of Lanka, 'Tell me what has happened,
Who has cut off your nose and ears?'
'The sons of Dasharath, the king of Avadh,

---

xxvii Ravan

Lions amongst men, have come to the forest for sport.
I have understood from their actions
That they are out to rid the earth of demons.
Protected by the might of their arms, Dashanan,[xxviii]
The munis roam free of fear in the forest.
They look like children, but are like Death himself,
They are supremely courageous, skilled archers and accomplished
    in many ways.
Unequalled in might and majesty are the two brothers,
Devoted to the extermination of the wicked, they bring joy to gods
    and munis.
The abode of beauty, his name is Ram—
With him is a young woman.
Vidhi made this woman so supremely beautiful
That she outshines a hundred million Ratis.
His younger brother cut off my ears and nose,
And hearing that I was your sister, he laughed at me in derision.
Hearing my call, Khar and Dushan came,
But Ram killed their whole army in an instant.'
Hearing of the death of Khar, Dushan and Trishira,
The ten-headed one burned all over with rage.

> He comforted Supnakha,
> And bragged about his strength in many ways,
> But retired to his palace exceedingly worried,
> And could not sleep all night.   (22)

'Amongst gods, men, Asurs, Nagas and birds,
There is no one who can stand firm against my soldiers.
Khar and Dushan were as strong as I am,
So who could have killed them except the Lord himself?
If the Lord who delights the gods and bears the weight of the world

---

[xxviii] Ravan

Has indeed descended upon earth,
I will go and, insisting upon it, fight him—
Losing my life by an arrow of the Lord, I will cross the ocean of
    this existence.
This body of darkness and vice is incapable of worship,
So this is my firm resolve—in thought, word and deed.
And if they turn out to be some earthly king's sons,
Then I will take their woman and vanquish them in battle.'
He mounted his chariot and set off alone to the spot
Where lived Marich by the seashore.
At this point, Uma, listen to the charming tale
Of the plan that Ram devised.

    When Lakshman went into the forest
    To gather roots, fruits and tubers,
    Ram, accumulation of mercy and joy,
    Said with a smile to Janak's daughter,   (23)

'Listen, beloved, my beautiful, devoted, good-natured wife,
I am now going to put on a charming act of being human.
So let fire be your abode
Till I have completed the destruction of the night-wandering
    demons.
As soon as Ram finished explaining all this to her,
Sita entered the fire, holding the Lord's feet in her heart.
She left behind her own shadow image,
As good-natured, beautiful and gentle as herself.
Even Lakshman did not know this secret,
Of what the Lord had done.
Meanwhile, intent upon his own objective, that vile wretch,
Dashmukh,[xxix] went where Marich resided, and bowed his head.
The bending of a vile creature gives rise to great suffering,

---

[xxix] Ravan

Like the bending of an elephant-goad, a bow, a serpent, or a cat,
And terrifying is soft speech by a rogue,
Like flowers that bloom out of season, Bhavani.

> Marich paid homage to him,
> Then reverently asked,
> 'What is it that disturbs you so much,
> That you have come here all alone, my son?'   (24)

The ten-headed one, unfortunate wretch, told him the whole story
And then arrogantly said,
'Assume the false form of a wily deer,
By means of which I can carry away that princess.'
Marich replied, 'Listen, Dashashish,[xxx]
Though in the form of a man, he is the god of all creation, animate
     or inanimate.
Do not quarrel with him, son,
For when he kills, we die, and it is when he gives life that we live.
These were the princes who had gone to protect the
     muni's sacrifice,
When Raghupati shot me with a headless arrow,
So that I was hurled a hundred yojans in an instant—
It is not good to pick a quarrel with him.
My state is like that of an insect caught by a bird—
Wherever I look I see the two brothers.
And son, even if they are men, they are exceedingly valiant,
So opposing them will not lead to success.

> He who killed Taraka and Subahu,
> Broke Har's bow and slew
> Khar, Dushan and Trishira—
> Can one so mighty be a mortal man?   (25)

[xxx] Ravan

Consider the welfare of your clan and go home.'
Hearing this, Ravan flew into a rage and called him many names.
'Fool, you instruct me as though you were my guru!
Tell me, is there in this world a warrior to equal me?'
Then Marich considered in his heart,
'One who is armed, or knows one's vulnerabilities, one who is a
    king, a fool, or very wealthy,
A physician, panegyrist, poet, or skilled cook—
There is no benefit in opposing these nine.'
Realizing that he would die either way,
He looked towards Raghunayak as his refuge.
'If I answer him back, this unfortunate wretch will kill me,
So why should I not die by Raghupati's arrow?'
Considering thus in his heart, he went with Dashanan.
In him was immutable love for Ram's feet,
His heart was full of great joy—which he concealed from Ravan—
'Today I will see my greatest friend!

With the sight of my most beloved
I will reward my eyes and be happy.
I will take into my heart the feet of the compassionate Lord
With Shri and his younger brother too.
He, whose wrath confers freedom from rebirth,
And who, though subject to none, surrenders himself to his devotees,
That same Hari, the ocean of bliss, will, with his own hands,
Make ready an arrow and slay me.

        As he runs after me,
        Holding his bow and arrow,
        I shall turn again and again to behold my Lord—
        There is no other as blessed as I!'   (26)

As Dashanan drew near the forest,
Marich assumed the false form of a deer
So extraordinary that it cannot be described,

With a body made of gold, inlaid with jewels.
Sita saw this most beautiful deer,
Enchanting in every part,
And said, 'Listen, Raghubir, my compassionate lord,
This deer has an exceedingly lovely hide.
Lord, you who are ever true to your word, kill this creature
And bring me its skin.' So did Vaidehi ask.
Then Raghupati, who knew all the reasons,
Joyfully rose to accomplish the work of the gods.
Seeing the deer, he tightened the sash around his belt,
Picked up his bow and made ready a bright arrow.
The Lord then called Lakshman and explained,
'Many night-wanderers roam the forest, brother,
So protect and take care of Sita
Using judgement and discernment, keeping in mind your strength
    and circumstances.'
The deer, seeing the Lord, took flight,
And Ram ran after it, his bow at the ready.
He whom the scriptures describe as 'Not this, not this', and whom
    even Shiv is unable to grasp by meditation,
Ran after an illusory deer.
Sometimes close, sometimes running far away,
Sometimes visible, sometimes hidden,
Revealing and concealing itself, and practising every kind of deceit,
It led the Lord far away.
Then Ram took aim and let fly the cruel arrow—
The deer fell to the ground and let out a terrible cry.
It first called out Lakshman's name,
Then remembered Ram in its heart.
As it gave up its life-breath, it revealed its own true form
And lovingly invoked Ram.
The all-knowing one recognized his inner love
And conferred upon him the ultimate state that even munis find
    hard to attain.

The gods rained down flowers in abundance
And sang the Lord's virtues, saying,
'Raghunath is such a friend of the lowly
That he conferred his own state upon an Asur.'   (27)

Slaying the wretch, Raghubir turned back at once,
His bow shining in his hand and at his waist his quiver.
When Sita heard the Asur's wounded cry,
She grew terribly afraid, and said to Lakshman,
'Go quickly, your brother is in great danger!'
Lakshman laughed and replied, 'Listen, Mother,
At the play of whose eyebrow all creation is destroyed,
Can he, even in dream, be in danger?'
But when Sita spoke harsh and hurtful words,
Lakshman's heart, impelled by Hari, grew restless.
Delivering Sita into the care of all the gods of the forest and the
    eight quarters,
He went to find Ram, the Rahu to Ravan's moon.
Meanwhile, with the hermitage deserted, Dashkandhar saw
    his chance,
And drew near in the guise of an ascetic.
He, for fear of whom gods and demons tremble,
And cannot sleep by night or eat by day,
That same ten-headed one came, glancing this way and that
As furtively as a dog bent on stealing.
In this way, even as one sets foot on the wrong path, Khagesh,[xxxi]
Not a trace remains of the body's radiance, or of intellect
    or strength.
Making up alluring tales of many kinds,
He tried to persuade her with a display of diplomacy, threats
    and love.
Said Sita, 'Listen to me, holy ascetic,

[xxxi] 'King of the birds', i.e., Garud

You have spoken like a scoundrel!'
Then Ravan showed his own form
And when he told her his name, Sita grew afraid.
But gathering up all her courage, she said,
'Stay where you are, wretch! My lord is almost here!
Like an insignificant hare that desires the lion's bride,
You, king of demons, have doomed yourself to die.'
Hearing her words, the ten-headed one grew furious,
But in his heart he paid homage to her feet and rejoiced.

Then, raging with anger, Ravan
Seized her and forced her into his chariot,
And set off in a great hurry through the sky.
But he was so afraid he could barely drive his chariot.   (28)

'Ah, Raghurai, unparalleled hero of the universe,
For what fault of mine have you forgotten mercy?
You who destroys all affliction, who bestows bliss upon
    your supplicants,
The sun to the lotuses of the Raghu line?
Ah, Lakshman! This is not your fault.
I had become angry, and am reaping its reward.'
Vaidehi wept and lamented in many ways,
'Though his mercies are many, my loving lord is far away.
Who will tell him of my misfortune?
A donkey wants to eat the offering meant for the gods.'
Hearing Sita's sorrowful lamentations,
All beings, moving and unmoving, grew deeply sad.
Jatayu, king of the vultures, too, heard her cries of distress,
And recognized the wife of the ornament of the Raghu clan
Being carried away by a vile night-wanderer,
Like a sacred kapila cow that had fallen into the hands of
    an unbeliever.
'Daughter Sita, do not be afraid!

I will annihilate this Rakshasa!'
The bird, full of fury, hurled himself at Ravan
Like a bolt of lightning at a mountain.
'Hey, you rogue, why don't you stop?
You proceed fearlessly, as though you know not who I am!'
Seeing him come like the god of death,
Dashkandhar turned and wondered,
'This must be the winged mountain, Mainak, or the king of the
     birds himself—
Though Garud and his master both know my strength.'
Then, 'This is only old Jatayu!
He will abandon his body at the pilgrimage site of my hands!'
At this, the vulture, enraged, flew even faster,
And said, 'Listen, Ravan, to my advice—
Let Janaki go and return home safely,
Otherwise, many-armed one,
Your entire clan will perish like insects
In the blazing fire of Ram's wrath.'
The ten-headed warrior did not reply.
Then the vulture flew at him in fury,
And, grabbing him by the hair, dragged him from his chariot so
     that he fell to the ground.
Placing Sita out of harm's way, the vulture returned,
And, attacking him with his beak, rent and tore at his body—
For a short while, Ravan lay senseless.
Then the Rakshasa, full of rage, gnashed his teeth,
And, drawing his dreadful sword,
Cut off Jatayu's wings so that the bird fell to the ground
Invoking Ram and his marvellous doings.
Placing Sita in his chariot once more,
Ravan drove off in a hurry, quite terrified.
Weeping and lamenting, Sita was carried through the air,
Like a frightened doe in a huntsman's snare.
Seeing some monkeys sitting upon a mountain,

She called out Hari's name and let drop her veil.
In this manner, Ravan carried away Sita,
And set her down in a grove of ashok trees.

> The scoundrel failed to gain his end
> Though he tried both intimidation and affection.
> Then, after making all arrangements,
> He left her under the ashok tree.   (29A)

> Sita held in her heart the radiant image
> Of Lord Ram as he had appeared
> When chasing the false kurang deer,
> And incessantly repeated Hari's name.   (29B)

When Raghupati saw his brother approaching,
He put on a show of concern.[9]
'You have left Janak's daughter alone, dear brother,
And come here disregarding my command!
Hordes of night-wandering demons roam the forest,
And I feel in my heart that Sita is not in the ashram!'
Lakshman clasped his lotus feet, and cried with folded hands,
'Lord, it is not my fault.'
With his brother, the Lord went
To his ashram on the banks of the Godavari.
When he saw the ashram bereft of Sita,
He was distraught and as distressed as an ordinary mortal.
'Alas, Janaki! Sita! Abode of virtue!
Of flawless beauty and disposition! Pure in her vows of austerity
    and devotion!'
Lakshman consoled him in every way he could,
But Ram, as he set off in search of her, questioned every vine and
    tree along the way.
'O birds and beasts, O swarms of bees,
Have you seen the doe-eyed Sita?

The wagtail, the parrot, the pigeon, the deer and the fish,
The swarming bees, the kokils so accomplished,
The jasmine buds, the pomegranate and the lightning,
The lotus, the autumn moon, the she-serpent,
Varun's snares and Kamdev's bow, the swan,
The elephant and the lion now can hear themselves praised!
Wood-apples and golden bananas now rejoice,
No doubt, no hesitation in their hearts!
Listen, Janaki, not seeing you today,
They are all as glad as if they have acquired a kingdom![10]
How can you bear such rivalry?
My beloved, why do you not quickly reveal yourself?'
In this manner the Lord searched and lamented,
Like a fond lover in great distress at being separated from
    his beloved.
Ram, who has no wish unfulfilled and is the accumulation of
    all bliss,
Unborn, uncreated, everlasting, performs the actions of
    a mortal man.
Further on, he saw the lord of the vultures lying,
Meditating upon Ram's feet, which were marked with the lines
    of divinity.

Raghubir, ocean of compassion,
Stroked his head with his lotus hands,
And, as Jatayu beheld Ram's beautiful face,
All his pain disappeared.   (30)

Then, summoning up all his strength, the vulture said,
'Listen, Ram, destroyer of the fear of rebirth!
Lord, it is Dashanan who has done this to me,
And he is the wretch who has carried off Janak's daughter.
He took her away to the south, master,
She was weeping as piteously as a kurari bird.

I held on to my life's breath because of my yearning to see you,
And now, abode of compassion, it wishes to depart.'
Ram replied, 'Stay alive, sire.'
But Jatayu, smiling, replied,
'He whose name spoken at the time of death,
Bestows salvation, as the Vedas declare, even upon a sinner,
Is present before me, visible to my eyes.
What want remains now, Lord, that I should keep this body?'
His eyes filling with tears, Raghurai replied,
'Sire, you have attained salvation through your actions.
There is nothing in this world that is unattainable
For those in whose hearts abides the good of others.
Giving up your body, sire, enter into my realm—
What more can I give you, who have fulfilled all your desires?

But sire, reaching there, do not tell my father
About Sita's abduction.
If I am indeed Ram, Dashanan himself
With all his clan, will go there and tell him of it.'   (31)

Jatayu gave up his vulture's body and took on Hari's form,
Adorned with jewels and attired in yellow robes of
      matchless splendour,
With dark-hued body, and four mighty arms,
And his eyes full of tears, he sang this song of praise.

Glory to Ram, of incomparable beauty,
Formless, embodied, the true impeller of all the gunas,
The ornament of the earth,
Whose fierce arrows cut to pieces Dashashish's dreadful arms.
With his body dark as a raincloud, his lotus face,
And large, lotus eyes,
I unceasingly worship Ram, the compassionate,
The long-armed one, who destroys the fear of rebirth.

Of immeasurable strength, without beginning, unborn, the one,
Without form, imperceptible, transcending the senses,
But attainable through the songs of the Vedas, the remover of dualities,
The sum of all wisdom, upholder of the earth,
And bestower of joy upon the countless saints and devotees
Who repeat the mantra of Ram's name—
I unceasingly worship Ram, who loves and is loved by those free
*   from desire,*
And holds in contempt lust and the multitude of other sins.

He whom the Vedas praise as free from delusion, the Absolute,
The all-pervading brahm, passionless, unborn,
To whom the munis attain through infinite contemplation,
*   spiritual knowledge,*
And the practice of detachment and rigorous penance and
*   self-discipline—*
That accumulation of compassion and beauty has become manifest
To captivate and enchant all creation, animate and inanimate.
He is the bee in the lotus of my heart, and his limbs are radiant
With the beauty of countless gods of love.

He who is at once inaccessible and accessible, inherently pure,
Partial and impartial, and always calm and tranquil,
Whom the ascetics perceive only with great and tireless effort
Upon subduing their minds and senses—
That Ram, who dwells in Ramaa's heart,
Who is the lord of the three worlds and ever subject to his devotees,
May he reside in my heart, he, whose pure renown
Destroys the cycle of birth and rebirth.

Asking for the boon of uninterrupted devotion,
The vulture ascended to Hari's realm.
Ram, with his own hands, performed
His last rites in the proper manner.   (32)

Exceedingly soft-hearted and compassionate to the humble,
Raghunath, who is gracious even to the undeserving,
Bestowed upon a vulture, an impure, flesh-eating bird,
That state of salvation which ascetics desire.
Listen, Uma, unfortunate are those
Who abandon Hari and become attached to worldly pleasures.
The two brothers once again set off in search of Sita,
Noticing how the forest grew thicker as they went.
That forest was dense with creepers and trees,
And home to many birds, deer, elephants and lions.
Along the way they killed the Rakshasa Kabandh,
Who related the full story of his curse.
'Rishi Durvasa had cursed me,
But now, upon seeing the Lord's feet, my sin has been wiped out.'[11]
'Listen, Gandharva, I tell you this—
I do not like those who are hostile to Brahmans.

> He who, abandoning deceit, in thought, word and deed
> Serves these gods upon earth,
> Makes subject to himself, along with me, Viranchi, Shiv
> And all the other gods.   (33)

Whether he curse or beat or hurl abuse,
A Brahman is worthy of worship—so declare the saints.
A Brahman must be revered, though devoid of goodness
    and virtue,
But a Shudra never, though learned and wise and possessing
    every virtue.'
So saying, the Lord explained to him his own doctrine
And was pleased to see his love for his feet.
The Gandharva bowed his head at Raghupati's lotus feet
And rose into the sky, having regained his own form.
The generous Ram, having given him back his Gandharva form,
Turned his feet towards Sabari's hermitage.

When Sabari saw that Ram had come to her home,
She remembered Muni Matanga's words and rejoiced.[12]
With lotus eyes, long arms,
Crowns of matted hair upon their heads, upon their breasts
    garlands of wildflowers,
One dark-complexioned, the other fair, were the two
    handsome brothers.
Sabari fell and clung to their feet
Immersed in love, she could not speak,
And again and again bowed her head at their lotus feet.
Reverently, she took some water and washed their feet,
And then conducted them to handsome seats.

> She brought and gave to Ram the most
> Delicious tubers, roots and fruits.
> The Lord ate them with love,
> Praising them again and again.   (34)

With folded hands, she came and stood before him,
And as she gazed upon the Lord, her love grew even greater.
'In what manner shall I sing your praises?
I am of mean descent and very stupid
The lowest of the low, low even amongst women,
And even amongst the lowest of women, O destroyer of evil, I am
    most dull-witted.'
Said Raghupati, 'Listen to me, respected lady,
I acknowledge only the kinship of devotion.
Though endowed with caste and class, lineage, religion, rank,
Wealth, power, connections, virtue and ability,
A man without devotion is like a raincloud without water.
I will now explain to you the nine forms of bhakti,
Listen carefully and hold what I say in your mind.
The first form of bhakti is the company of holy men,
The second is love for the stories and legends about me.

Serving the guru's lotus feet
Without arrogance is the third,
While the fourth form of bhakti is singing
My praises without guile or deceit.   (35)

Repeating the mantra of my name and unshakeable faith in me
Is the fifth form of bhakti, revealed in the Vedas;
The sixth is self-restraint, good conduct, renunciation of the many
     demands of the world,
And unceasing pursuit of the dharma of the good;
The seventh is seeing the whole world equally full of me
And regarding the saints as being more than me;
The eighth is being content with whatever one receives
And not finding fault in others even in dream;
And the ninth is simplicity and honesty towards all,
Implicit faith in me, and no matter the circumstance, to be neither
     jubilant nor sad.
Whoever—whether man or woman, animate or inanimate—
Practises even one of these nine forms of devotion,
Is exceedingly dear to me, respected lady,
And all these forms of bhakti are unshakeably present in you.
The ultimate state, difficult even for ascetics to attain,
Has today become easily attainable for you.
The fruit, most incomparable, of beholding me
Is that the soul attains its own natural form.
But, dear lady, if you have any tidings of Janak's daughter,
That most graceful one, tell me all that you know.'
'Go to the Pampa Lake, Raghurai,
And there make friends with Sugriv—
He will tell you all, divine Lord Raghubir.
You, of steadfast mind, know everything, yet you ask me!'
Again and again she bowed her head at the Lord's feet,
And lovingly told him her whole story.

After relating her whole story, she gazed upon the Lord's countenance
And took his lotus feet into her heart.
Abandoning her body in yogic fire,
She became absorbed in Hari's state, from which there is no return.
Men, your varied activities, your sins, your many creeds—
These give rise to sorrow, abandon them,
And with true faith be devoted to Ram's feet—
So says Tulsidas.

> The divine one who bestowed salvation even upon
> A woman without caste, and of low and sinful birth—
> O foolish heart, do you seek bliss
> By forgetting such a Lord?   (36)

Ram left that forest and they continued on their way,
Two lions amongst men, of matchless strength.
The Lord, lamenting like a grief-stricken lover separated from
    his beloved,
Related many stories and discoursed on many things.
'Lakshman, look at the splendour of the forest,
Whose heart will not be moved to look upon it?
The birds and deer, all with their mates,
Seem to reproach and mock me.
When, seeing me, the stags would run away,
The does say, "You have nothing to fear,
So enjoy yourselves, you who are born of deer,
For it is a golden deer that he comes searching for!"
The elephants keep the she-elephants close to them
As though instructing me.
The Shastras, however well studied, must be read again and again,
And a king, however well served, must never be considered under
    one's sway.
And though you keep your wife in your heart,

A young woman, like the Shastras and the king, is never under
    one's control.
Look, dear brother, how beautiful spring is,
Yet to me, without my beloved, it is frightful.

    Thinking that I am distracted with the grief of separation,
    And powerless and completely alone,
    Madan, with the forest, the honeybees, and the birds
    All at once, is attacking me.   (37A)

    But his spy, the wind, has seen that I am with my brother,
    And taking heed of his report,
    The mind-born god of love
    Has halted his legions and made camp.   (37B)

The tangled creepers entwined around enormous trees
Seem like the tents and pavilions that he has spread,
While the palms and plantain trees are his noble flags
    and pennants—
Looking upon these, only the most resolute can resist their beauty.
The many trees blooming with flowers of various kinds,
Are like archers arrayed in livery of many kinds.
Magnificent trees stand resplendent here and there,
Like army commanders severally encamped.
The sweet-voiced kokil's call is the trumpeting of his fierce
    war-elephants,
While cranes and coucals are his camels and mules.
Peacocks, chakors and parrots are his noble war-horses,
All pigeons and swans, his Arab steeds,
And quails and partridges his troops of foot soldiers—
Love's legions are beyond description.
The mountain peaks are his war chariots, waterfalls his war drums,
And chataks the minstrels singing his praises.
The humming honeybees are his bugles and clarinets,

While soft, cool and fragrant breezes blow as his ambassadors.
His fourfold army with him,
He roams around challenging all to battle.
Lakshman, only those who remain steadfast upon beholding
    Kamdev's host
Are respected in this world.
Love has one great strength, and that is woman—
The one who can escape her is indeed a mighty warrior!

Dear brother, there are three mighty evils—
Love, anger and greed.
They disturb the hearts of even the wisest munis
In the twinkling of an eye.   (38A)

Greed's might lies in desire and pride,
Love's strength is woman alone,
While anger's power is rough speech—
So the great munis have declared upon reflection.'   (38B)

Transcending the three gunas, and lord of all creation, moving
    and unmoving,
Ram pervades the inner hearts of all, Uma.
But he displayed the misery of a lover
And strengthened dispassion in the hearts of the resolute.
Anger, love, greed, pride and delusion,
May be got rid of only by Ram's favour.
He who has the favour of that divine performer,
Never gets lost in his illusion.
Uma, I speak from my own experience—
The worship of Hari is real, and all the world only a dream.
The Lord then went to the shore of that deep
And lovely lake called Pampa.
Its water was as pure as the hearts of holy men,
It had four heart-enchanting ghats,

And drinking at it here and there were animals of various kinds,
Like a crowd of beggars at the home of a generous man.

> Under its cover of dense lotus leaves
> The water could not be quickly found,
> Just as, concealed by maya,
> The nirgun brahm cannot be seen.   (39A)

> The fish were all uniformly happy
> In its exceedingly deep waters
> Like the days of the pious,
> That pass in tranquillity.   (39B)

Lotuses of many colours opened their petals
While swarms of bees sweetly hummed.
Geese and water-hens called
As though, seeing the Lord, they were praising him.
The flocks of storks, chakravaks,[xxxii] and other birds
Could only be seen and not described.
The cries of these beautiful birds were very pleasing
And seemed to be calling out to travellers passing by.
Close by the lake, munis had built their hermitages,
And all around were beautiful forest trees.
Champak, bakul, kadamb, tamal
Patal, panas, palash, mango—
The many kinds of trees had put forth new leaves and flowers,
Upon which swarms of bees buzzed and hummed,
While a pleasing breeze blew,
Naturally cool, soft and fragrant.
'Kuhoo, kuhoo' the kokils sang—
Hearing their sweet cries even a muni's meditation would break.

---

xxxii Kok birds

The trees, heavy with fruit
Bowed down low to the ground,
Like generous men who humbly bow
Upon receiving a large fortune.   (40)

When Ram saw this very beautiful lake,
He bathed in it with great joy,
And then, with his younger brother,
Sat down in the pleasing shade of a noble tree.
There again came all the gods and munis,
And after singing his praises, returned to their own abodes.
The compassionate one rested there in supreme delight
And narrated pleasant tales to his younger brother.
When he saw the divine Lord suffering the pain of separation from
     his beloved,
Narad grew deeply concerned in his heart.
'He submitted to my curse, and now because of it,
Ram is bearing the weight of so many sorrows.
I must go and look upon such a Lord,
For this chance may never come again.'
Thinking this, Narad, vina in hand,
Went where the Lord sat at ease.
Singing of Ram's holy acts in a sweet voice,
He lovingly praised him in many ways.
As he reverently prostrated himself, Ram raised him up
And clasped him to his heart again and again.
Asking about his welfare, he seated him by his side,
And Lakshman washed his feet with reverence.

After supplicating him in many ways,
And perceiving that the Lord was pleased in his heart,
Narad folded his lotus hands
And spoke these words: (41)

'Listen, Raghunayak, you who are by nature generous,
You are the giver of delightful boons, both otherwise unattainable
    and attainable.
Grant me this one boon that I ask, master—
Though you already know what it is, for you know the inner secrets
    of all hearts.'
'Muni, you know my disposition,
When do I ever conceal anything from my devotees?
What object do I love so much,
That you, noble muni, may not ask it of me?
There is nothing of mine I would not give a devotee,
Never abandon this confidence in me even by mistake.'
Then Narad, rejoicing, said,
'This is the boon I presume to ask—
Though the names of the divine Lord are many,
And though the Vedas declare that each is greater than the other,
May "Ram" be greater than all the other names, Lord,
The hunter that destroys the flock of birds that is sin.

    Devotion to you is a full-moon night—
    May the name of Ram be that full moon
    And the other names the stars
    In the clear sky of your devotee's heart.'   (42A)

    Raghunath, ocean of compassion,
    Said to the muni, 'So be it.'
    Then Narad, with great joy in his heart,
    Bowed his head at the Lord's feet.   (42B)

Seeing Raghunath so pleased,
Narad said again in sweet tones,
'Ram, when you had sent forth your maya
And beguiled and bewildered me,
Then, Raghunath, I had wanted to marry.

Why, Lord, did you not let me?'
'Listen, muni, I tell you most emphatically,
I always protect those
Who worship only me,
Like a mother protects her child.'

When a small child rushes to grab hold of the fire or a snake,
The mother protects it by pulling it away.
But when her son becomes an adult,
She loves him, but does not rush to protect him as before.
The wise are like my grown-up sons,
And humble, simple devotees my infant sons.
My devotees depend on my strength, the wise upon their own,
But lust and anger are the enemies of both.
Considering this, those endowed with understanding worship me,
And even upon acquiring wisdom, they do not abandon bhakti.

> Lust, anger, greed, pride and other passions
> Form delusion's mighty army,
> But among them all, the most pitiless, and giving greatest pain
> Is Woman, that personification of maya.   (43)

Listen muni, the Puranas, Vedas and holy men declare—
Woman is like spring to the forest of delusion,
And, becoming scorching summer, she renders dry
The lakes and waterfalls of prayer, meditation and penance.
Like the season of rains, she is the one that brings delight
To the frogs of lust, anger, greed and pride,
And to the clusters of lilies that are evil desires,
She is autumn, ever agreeable to them and beneficent.
The multitude of lotuses are all the virtues
That vile Woman, becoming winter frost, blights,
And at other times, she is the cool season of dews that makes
The javas of attachment flourish and grow in profusion.

To the flocks of owls that are sins and evil deeds,
Woman is the benevolent night, deep and dark.
Intelligence, strength, goodness and truth are all fish,
And Woman the fishing-hook—so declare the wise.

    The root of evil, a giver of pain,
    And the receptacle of all sorrow is a young woman.
    That is why, muni, knowing this is in my heart,
    I stopped you from getting married.'   (44)

Upon hearing Raghupati's pleasing words,
The muni's body trembled with happiness and his eyes filled with tears.
'Tell me, is there any other master who
Showers such concern and love upon a servant?
Those who do not worship such a Lord abandoning all delusion,
Are devoid of wisdom, dull-witted and unfortunate.'
Muni Narad then reverently said,
'Listen, Ram, versed in knowledge,
My master, destroyer of the terror of rebirth, tell me—
What are the marks of holy men, Raghubir?'
'Listen, muni, as I tell you the qualities of holy men,
Because of which I remain subject to them.
They have overcome the six passions,[13] and are sinless, without desires,
Unwavering, without worldly possessions, pure in every way,
    abodes of bliss,
Of unbounded wisdom, disinterested, temperate in food,
Truthful, sagacious, learned, versed in meditation,
Circumspect, bestowing honour upon others, without pride or conceit,
Resolute, supremely wise in the ways of dharma.

    They are abodes of virtue, free from the sorrows
    Of this world, and devoid of doubt.
    They love only my lotus feet,
    Abandoning even their own bodies and their homes.   (45)

They are abashed to hear their own virtues related,
And rejoice to hear the virtues of others being sung.
They are even-tempered and calm, and never abandon what
    is right.
Straightforward by nature, they have affection towards all.
They remain absorbed in prayer, penance, religious observances,
    self-denial, self-restraint and pious vows
And are devoted to the feet of their guru, the Lord and Brahmans.
Full of faith, forbearance, goodwill, compassion,
And joy, they have guileless love for my feet.
Distinguished by dispassion, discernment, humility, knowledge,
And with true understanding of the Vedas and Puranas,
They never give in to ostentation, pride or arrogance,
And do not, even by mistake, set their foot upon an evil path.
They incessantly sing and listen to my holy acts,
And, without self-interest, are devoted to the good of others.
Listen, muni, the virtues of holy men are so many
That not even Sharada or the Vedas can tell them all,

No, not Sharada nor Shesh can relate them!'
As soon as he heard this, Narad clasped the Lord's lotus feet.
Thus did the compassionate Lord, the friend of the lowly,
Relate with his own mouth the virtues of his devotees.
Bowing his head again and again at the Lord's feet,
Narad returned to Brahma's abode.
Blessed, say Tulsidas, are they who place their faith in no other,
But immersing themselves in Hari, become one with him.

    Those who sing or hear
    The pure fame of Ravan's foe,[xxiii]
    Will receive steadfast faith in him
    Without detachment, prayer, or meditation.   (46A)

[xxiii] Ram

A young woman's body is like the flame of a lamp.
O heart, do not be the moth!
Worship Ram, giving up lust and pride,
And ever seek the company of the good.   (46B)

Thus ends the third descent into the Manas lake of Ram's acts that destroys all the impurities of the age of Kali.

Glossary

abir: Red powder, thrown into the air in celebration.

Aditi: The mother of the gods. In the Rig Veda, she
                 is represented as being the mother of Daksh as
                 well as the daughter of Daksh. She is addressed
                 as 'the mother of the gods' and 'the mother of the
                 world'. She gave birth to eight sons, of which she
                 abandoned the eighth, the Sun. The other seven
                 became the Adityas. In the Yajur Veda, she is
                 called the wife of Vishnu, but in the Ramayana,
                 the Mahabharata and the Puranas, Vishnu is
                 called the son of Aditi; therefore, he is also
                 sometimes called Aditya. In the Vishnu Purana,
                 she is the daughter of Daksh and the wife of the
                 sage Kashyap, by whom she was the mother of
                 Vishnu in his Vaman, or dwarf, incarnation, and
                 also of Indra. In the *Ramcharitmanas*, Aditi is
                 reborn as Kaushalya and Kashyap as Dasharath,
                 and in that form, they are the mother and father
                 of Ram, who is Vishnu in his seventh incarnation.

Agahan: The eighth month of the Hindu calendar
                 equivalent to November–December.

Agastya: A rishi, and the author of several hymns in the Rig
                 Veda. It is said that he was born in a water-pitcher

285

as 'a fish of great lustre'. He is therefore also known as 'Ghatjoni' and 'Kumbhaj' or 'pitcher-born'. He is supposed to have drunk up the ocean because it had offended him, and because he wanted to help the gods in their wars with the Daityas when the latter had hidden themselves in the sea. He is therefore also called 'Samudra-chuluk' or 'ocean-drinker'.

ages of the world; yuga:	The duration of the world is said to be 4,320,000,000 human years (equal to a day for Brahma); this period consists of a thousand epochs, and each epoch is made up of four ages, or yugas. These are: (i) Krit or Satyayug (the golden age); (ii) Tretayug (the silver age); (iii) Dwaparyug; (iv) Kaliyug. The first age comprises 1,728,000 years; the second 1,296,000 years; the third 864,000 years; and the fourth 432,000 years. The duration of the Dwapar is twice the length of the Kali, that of the Treta is thrice that of the Kali, and that of the Satyayug is four times that of the Kaliyug. In the current epoch, the first three ages have already elapsed, while the Kali is that in which we live. Ram's incarnation took place towards the end of the Tretayug.
Agni:	Fire, one of the most ancient and sacred objects of worship in Hinduism. He appears in three places—in the sky as the sun, in air as lightning, and upon earth as ordinary fire. He is one of the chief deities of the Vedas, and, through the fire-sacrifices, the mediator between gods and men.
Ahalya:	Wife of the Rishi Gautam, and a very beautiful woman. She was the first woman created by Brahma, who gave her to Gautam. Ahalya's exceptional beauty caught Indra's eye. Determined to seduce her, he enlisted the help of the moon, who turned into a cock and crowed at midnight.

Gautam, thinking it was time for his morning worship, went off to the river to bathe. Then Indra, taking the form of the rishi, entered his hermitage and seduced his unsuspecting wife. The sage, returning, caught him and in his fury cursed him. He also threw out Ahalya from the hermitage, and depriving her of the prerogative of being the most beautiful woman in the world, turned her into a block of stone. She was restored to life by the touch of Ram's feet.

Amaravati: Indra's capital city, renowned for its magnificence and splendour.

amla: The plant known as the Indian gooseberry and its fruit. The fruit is small and green and quite sour, but greatly valued for its medicinal properties. 'Holding an amla in the palm of your hand' signifies understanding something clearly and from every angle, just as the small and round amla fruit can be seen when held upon one's palm.

amrit: Nectar conferring immortality, produced at the churning of the ocean by the gods and demons.

Anasuya: The wife of the Rishi Atri, and by him, the mother of the sage, Durvasa. She was also one of the daughters of Daksh. She was exceedingly pious and practised intense austerities, which gave her miraculous powers.

anchal: The flowing, free end of a sari.

Angad: Son of Baali, the monkey king of Kishkindha.

apsara: The apsaras are the nymphs of Indra's court. They are beautiful, fairy-like beings, and are the wives or mistresses of the Gandharvas. They are also famous for their liaisons with mortal men. The

Ramayana and the Puranas attribute their origin
to the churning of the ocean. It is said that when
they appeared out of the ocean, neither the gods
nor the Asurs could have them, so they became
common to all. They are also called Suranganas,
or 'the wives of the gods'.

arghya: A libation of water and milk, flowers, kush grass
                          and other auspicious ingredients made to a deity,
                          or an honoured guest.

ark: The plant known as the crown flower. Native to
                          India and South-east Asia, it grows to about 4 m
                          in height, and has waxy white or lavender flowers.
                          Its leaves and stem gives a thick, milky sap if
                          broken. The seed follicles are small and hard.
                          The plant is poisonous, but has several medicinal
                          uses in Ayurveda. It is often grown in temple
                          compounds and is believed to be particularly liked
                          by Lord Shiva.

arti: A ceremony performed in welcome of an
                          honoured guest, by moving circularly around his
                          head a platter containing lamps, incense, flowers,
                          etc.

Arundhati: The morning star, personified as the wife of the
                          Rishi Vasishtha.

Ashvamedha: 'The sacrifice of a horse'; a sacrifice performed
                          only by the greatest and most powerful of kings.
                          It was believed that the performance of a hundred
                          such sacrifices would enable a mortal king to
                          overthrow Indra and become the ruler of the
                          universe. A horse was selected and consecrated
                          by the performance of certain ceremonies; it was
                          then let loose to wander wherever it wanted for
                          a year. The king, or his representative, followed
                          the horse with an army, and if the horse entered

another country, the ruler of that country had to either fight or submit. If the king who had released the horse was victorious over the kings through whose lands the horse passed, he would return home triumphant after a year, with the defeated kings behind him; if he failed in this, he was ridiculed and disgraced. After a king returned home successful, a great festival was held, during which the horse was sacrificed, either really or metaphorically.

Ashvins; Ashvin twins; Ashvinkumar: Two Vedic deities, twin sons of the Sun by a nymph who concealed herself in the form of a mare (*ashva* in Sanskrit)—hence, Ashvini, and her sons, Ashvins. The Ashvins are ever young and handsome, and shine with the radiance of gold. Swift as falcons, they ride in a golden chariot drawn by horses or birds, and, as personifications of the morning twilight, they are the first bringers of light in the morning sky. They also have great healing powers, and are the physicians of heaven.

Astagiri: This is the western mountain behind which the sun is supposed to set; it is also called Astachal.

Asur: Literally, 'not a god', so 'enemy of the gods', or generally 'demons'. The word is used as a general term for the enemies of the gods, including Daityas and Danavs, who are descended from the sage Kashyap. It does not include the Rakshasas, who are descended from the sage Pulastya. The Asurs are in constant conflict with the gods.

Atri: A rishi, and author of many Vedic hymns. In the Vedas, he appears in hymns in praise of Agni, Indra, and the Ashvins; later he is regarded as one of the ten Prajapatis, or lords of creation, engendered by Manu for the creation of the world; and still later, he appears as one of the mind-born sons of Brahma. He is also one of the Saptarishi, the seven great sages who preside over the world, and as one of them, he is one of the seven stars of the Great Bear. He married Anasuya, one of the daughters of Daksh, and their son was the sage Durvasa. In the Puranas, he was also the father of Soma, the moon, and the ascetic Dattatreya by Anasuya.

Ayodhya:

The capital city of the kingdom of Koshal. It was the city from which ruled Ikshvaku, the founder of the solar dynasty. It later became the capital city of Dasharath and then of Ram. It is also the city of Ram's birth. It is also called Avadh.

Baali:

The monkey-king of Kishkindha. He was the son of Indra, and said to have been born from his mother's hair (*baal*), hence his name. He was killed by Ram, and his kingdom given to his brother, Sugriv. His wife was Tara, and his sons were Angad and Tar.

Baitarni:

'(The river) to be crossed'; it is the river that must be crossed before hell can be entered. The river is described as being filled with blood, excrement and all kinds of filth. It flows fast and with great force.

bakul:

A medium evergreen tree native to India. The tree gives thick shade and bears fragrant flowers. Its fruit is also edible and is used in traditional medicine. It is also called maulsari.

Bali:

A good and virtuous Daitya king, he was the son of Virochan, who was the son of Prahlad, the son of Kanakakasipu. Through devotion and penance, Bali became so powerful that he defeated Indra and the other gods, and extended his rule over the three worlds. The gods appealed to Vishnu for help, and he took on his Vaman or dwarf avatar to restrain the king. (See Vishnu, fifth avatar.) He asked the generous king for three steps of land. The king granted him the boon. Vishnu then stepped over the earth with his first step, the heavens with his second, and when he asked where he should place his foot for the third step, Bali offered his own head. Out of respect for Bali's goodness and generosity, Vishnu stopped short and gave him the infernal region of Patal to rule. Bali is also called Mahabali, and his capital city was Mahabalipuram.

Bana; Banasur: A powerful Daitya, the eldest son of the Daitya king, Bali; he had a thousand arms and was a devotee of Shiv and an enemy of Vishnu. He is also called Vairochi.

ber: The jujube tree and its fruit. This is cultivated as well as grows wild in India; every part of the tree has medicinal uses, and its small and somewhat acid fruit is very popular and is eaten pickled, cooked or raw. 'Holding a ber in the palm of your hand' signifies understanding something clearly and from every angle, just as the small and round ber fruit can be seen when held upon one's palm.

Bhadon: The sixth month of the Hindu calendar, equivalent to August–September.

Bhagirath: A king of the Ikshvaku dynasty, and a descendent of Sagar; he brought the sacred River Ganga to earth from heaven. King Sagar of Avadh married two women, the princess Keshini, and Sumati, the daughter of the sage Kashyap. With Keshini, he had one son, Asamanjas; through him the royal line was continued. With Sumati he had sixty-thousand sons. Now Asamanjas

grew up into such a wild and immoral man
that Sagar abandoned him. Unfortunately, the
sixty-thousand also followed in their brother's
footsteps, and became so known for their impiety
that the gods complained about them to Vishnu
and to the sage Kapil. Once, Sagar decided to
hold the Ashvamedha or horse-sacrifice. Though
the horse was guarded by his sixty-thousand sons,
it was carried off to Patal, the underworld. They
dug their way to the underworld, where they
saw the sage Kapil seated in meditation, and the
horse grazing close by. Thinking that he was the
thief, they threatened him with their weapons.
This disturbed the sage in his meditation, and
so enraged him that a single glance from him
reduced them to ashes. Their remains were
found by Anshumat, the son of Asamanjas, who
begged Kapil that his uncles be raised to heaven
through his favour. Kapil promised Anshumat's
grandson would be the means of accomplishing
this by bringing down Ganga, the river of
heaven. Anshumat returned to Sagar, who then
completed the sacrifice. The deep chasm that his
sons had dug became the ocean, which is called
'saagar' after his sons. The son of Anshumat was
Dilip, and his son was Bhagirath. Determined
to free the souls of his ancestors, Bhagirath left
his kingdom in the care of his ministers and
retreated to the Himalayas, where he practised
severe austerities in order to please Brahma. After
a thousand years of prayer and penance, Brahma
appeared before him. When Bhagirath told him
that he wanted to bring down the divine river,
Ganga, so that he may perform the appropriate
rites for his ancestors, Brahma told him to pray
to Shiv, for only he could withstand the force of
the river's descent. So Bhagirath prayed to Shiv.
The compassionate god was quickly pleased, and
agreed to help him, promising to hold the Ganga

in his matted locks and so reducing the force of her descent. Ganga agreed to come to earth, and as she fell, Shiv stood beneath her cascading waters and caught them in his hair, letting only a trickle escape. This trickle was as much as the earth could bear, and this became the mighty River Ganga upon earth. She followed Bhagirath, and he guided the river from the Himalayas, across the plains of northern India, into the sea, and from there to Patal, where the ashes of Sagar's sixty-thousand sons were washed with her waters and purified.

bhakti: A many-nuanced idea meaning at one time all or any one of the following: faith, belief; devotion, adoration, worship; attachment, devotedness, service. In the Hindu context, it means devotion to and love for a personal god. There are nine forms of bhakti, which are explained by Ram to Sabari in the Aranyakand (35-36).

Bharadvaj: An eminent rishi to whom are attributed many hymns from the Vedas.

Bharat: 'He who supports, bears, or carries'; son of Dasharath and Kaikeyi, younger brother to Ram.

Bhogavati: The magnificent, subterranean capital city of the Nagas in Patal.

Bhrigu: A Vedic sage. He is one of the Prajapatis and the great Rishis, and regarded as the founder of the race of Bhrigus or Bhargavas, in which were born Jamadagni and his son, Parashuram. He officiated at Daksh's sacrifice.

Bhringi: A sage, especially devoted to Shiv. It is said that Bhringi was so deeply devoted to Shiv that he even refused to honour Parvati, maintaining that he would worship Shiv and Shiv alone. He attempted to circle Shiv in homage, leaving out Parvati, so Shiv took Parvati upon his lap; Bhringi then turned himself into a snake and tried to slither between the two. At that, Shiv made Parvati a part of himself, taking on the form of Ardhanarishvar. Bhringi then turned himself into a bee and tried to separate the two. At this Parvati was so angry that she cursed him, so that he lost all flesh and blood and, turning into a bag of bones, collapsed upon the ground. Bhringi then realized that he could not separate Shiv from Parvati, for they were not separate, but together made up the whole. Bhringi was forgiven, and given a third leg by which to support himself.

Bhushundi;
Kak Bhushundi:

The crow, Bhushundi. He is a sage in a crow's body, and a great devotee of Ram. He is also one of the four narrators of the *Ramcharitmanas*, and relates the story of Ram to Garud.

birth, modes of:

According to Hindu tradition, there are four modes of birth: (i) born from the womb (such as man and other mammals); (ii) born of an egg (such as birds, fish and so on); (iii) engendered by heat and moisture (such worms, insects, lice, etc.); and (iv) born by sprouting or germinating (trees, plants, vegetables, etc.). From these four modes of birth are generated eighty-four lakh (1 lakh = 100,000) forms of life.

blue-throat:

The Indian roller. This bird has a blue crown and blue wings and tail, and a pale-brown breast. Though it does not have a blue throat, it is called nil-kanth (literally 'blue-throat' in Hindi), which is also a name for Shiv. It can be easily seen in India, and is believed by many to be sacred to Vishnu.

brahm:	The Absolute, the Eternal, the Self-existent, the divine essence and source of all being from which all created things emanate and to which they all return (not to be confused with Brahma who is the Supreme Spirit personified as the Creator).
Brahma:	The Supreme Spirit manifested as the Creator of the universe. He is the first god of the Hindu triad of the Creator, the Preserver and the Destroyer. He is represented as red in colour, with four heads. He wears a pointed beard, usually white in colour. He has four arms, in which he variously holds his sceptre, a spoon, a rosary of beads, a waterpot, a lotus, his bow Parivita and the Vedas. His consort is the goddess Sarasvati. His vehicle is the hansa, or swan. Brahma is also called 'Aj', the unborn; Chaturanan or Chaturmukh, 'having four faces'; Sanat, 'the ancient'; Vidhi, as providence, or the one who ordains what will be; Vidhatra or Vidhata 'disposer' or 'arranger'; Viranchi, the Creator.
Brahman:	The first of the four castes of Hinduism. It is the priestly caste, though its members may not necessarily be priests. In Hindu belief, a Brahman is the chief of all created beings. His person is inviolate, he is entitled to every honour and causing harm to a Brahman results in the severest consequences, in this life and the next. The chief duty of a Brahman is the study and teaching of the Vedas, and the performance of fire-sacrifices and other ceremonies. Hindus believe that there are two kinds of gods: the gods themselves, and then the Brahmans who have learnt the Vedas—they are gods upon earth.
chakor; chakori (f.):	A mythical bird, which is believed to subsist only upon moonbeams and to eat fire at the full moon.

chatak; chataki (f.):   A mythical bird that subsists only on raindrops that fall in autumn, when the sun is at the same longitude as the star Svati.

Chintamani: The 'wish-jewel'. It has the power of granting all desires. It belongs to Brahma, who is himself sometimes called by this name.

Chitrakut: 'Bright peak'; one of the peaks of the Vindhya range, and the first dwelling-place of Ram and Sita during their exile.

Dadhichi: A Vedic rishi. Once, Indra had been driven out of his kingdom by the Asur, Vritra, who was invulnerable to any known weapon. Vritra also stole all the water in the world for his own use and that of his army. Indra turned to Vishnu for help, who revealed that Vritra could be defeated only by a weapon made from the bones of the sage Dadhichi, who was practising penance in the Naimisha forest. Indra and the other gods went to Dadhichi and appealed to him for help. The sage agreed, and gave up his life immediately. From his bones, Vishvakarma, the smith of the gods, fashioned the thunderbolt and other weapons, with which Indra and the gods defeated Vritra and his army.

Daityas: A race of demons and giants, the sons of Diti, daughter of Daksh, by the sage Kashyap. They warred against the gods, and were often victorious. They are very similar to their cousins, the Danavs.

Daksh: 'Competent, intelligent'; Daksh is one of the mind-born sons of Brahma, and is generally associated with male energy or creative power. Depending on the source consulted, he had twenty-four, fifty, or sixty daughters. The Ramayana and the Mahabharata agree on the larger number. According to the Mahabharata, ten of his daughters married Dharma, and thirteen married the sage Kashyap, becoming the mothers of gods and demons, men, birds, serpents and all living things. Twenty-seven married Soma, the Moon, and these became the twenty-seven Nakshatras or lunar asterisms. His daughter Sati married Shiv and killed herself because of a quarrel between her father and her husband. Daksh was also one of the Prajapatis, and is often regarded as their chief. He is also called Prajesh (lord of creatures).

damru:

A small drum shaped like an hour-glass, which is held in one hand; it is said to have been created by Shiv, and by beating it, Shiv produced the very first sounds. Shiv also performs his cosmic dance of regeneration to the beat of the damru.

Danav; Danuj:

A clan of demons, giants who warred against the gods; they are the sons of Danu, daughter of Daksh, by the sage Kashyap. They are associated with and very similar to the Daityas.

Dandak:

A vast forest between the rivers Godavari and Narmada. Some passages in Valmiki's Ramayana describe it as beginning immediately south of the Jamuna. It is described as a wilderness, with scattered hermitages, and full of wild beasts and Rakshasas.

Dasharath:

A prince of the solar dynasty, descendant of Ishkvaku, the king of Koshal, and the father of Ram and his brothers, Bharat, Lakshman and Shatrughna. Dasharath had three wives, Kaushalya, Sumitra and Kaikeyi.

Dharma:

Literally, 'that which is to be held fast or kept'. It is a many-layered concept, and can variously mean statute, law, rule, or custom; customary observances of caste, sect, or social class;

prescribed course of conduct, duty, or obligation; virtue, morality, morals; righteousness, good works; religion, piety, or religious observances.

Dhruv: The Pole star; son of Uttanapad and his wife Suniti, he was a staunch devotee of Vishnu. According to the Vishnu Purana, King Uttanapada was one of the sons of Manu Swayambhuva. He had two wives: Suruchi, who was his favourite, and was haughty and cruel, and Suniti, the second queen, who was gentle and kind. Suruchi had a son called Uttam, and Suniti's son was Dhruv. Suruchi demanded that her son Uttam should alone succeed to the throne. Uttanapad agreed, and Suniti and Dhruv left the palace for the forest. Dhruv, rejected by his father, declared he wanted no honours except those that he attained by his own actions. In his grief he meditated upon Vishnu, and in return for his unwavering devotion, Vishnu raised him up to the heavens as the Pole star.

Diti: One of the daughters of Daksh, wife of Kashyap, and mother of the Daityas.

Durvasa: 'Ill-clothed'; a sage known for his fiery temper and irascible nature. According to some sources, he is the son of Atri and Anasuya; but some authorities say that he is a son or an emanation of Shiv. Many fell under the curse of his anger, including Indra, whom he cursed for disrespecting him, and by his curse, the gods under Indra became weak and were overpowered by the Asurs. This state of affairs ultimately led to the churning of the ocean by the gods and demons to recover amrit and other precious things.

Dushan: A man-eating Rakshasa, the younger brother of Ravan; he was killed by Ram.

elephants, celestial:	The eight elephants who protect the earth and support it at the eight points of the compass. They are Airavat, Pundarik, Vaaman, Kumud, Anjan, Pushpadant, Sarvabhaum and Supratik. (See also guardians of the eight quarters).
food, flavours of:	There are six kinds of flavours in food. These are: sweet, sour, salt, bitter, acrid and astringent.
food, kinds of:	There are four kinds of food, classified according to the way in which they are ingested: (i) food that is chewed; (ii) food that is swallowed; (iii) food that is sucked; and (iv) food that is lapped up or drunk.
Galav:	A pupil of Rishi Vishvamitra. At the end of his studies, he asked Vishvamitra what fee he should give him. Vishvamitra refused to ask for anything, but when Galav insisted, he grew annoyed, and to get rid of him, asked him to bring him a thousand white horses with one black ear. After a long search, Galav found three kings who each had two hundred of the kind of horses he wanted. The kings, all of whom were childless, agreed to let him have the horses if he could somehow ensure they had a son. Galav appealed to Garud for help, who took him to see King Yayati. The king gave him his daughter, Madhavi, who, by a special boon, was able to bear sons and still remain a virgin. Galav gave her in marriage one after another to the three childless kings, Haryashwa, king of Ayodhya, Divodas, king of Kashi, and Ushinar, king of Bhoj; to each of the kings, Madhavi bore a son, and in return, Galav received 200 of the horses he wanted. Galav then presented Madhavi and the 600 horses to Vishvamitra. The sage accepted them and had a son by Madhavi, who was named Ashtaka. When Vishvamitra retired to the forest, he gave his hermitage and the horses

	to Ashtaka. And Galav, having taken Madhavi back to her father, also retired to the forest, like his guru.
Gandharva:	The Gandharvas are heavenly beings, who have their home in the sky or atmosphere; many of them live in Indra's heaven. They are entrusted with the task of preparing soma for the gods, are skilled in medicine, and are singers and musicians.
Ganesh:	Lord of the ganas, the troops of lesser deities attendant upon Shiv; the son of Shiv and Parvati. As the god of wisdom and the remover of obstacles, he is propitiated at the beginning of any endeavour. He is represented as a short man, with a yellow body, four hands, and the head of an elephant, with one tusk. He has a pot belly, signifying his love of food. In one hand he holds a shell, in another a discus, in the third a club, and in the fourth a lotus. His steed is a rat. He is also called Ganpati, 'chief of the ganas'; Ganraja, 'king of the ganas', Gajanan, 'elephant-faced'; Vinayak, 'leader of the Shiv's retinue' or 'remover of obstacles'.
Ganga:	The sacred river Ganges. According to the Puranas, the river flows from the toe of Vishnu, and was brought down to earth by the actions of Bhagirath, to purify the ashes of the sixty-thousand sons of King Sagar, who were burnt by the angry glance of the sage Kapil. Thus the river is also called Bhaagirathi. To save the earth from the shock of her fall, Shiv caught the river upon his head and checked the force of her waters with his matted hair. (See also Bhagirath.) Personified as a goddess, she is the daughter of Himvat and Maina, and her sister is Uma, the goddess Parvati.

Garud:	King of the birds and the steed of Vishnu. He is represented with the head, wings, talons and beaks of an eagle, and the body and limbs of a man. His face is white, his wings red and his body golden. When he was born, he was so bright that people mistook him for Agni. He is the son of the rishi Kashyap and Vinata, one of the daughters of Daksh. From his mother he is called Vainateya, 'Vinata's son'; as Vishnu's mount he is called 'Hariyan'; as the enemy and devourer of snakes he is called Urugari, Uragari, Pannagari, Uragad; and as king of the birds he is Khagesh, Khagapati.
Godavari:	Revered by Hindus, this is India's second-longest river after the Ganga; it rises in Trimbakeshwar in Maharashtra and flows east for 1465 kilometres to empty into the Bay of Bengal.
Gomati:	River in northern India; it is a tributary of the Sarju. It is also called the Dhenumati.
gorochan:	A bright yellow pigment, found as a bezoar in cattle; this is considered very rare and holy and has various ritual uses in Hindu practice, and is specially used for marking the foreheads of Hindus with the tilak. It is also supposed to have medicinal properties, including as a sedative and an antidote to poisons.
guardians of the eight quarters:	The eight points of the compass (the four cardinal and four intermediate points) are guarded and presided over by eight guardian deities. They are: (i) Indra, king of the gods, guards the east; (ii) Agni, or Fire, the south-east; (iii) Yama, god of death, the south; (iv) Surya, the Sun, the south-west; (v) Varun, the Sky, the west; (vi) Vayu, the Wind, the north-west; (vii) Kuber, god of wealth, the north; (viii) Soma, the Moon, the north-east. Some substitute Shiv in his form as Ishan, for Soma.

Each of these guardian deities has an elephant who helps to defend and protect the quarter; together these eight celestial elephants support the earth upon their backs. Indra's elephant at the east is Airavat; Agni's elephant at the south-east is Pundarik; Yama's at the south is Vaaman; Surya's at the south-west is Kumud; Varun's at the west is Anjan; Vayu's at the north-west is Pushpadant; Kuber's at the north is Sarvabhaum; and Soma's elephant at the north-east is Supratik.

Guha:

Chief of the Nishads, and a devotee and friend of Ram.

guna:

A quality, or an ingredient or constituent of nature, of which there are three in particular, viz., Sattva, Rajas, and Tamas, or 'goodness, passion, and darkness', or 'virtue, foulness, and ignorance'.

gunj seeds:

The tiny, bright red and black seeds of the shrub known as the jequirity bean or the rosary pea; they form the smallest of a jeweller's weights.

Hanuman; Hanumant;
Hanumat:

Literally, 'he who has large jaws'; the monkey chief who helped Ram in his search for Sita and fought with him in his war against Ravan. The son of Pavan, the Wind, he was of divine origin and endowed with magical powers. His mother was Anjana, the wife of a monkey called Kesari. He was enormously strong, he could also fly and change his size at will. In his true form he is as vast as a mountain and tall as a tower. His body is yellow and glows like molten gold. His face is as red as a ruby and his tail is so long that no one can measure its length. At the end of the war with Ravan, he went back with Ram to Ayodhya; there, Ram gave him the reward of perpetual life and youth. He epitomizes devotion to Ram. He is known by many names. For setting Lanka on fire, he is called Lankadahi; as the son of the wind he has the patronymics Pavanputra, Anili and Maruti; from his mother he is called Anjaneya; for his magic powers and knowledge of the healing arts, he is called Yogachara and Rajat-dyuti, 'the brilliant'. He is also a grammarian, and rivals Brihaspati, the guru of the gods, in his knowledge of all the sciences.

Harishchandra:

Son of Trishanku and king of Ayodhya, the twenty-eighth in descent from Ishkvaku, founder of the solar dynasty. He was a just and virtuous king, and famed for his generosity. There are several legends about him. The Mahabharata says that he was raised to Indra's heaven for his performance of the Rajasuya sacrifice (a fire-sacrifice that may be performed only by the greatest of kings) and his immense generosity. The Markandeya Purana gives a fuller version of the story: One day, while Harishchandra was out hunting, he heard the cries of several women in distress. The king rushed to help, but the cries were an illusion created by Vighnaraj, the god of obstacles. At that time, the sage Vishvamitra was observing strict penance in the forest. Vighnaraj, to test Harishchandra's goodness, entered his body, and the moment he did so, the king lost his temper and began to loudly curse and hurl abuse at Vishvamitra. This angered the sage, who, because of his anger lost all the power he had acquired through years of penance. Vishvamitra was now furious with Harishchandra, and the king, seeing his wrath, begged for forgiveness. In return, the sage demanded the sacrificial gift that would be due to him as a Brahman for the performance of a Rajasuya sacrifice. The king agreed, and promised to give him whatever he would choose to ask. Vishvamitra demanded that the king give him everything he possessed. The king agreed

and handed over all his material possessions to
the sage, including his kingdom and the clothes
he wore, so that he had remaining only his own
body, a garment of bark, his wife, Shaivya, and
his son, Rohit. The king, now destitute, left for
the city of Banaras. But the sage was waiting
for him there, and demanded that the gift be
completed. In despair, Harishchandra sold his
wife and his son, and handed over the proceeds to
Vishvamitra. Now there remained only himself.
Just then, Dharma, the god of justice, appeared
in the form of a low-caste Chandal, and offered
to buy him. When Vishvamitra still insisted upon
the completion of his gift, the king sold himself
to the Chandal and gave the money to the sage.
His new master put Harishchandra in charge of
a cremation ground, with strict instructions to
be always present there and to allow cremation
only after the payment of a toll. The honest king
did exactly as his master commanded. As the
months passed, his appearance grew dishevelled,
and he lost all hope of ever seeing his wife and
son again. One day, Rohit was bitten by a snake
and died. His grieving mother carried his body to
the cremation ground. The king and the queen
recognized each other, and exchanging stories,
were overcome with grief. They decided to
immolate themselves upon the funeral pyre of their
son. Harishchandra made ready a great pyre upon
which he placed Rohit's body, and once all was
done, he lost himself in contemplation of Vishnu.
At this, the gods all appeared and asked him to
stop, and bringing Rohit back to life, told him
that he, his wife and his son had all won a place
in heaven because of his steadfastness in fulfilling
his promise to Vishvamitra. But Harishchandra
was hesitant. He could not go to heaven without
his master, the Chandal's permission. At this,
the Chandal appeared and revealed himself to

be Dharma. Harishchandra still refused, saying he could not leave behind his faithful subjects, in turmoil without a king. So Indra, Dharma and Vishvamitra took the king, his wife and his son to Ayodhya. There, Vishvamitra crowned Rohit king of Koshal, after which Harishchandra and his wife Shaivya were taken to heaven.

Hataklochan: 'The golden-eyed', a powerful Daitya chief, son of Diti by the sage Kashyap, and twin brother of Kanakakasipu; he was killed by Vishnu in his third, Boar, incarnation. Hataklochan had dragged the earth to the bottom of the sea. In order to recover the earth, Vishnu took the form of a boar, and after a battle that lasted a thousand years, he killed Hataklochan and carried the earth back to the surface on his tusks. He is also known as Hiranyaksh and Kanakalochan.

Himvat; Himvant;   'Snow-clad'; the personification of the Himalaya
Himalaya: mountains, husband of Maina, and father of Ganga and Uma (Parvati). He is also called Himachal, Himbhudar, Himgiri, Tuhinachal, Tuhingiri, 'snowy mountain'; Girish, 'mountain king' or 'king of the mountain', a title he sometimes shares with Shiv.

humours of the body: In the Indian Ayurvedic system of medicine, the body is regarded as having three humours (or bodily fluids) in addition to blood. The three humours are vat or (wind), pitt (bile) and kaph (phlegm). All organic disorders of the body arise from an imbalance in these humours.

Ikshvaku: Founder of the solar dynasty, and king of Ayodhya at the beginning of the Tretayug or second age of the world. He had a hundred sons, of whom one was Nimi, who founded the Mithila dynasty.

Indra: God of the firmament, personification of the atmosphere; king of the gods. His consort is Indrani (also known as Shachi); he has a son by her, called Jayant. His heaven is Swarga; his capital is Amaravati; his elephant is Airavat; and his horse is Uchchaihsravas. His charioteer is Matali. In the Vedas, he is one of the most important of the gods, though he is not unbegotten/uncreated but has a father and a mother. He is described in the Vedas as a being of golden colour, with arms of enormous length. His forms are infinite and he can take any shape at will. He rides in a golden chariot drawn by two ruddy horses with flowing tails and manes. His weapon is the thunderbolt, which he carries in his right hand; he also uses arrows, a hook and a net in which he entangles his enemies. His chief delight is soma ras, the extremely potent juice of the soma plant, which he drinks in enormous quantities. He controls the weather, dispenses rain, and sends down lightning and thunder. He is constantly at war with Vritra, the demon of drought and bad weather, whom he ultimately overcomes with his thunderbolts. In the later centuries, Indra's importance decreased. He became less than the triad of Brahma, Vishnu and Shiv, but remained chief of all the other gods. According to the Mahabharata, he is the son of Aditi by Kashyap, and the foremost of the Adityas. He is the regent of the atmosphere and the guardian of the east quarter of the compass. He sends the lightning and hurls the thunderbolt, and the rainbow is his bow. He is represented as a fair-skinned man, riding a white horse or an elephant, and holding the thunderbolt in his hand. He is constantly at war with the Asurs, and is often defeated by them. He killed Vritra, but because Vritra was a Brahman, Indra had to go into hiding and perform penance till his guilt was purged away. There are many stories of his lack of self-restraint. He became infatuated with Ahalya, the beautiful and virtuous wife of the sage Gautam, and in his arrogance, decided to seduce her. He tricked the sage to leave the hermitage, and then taking on his form, seduced the unsuspecting Ahalya. The sage returned to see him leaving his house, and in fury cursed him so that he would be covered with the marks of a thousand yonis (the female organs of reproduction). Thus he was called Sa-yoni. But these marks were later changed to eyes, because of which he is also called Netra-yoni or Sahasraksha 'the thousand-eyed'. He was defeated and carried off to Lanka by Ravan's son, Meghnad (who thus received the title of Indrajit, 'vanquisher of Indra'). Brahma and the other gods had to beg Meghnad to release him, which Meghnad did, in return for the boon of immortality. Brahma then tells Indra that his defeat was his punishment for seducing Ahalya. He is also known as Sakr, 'the powerful'; Purandar, 'destroyer of cities'; Pakripu, 'destroyer of the demon Pak'; Maghva or Maghvan, 'endowed with riches, wealthy'; Basav or Vasava, 'lord of the Vasus'.

Jabali: A Brahman, and a priest of King Dasharath. He is also called Javall.

Jadu: One of the sons of King Yayati, from his wife Devyani. Jadu (or Yadu) refused to relieve his father of the curse of old age passed on to him by the Rishi Sukra, and was therefore cursed in turn by Yayati that his children will not have a kingdom to rule. He was the founder of the line of Jadavas (or Yadavas), in which Krishna was born. He did ultimately receive the southern part of his father's kingdom, which the Jadavas went on to successfully rule.

Jagbalik: A celebrated sage. To him is attributed the code of law called *Yajnavalkyasmriti* (from 'Yajnavalkya', the Sanskrit rendering of his name). He is believed

	to have flourished at the court of Janak, king of Videha and Sita's father.
Jam, Jamraj; Yam, Yamraj:	The god of death. He is the son of the sun god Surya and his wife Saranyu, and twin brother of the river Jamuna. He is represented as a man green in colour and clothed in red; he is armed with a huge mace and a noose. He rides upon a buffalo, because of which he is also called as Mahishesh, 'the god whose steed is a mahish, or buffalo'. He is sometimes also called Shaman, 'the destroyer'.
jamana:	From the Sanskrit *yavana*; originally denoted a Greek, an Ionian, and then came to mean any barbaric foreigner from the West.
jambu:	The rose-apple tree, also called jamun in Hindi.
Jamuna; Yamuna:	The river Jamuna (or Yamuna) is the daughter of the sun god Surya and his wife Saranyu, and the twin sister of Jam (or Yama), the god of death. While Jamraj is death, Jamuna is life and bathing in her waters absolves one of sin.
Jamvant:	King of the bears. With his army of bears, he helped Ram in his war against Ravan and was always ready with sage advice and good counsel. He is also called Jambavat.
Janak:	A prince of the solar dynasty, king of Mithila/ Videha, and the father of Sita. Amongst his ancestors are the kings Ishkvaku and Nimi. Janak was known for his great knowledge and good works. It is said that Janak refused to submit to the hierarchical superiority of the Brahmans and insisted upon his right to perform fire-sacrifices without their intervention. He is also called Siradhwaja, 'he whose banner is the plough',

because his daughter Sita appeared as a baby in the furrow he was ploughing in preparation for a fire-sacrifice to obtain children. He is also known as Videh, the title used for the kings of Videha. 'Janak' is also the name of a royal dynasty of Mithila to which he belonged. He is therefore also called Janakpati, or 'lord of the Janak dynasty'.

Jatayu: King of the vultures, and son of Garud, Vishnu's steed. He is a friend of King Dasharath, and became an ally of Ram. He saw Ravan carrying away Sita and tried to stop him. In the ensuing battle, he was mortally wounded. Ram found him in time to hear his dying words and learn what had happened to Sita. Ram and Lakshman performed his last rites, and he ascended to heaven in a chariot of fire.

javas: The camel thorn. A small and prickly plant, it grows to about four feet in height. It has long spines along its branches and bright pink or reddish flowers. It is said to wilt at the coming of the rains and flourish only in dry soil.

Jayant: Son of Indra, also called Jaya.

jiva: The individual soul.

jubaraj: Literally 'young king'; an heir-apparent associated with the reigning sovereign, who assumes kingly duties while the king is still living.

Kabandh: A hideous Rakshasa killed by Ram. He was originally a Gandharva, the son of the goddess Lakshmi. He is described as being covered with hair, as huge as a mountain, without head or neck, a mouth full of immense teeth in the middle of his belly and a single eye in his breast. According to some accounts, he was turned into this hideous monster as the result of a quarrel with Indra, who struck him with his thunderbolt and drove his head and thighs into his body. Another account says that he was cursed by the sage Durvasa. When mortally wounded, he asked Ram to burn him, and from that fire he came out in his original form as a Gandharva. He is also called Danu.

kadamb: A tall, evergreen tree, with fragrant, globe-shaped orange flowers which are used in the preparation of perfumes; the tree also has great mythological and religious significance in India.

Kadru: A daughter of Daksh, and one of the thirteen wives of the sage Kashyap. She is the mother of the serpents, including Sheshnag. Her offspring bear the metronymic Kadraveya.

Kaikeya: A kingdom in the west, beyond the rivers Saraswati and Beas, and from which came Dasharath's queen, Kaikeyi.

Kaikeyi: A princess of Kaikeya, King Dasharath's favourite queen, and the mother of Bharat, his second son.

Kailash: A mountain in the Himalayas, north of the Mansarovar; it is the abode of Shiv, and also of Kuber, the god of wealth.

Kalnemi: A Rakshasa, and Ravan's uncle. At Ravan's behest, he attempts to kill Hanuman.

kalpa: A period of 4,320,000,000 years, equal to a day for Brahma. This is one cosmic cycle of creation, and is made up of a thousand cycles of the four ages, or yugas. (See also 'ages of the world'.) According to the Puranas, there are innumerable such cycles of creation, and within them, in each cycle of the four yugas, there occurs one incarnation of Ram.

Kalpataru:

A tree in Indra's paradise that grants all desires. It is also called Kamtaru, 'tree of desire'.

Kam:

Literally, wish, desire, longing; affection, love, passion; sexual passion; lust; love of pleasure; and personified, the god of love, Kamdev. He is the son of Vishnu by Rukmini, and the husband of Rati, the goddess of desire. He is lord of the celestial nymphs, the apsaras. He is armed with a bow and five arrows: the bow is of sugarcane, the bowstring a line of bees, and each of his five arrows is tipped with a particular flower (the white lotus, the ashok flower, the mango blossom, the jasmine and the blue lotus), which pierce the heart through the five senses; his favourite arrow is the one tipped with the mango blossom. His helpers are Vasant or Spring, and Malayanil, the southern winds or the cool and fragrant winds that blow from the Malay mountain. He is usually represented as a handsome young man riding on a parrot, and attended by apsaras; one of the apsaras bears his banner, which displays the Makar (a fabulous sea creature that represents Capricorn in the Hindu zodiac, and is depicted with the head and forelegs of an antelope and the body and tail of a fish), or a fish on a red background. He is therefore also called Jhashketu, 'one with a fish on his banner'. Once, as Shiv sat in meditation, Kamdev inspired him with thoughts of Parvati; Shiv, greatly angered by this impertinence, opened his third eye and reduced Kamdev to ashes. Later, Shiv relented and allowed him to be reborn as feelings. Kamdev therefore does not have a substantial form or body. He is thus called Anang and Atanu, or 'bodiless'. He is also known as Hridayniket, 'one whose abode is the heart'; Mayan or Madan, 'passion, lust or love (or the act of intoxicating or exhilarating, or gladdening)'; Manmath, 'he who churns the heart'; Manobhav, 'mind-born'; Manoj, 'born of the mind'; Mansij, 'born or generated in the mind, mind-born, heart-born'; Mar, the passion of love, personified. As husband to Rati, he is known as Ratinath, 'Rati's lord'. He is also called Kandarp.

Kamadgiri: Literally, 'the mountain that fulfils all desires'; the hill in Chitrakut upon which Ram stayed.

Kamdhenu: 'The cow that grants all desires'; she belongs to the sage Vasishtha and was one of the fourteen precious objects recovered at the churning of the ocean.

Kanakakasipu: 'Golden-robed'; a powerful Daitya chief, son of the sage Kashyap and his wife Diti, and twin brother to Hataklochan. As the result of practising severe austerities, he obtained from Shiv sovereignty over the three worlds for a million years, as well as immunity from death by man and beast. He grew so arrogant in his power that he declared that no one may worship any god but him. When his son, Prahlad, remained steadfastly devoted to Vishnu, he punished him and tried to kill him several times, but in vain. He was finally killed by Vishnu in his fourth avatar as Narsingh or Narkeshari, who was half-man, half-lion, and thus neither man nor beast. He is also called Hiranyakashipu.

kanji: A sour drink made by steeping mustard seeds in water and letting it ferment.

Kapil: A celebrated sage, the founder of the Sankhya philosophy. He reduced the sixty-thousand sons of King Sagar to ashes with a single glance.

kapila cow: A brown or reddish-coloured cow, considered in Hinduism to be the most sacred of all cows. A number of Hindu pilgrimage sites are linked to cows, some specifically to the brown cow. Several of these sites are mentioned in the Mahabharata and the Puranas. According to the Puranas, the gift of a kapila cow is equal to the giving away of a whole world in charity and confers upon the giver an assured place in Vishnu's heaven for as many thousand years as there are hairs upon the body of that cow and her calf, and after that time is over, it guarantees rebirth into a rich and wealthy family. Gifts of land, horses, gold, etc., do not equal in virtue even a sixteenth of the gift of a kapila cow.

Karamnasa: A river that flows through the holy city of Kashi; bathing in its waters destroys all merit (as opposed to bathing in the waters of the Ganga, which destroys all sin).

karila: A thorny, leafless shrub that grows in arid regions.

karma: Fate, or the certain consequence of previous acts; destiny.

Kashi: The city of Varanasi. It is sacred to Shiv, and one of the most holy of all pilgrimage places for Hindus. It is believed that those who die in Kashi immediately attain liberation from the cycle of birth and rebirth.

Kashyap: A Vedic sage, to whom are attributed some of the Vedic hymns. According to the Atharva Veda, he was 'self-born' and sprang into existence from Time. According to the Mahabharata, the Ramayana, and the Puranas, he was descended from Brahma. All authorities agree that he played a significant role in creation. The Mahabharata and later sources say that he married Aditi, and twelve other daughters of Daksh. From Aditi were born the celestial Adityas, headed by Indra, and also Visaswat, from whom was born Manu, the progenitor of all mankind. The Ramayana and Vishnu Purana state that Vishnu in his dwarf incarnation was the son of Aditi and Kashyap. From Kashyap's twelve other wives were born demons, serpents, reptiles, birds and all living things. He is also one of the Saptarishi, the seven great sages.

Kaushalya: King Dasharath's chief queen, and Ram's mother.

Kaustubh: A precious jewel, obtained at the churning of the ocean and worn by Vishnu upon his breast.

Ketu: A comet or meteor, and the ninth of the planets; and in Vedic astronomy, the descending lunar node, represented by a dragon's tail. He is personified in mythology as the lower half of the Danav, Rahu. See Rahu.

Khar: A man-eating Rakshasa, the younger brother of Ravan; he was killed by Ram.

Khasiya: A tribal, hill people of northern India.

Kinnara: Literally, 'What men?' in Sanskrit; they are mythical beings with the body of a man and the head of a horse. They are singers and musicians, and live in the paradise of Kuber, the god of wealth, on Mt Kailash. According to some sources, they sprang from the toe of Brahma together with the Yakshas; but others say that they are the sons of Kashyap.

kinshuk: A tree native to India. When in bloom, it is covered with a profusion of bright red, flame-coloured flowers. It is also known as the palash, the dhak, or the flame-of-the-forest.

Kirat: A mountain tribe that lives by hunting; a man of that tribe.

kodo:

A kind of small grain (like millet), considered inferior to rice and usually eaten by the poor.

kok; koki (f.):

These birds are a symbol of love and fidelity. Legend says that they are doomed to spend every night apart because of a curse pronounced upon them by a sadhu. They spend the day together, but every night they must separate; the birds spend the night calling to each in sad and mournful tones. Since they can be together only during the day, the birds are full of joy in the light of the sun, and grow sorrowful in the light of the moon. They are also called chakravak birds, or chakwa (male) and chakwi (female). They are also identified with the rathang birds, the ruddy or Brahmany geese.

kokil; koel:

The black or Indian cuckoo. This bird is prominent in Indian poetry; its musical cry is supposed to inspire pleasing and tender emotions.

Kol:

A tribe that lives the hills and forests of central India; a man of that tribe.

kos:

A measure of distance, equivalent to about 2 miles.

Koshal:

A country on the Sarju river, with Avadh its capital city. This was the kingdom ruled by Dasharath, and later by Ram.

Kshatriya:

The second of the four castes of Hinduism. It is the regal or warrior caste.

Kuber:

The god of wealth, and the king of the Yakshas. He is also regent of the north, and the keeper of gold and silver, pearls and precious stones, and all the treasures of the earth. He is the son of Vishravas (the son of the sage Pulastya), and the half-brother of Ravan. His consort is called

Yakshi. Kuber's city is Alaka in the Himalayas, and his garden is on Mount Mandar, where he is waited upon by the Kinnaras. Some authorities place his abode on Mount Kailash, in a palace built by the divine architect, Vishvakarma. According to the Ramayana and Mahabharata, he once ruled in the city of Lanka, also built by Vishvakarma, and from which he was thrown out by Ravan. He is the owner of the self-moving flying chariot, Pushpak, given to him by Brahma. He is also the keeper of the nine Nidhis, nine treasures considered precious beyond compare. They are called padma or the lotus flower, maha-padma, sankha, makar, kachhapa, mukunda, kunda, nila, kharba. Their nature and purpose are not clearly defined. Each treasure is also personified as a spirit that is also the guardian of that particular treasure. These guardian spirits are worshipped by some tantrics. Kuber is represented as a fair-skinned man, deformed in body, with three legs and only eight teeth. His body is covered with jewelled ornaments. He receives no worship. He is also known as Dhanesh, 'god of wealth'; Dhandhari, 'holder of wealth'; and 'Dhanad, 'one who grants wealth, the munificent'.

Kumbhakaran: A Rakshasa, the son of Vishravas (the son of the sage Pulastya), and brother of Ravan. As the result of a boon (or, as variously told, a curse) by Brahma, he slept for six months at a time and remained awake for only a single day.

kush: A kind of grass used in sacrifices and rituals. It is also called darbh.

Kushaketu: King Janak's younger brother, the father of the princesses Mandavi and Shrutakirti. He is also known as Kushadhvaja.

Lakshman:	'Possessed of lucky signs or marks, fortunate, prosperous'; son of Dasharath and Sumitra, Ram's younger brother and Shatrughna's twin. For his mother, Sumitra, he is also called Saumitri, 'Sumitra's son'. He is often considered to be the incarnation of the celestial serpent, Sheshnag.
Lakshmi:	The goddess of wealth and beauty, Vishnu's consort, and the mother of Kamdev, the god of love. According to the Ramayana, she sprang from the the froth of the ocean, in all her beauty, when it was churned by the gods and the Asurs. The Vishnu Purana says that she accompanied Vishnu in all his incarnations, and when Vishnu was born as Ram, she became Sita. She is also known as Shri; Indira; and Ramaa, 'Ram's consort'.
Lanka:	Ravan's kingdom. Also known as Singhal.
life, ends, fruits, rewards of:	These are four: (i) kama or sensual pleasure; (ii) artha or wealth; (iii) dharma or religious merit; and (iv) moksha or nirvana, i.e., liberation from worldly existence and rebirth.
life, four stages of:	For traditional Hindus, life is divided into four stages: (i) Brahmacharya, the student life, spent in study and obedience to one's guru; (ii) Grihastha, the stage of a householder, the married man living with his wife, and engaged in the ordinary duties of everyday life; (iii) Vanaprastha, the phase of a 'forest-dweller', who has discharged his duties in this world, and who, handing over his responsibilities to the next generation, has retired to the forest to devote himself to a life of simplicity and contemplation of the divine; and (iv) Sannyas, the period spent as a religious mendicant, who has renounced all worldly goods and desires and attained complete detachment from this material existence; freed from all forms and observances,

	he wanders about, subsisting only on alms, and striving for ultimate absorption into the divine.
lila:	Literally 'play, sport, pastime'. In Hindu belief, all creation is the Lord's lila, his sport or pastime.
Madhav:	Krishna (Vishnu) in his role as presiding deity of Prayag.
Magh:	The tenth month of the Hindu calendar, corresponding to January–February.
Mahishasur:	Literally, 'the buffalo demon', an Asur killed by the goddess Parvati in her form as Durga. Through intense austerities, he received a boon from Brahma and asked to be made immortal. Brahma refused the boon of immortality, but granted him the boon that no man would be able to kill him. The gods were powerless against him and were soundly defeated by him in battle. Then the goddess Parvati, who was Shiv's Shakti, the feminine manifestation of Shiv's cosmic energy, took on one of her fierce forms and killed him.
Mai:	A Daitya, the architect of the Asurs, as Vishvakarma was of the gods. He was the father of the demon Mayavi, and of Mandodari, Ravan's wife.
Maina:	The wife of Himalaya, and the mother of Parvati.
Mainak:	A winged mountain.
Makar:	Makar (equivalent to Capricorn) is the tenth sign of the zodiac, and is represented by a water-animal with the body and tail of a fish, and the forelegs, neck and head of an antelope.
Malaya, mountain range:	One of the seven mountain ranges mentioned in the Puranas; they are supposedly the southernmost

mountains of the Western Ghats in peninsular India. The mountains were famous for their sandal trees, which yielded the finest sandalwood in the world.

Manas; Manas lake; Mansarovar: A freshwater lake in modern Tibet, at the foot of Mt Kailash, the abode of Shiv. The lake is sacred to Hindus, Buddhists and Jains, and an important place of pilgrimage for them.

Mandakini: A sacred river that flowed by the hill of Chitrakut, where Ram and Sita spent part of their forest exile. It is also called Payasvini, 'water-giving'. It is said that the river was brought down from heaven to Chitrakut by Anasuya, the wife of the sage Atri, in order to alleviate a drought.

Mandar: The sacred mountain with which the ocean is said to have been churned by the gods and Asurs for the recovery of amrit and thirteen other precious things lost during the great flood.

Mandavi: Sita's cousin, the eldest daughter of Janak's younger brother Kushadhvaj (Kushaketu); she was married to Bharat.

Mandodari: The daughter of the Daitya Mai, she was Ravan's favourite wife, and the mother of Meghnad.

Manthara: Queen Kaikeyi's hunch-backed bondswoman, who roused the queen's jealousy and set her against Ram, which led to him being banished to the forest for fourteen years.

Manu: From the root *man*, 'to think'; this name belongs to fourteen mythological progenitors of mankind and rulers of the earth, each of whom rules for the period called a Manwantara (Manu-antara: the life or period of a Manu). There are fourteen

Manwantaras in any kalpa. The gods, the seven
great sages (Saptarishis) and Indra change from
one Manwantara to another. The first of these
Manus was Svayambhuva, who sprang from
Swayambhu, the self-existent.

Mar: The passion of love; personified, it is another
                            name for Kamdev, the god of love.

Marich; Marichi: A Rakshasa, son of Taraka; he was also one of
                            Ravan's ministers, and helped him to kidnap Sita
                            from the forest hermitage.

Maruts: The storm gods. They are armed with thunderbolts
Marut   and ride on the whirlwind and direct the storm.
                            Many origins are assigned to them – they are the
                            sons of Rudra, the sons or brothers of Indra, sons
                            of the ocean, sons of the earth. Their number
                            varies—according to one source they are twenty-
                            nine in number, according to another, three times
                            sixty; in the *Ramcharitmanas*, Tulsi says they are
                            forty-nine in number. In the singular, Marut is
                            also the god of the wind, and the presiding deity
                            of the north-west quarter.

Matali: Indra's charioteer.

maya; Maya: Illusion, deception; the unreality of worldly
                            things; in Hindu belief, a deception dependent
                            on the power of the Supreme Being, through which
                            mankind believes in the existence of the world which
                            is in fact mere illusion without reality. Personified,
                            Maya is a woman, the consort of the Supreme Being,
                            and the immediate operative cause of the creation.
                            It also means magical or supernatural power, such as
                            that possessed by the Rakshasa, Ravan.

Meghnad: Literally, 'the rumbling or thundering of clouds';
                            he was Ravan's eldest son by his chief queen,

Mandodari. When Ravan attacked Indra's forces, Meghnad accompanied him and fought most valiantly. He used the power of invisibility given to him by Shiv to capture, tie up and carry off Indra to Lanka where he kept him a prisoner. The gods, led by Brahma, went to Lanka to secure Indra's release, and Brahma gave Meghnad the title of 'Indrajit', 'conqueror of Indra'. He is also called Arindam, 'the destroyer of enemies'.

Mekal: A part of the Vindhya mountain range, in which rise the headwaters and several tributaries of the Narmada river.

Meru: A fabulous mountain in the centre of the earth, upon which is situated Swarga, Indra's heaven, containing the cities of the gods. It is also known as Sumeru.

Mithila: The capital city of Videha, the kingdom of King Janak; also known as Janakpur, or Janak's city, Tirhut, and Terahuti.

moksha: Ultimate freedom from birth and rebirth. There are four kinds of moksha possible: (i) living in the same world as the Supreme Being; (ii) living in close proximity to the Supreme Being; (iii) attaining a form similar to that of the Supreme Being; and (iv) complete union with the Supreme Being.

mridang: A double drum, broader in the middle than at the ends.

muni: A sage, a holy man who has attained almost divine status through penance and meditation. The term is also used as a title for the seven great Rishis and for other wise and learned men.

Naga: A semi-divine being belonging to the serpent
                        race, with a human face, the tale of a snake and
                        the expanded neck of the cobra. The Nagas are
                        said to have sprung from Kadru, one of the wives
                        of the sage Kashyap, for the purpose of populating
                        the underworld, Patal, where they rule in great
                        splendour.

Nahush: The son of Pururavas, and the father of Yayati;
                        he came into conflict with the Brahmans. His
                        story is told, with variations, in the Mahabharata
                        and the Puranas. Nahush was a good and
                        righteous king, and, through prayer and penance
                        and sacred study, he acquired the sovereignty
                        of the three worlds. Once, when Indra had
                        temporarily gone into hiding (for having killed
                        the demon Vritra, who was a Brahman), leaving
                        his throne vacant, Nahush was chosen to reign
                        in his stead. He ruled over the heavens wisely
                        and well for many years, but as time went by,
                        he became arrogant and haughty. One day, he
                        caught sight of Shachi, Indra's beautiful consort,
                        and wanted her for himself. Shachi, known for
                        her love and fidelity to Indra, was angered and
                        distressed by his advances, and complained to
                        the sage Brihaspati and sought his protection.
                        The gods remonstrated with Nahush, but
                        blinded by desire, he refused to listen to them,
                        and insisted upon having Shachi as his consort.
                        Brihaspati then advised Shachi to lay down a
                        condition—that she would accept Nahush as her
                        husband if he would come to her in a palanquin
                        carried by sages. Nahush, who had lost all sense
                        of propriety and was guided only by his stubborn
                        desire to possess Shachi, agreed at once. He
                        somehow convinced the rishis to carry him to
                        Shachi on his shoulders. The sages were not very
                        strong men, and walked slowly with frequent
                        stops. The king grew impatient, and kicked the

sage Agastya, who was one of the sages carrying him. The sage cried out in anger, 'Fall, you serpent!' and Nahush fell from his palanquin and turned into a huge python. Horrified, he begged Agastya to forgive him; relenting, Agastya put a limit on the curse, saying that he would regain his human form when he had learnt how to be a good king. According to one version of the story, he was released from his curse by the eldest Pandava, Yudhishthira, who lectured him on the qualities of a good king. Nahush, understanding these at last, was released from his serpent form and ascended to heaven.

Nar and Narayan: Two ancient sages; twin sons of Dharma (Brahma's son) and his wife Ahimsa (daughter of Daksh). The brothers are considered by some to be the fourth avatar of Vishnu.

Narad: A Devarshi, or divine sage or saint akin to a demigod, to whom some of the hymns of the Rig-Veda are ascribed. Various sources have different accounts of his life. He is regarded as one of the four sons of Brahma, and one of the ten principal and original Munis or Rishis. He is also the inventor of the vina or lute and lord of the celestial musicians, the Gandharvas. He was also one of the great writers on law, the author of the *Naradiya Dharmashastra*. Later, he is connected to the legend of Krishna. He is also regarded as somewhat of a mischief-maker, causing frequent quarrels among the gods by bearing tales.

Narmada: A sacred river, said to rise from the Mekal hills, and because of which the river is also known as 'Mekal's daughter'.

Nimi: Son of Ikshvaku, and the founder of the dynasty of Mithila. According to the Vishnu Purana, he was cursed by the sage Vasishtha to lose his corporeal form, and in response, he pronounced the same curse upon the sage. Both then abandoned their bodily forms. Though Vasishtha took birth again, Nimi's corpse was embalmed and preserved in death as he had been in life. The gods offered to restore him back to life, but Nimi refused, saying that the separation of the soul from the body was so painful that he did not want to have to experience it again. The gods respected his wishes, and instead, placed him in the eyes of every living creature, because of which their eyelids are always blinking. (A blink of the eye is called 'nimish'.)

nine poetic sentiments (navras):

The nine poetic sentiments or moods are: erotic, humorous, compassionate, astonishing, frightening, peaceful, disgusting, wrathful and heroic.

nirgun:

Devoid of all qualities or properties, without attributes; the Supreme Being, who has no attributes of any kind.

Nishad:

A forest tribe who lived along the banks of the Ganga; their main occupation was hunting and fishing.

Ocean of Milk:

In Hindu cosmology, one of the seven seas surrounding directional space.

ocean, churning of:

One of the most well-known stories in Indian mythology; from this was produced, amongst other things, amrit, the nectar of immortality, and Lakshmi, the goddess of wealth and beauty. Once, Indra displeased the sage Durvasa, who in his anger, cursed Indra that he and all the gods would lose their strength, energy and good fortune. Weakened by the sage's curse, the gods

were defeated in battle by the Asurs, who now
gained control over the universe. In despair, the
gods appealed to Vishnu. Vishnu directed them
to churn the ocean and thus to obtain from it
the nectar of immortality—this, if consumed,
would restore to them their strength and power.
The gods, rendered powerless by Durvasa's
curse, were unable to accomplish this task on
their own, and on Vishnu's advice, enlisted the
Asurs to help them, agreeing to divide with
them whatever was retrieved from the ocean.
Vishnu assured the gods that he would make
sure that the nectar of immortality would
remain with the gods. The ocean was then
churned, with Mount Mandar as the churning
stick, and Sheshnag, the celestial serpent as
the rope wound round it. The Asurs held the
head of the serpent, and the gods the tail, and
as they pulled back and forth on the serpent,
Mount Mandar began to sink into the waters.
So Vishnu took on the form of a kurma or
tortoise (his second avatar), and slipping into
the waters, supported Mount Mandar on his
back. From the churning of the ocean were
produced many precious objects, Lakshmi,
precious gems, the horse Uchhaishravas, and
a deadly poison (which Shiv swallowed and
held in his throat). At last, there arose from the
waters Dhanvantari (who became the physician
of the gods), bearing in his hands the pot of
amrit. The Asurs demanded their share of it,
but Vishnu's steed, Garud, grabbed the pot and
flew away with it. Then Vishnu took on the
form of the beautiful enchantress, Mohini, and
distributed the amrit amongst the gods, who
drank it and regained their strength. Only one of
the Asurs, called Rahu, managed to drink some
of the amrit, and though his head was cut off by
Vishnu as punishment, he had already attained

immortality and was thus placed amongst the stars. (See Rahu, and Vishnu—second avatar).

paan:
Betel leaves prepared with areca nuts, etc., used as a mouth-freshener after a meal and served to honoured guests.

pakar:
The Indian fig tree, also called gular in Hindi.

Panchavati:
A place in the Dandak forest, near the River Godavari, where Ram lived for a long period during his exile. It was here that Lakshman cut off Supanakha's nose (nasika). Hence, it is often identified with the modern city of Nasik.

Parashuram:
'Ram with the axe', the sixth avatar of Vishnu. He was born in the Tretayug, as the son of the Brahman, Jamadagni, to deliver the world from the tyranny of the Kshatriyas. His weapon is the axe. The Mahabharata relates that, at the command of his father, he cut off his mother's head. She had so infuriated her husband by her thoughts that he had asked each of his sons in turn to kill her. They had all refused, except Parashuram. His obedience pleased his father so much that he told him to ask a boon. Parashuram asked that his mother be restored to life, and that he himself become invincible in combat and enjoy a long life. When his father was pitilessly slain by the sons of Sahasrabahu (Kartavirya), king of the Haihayas, Parashuram vowed to wipe out the whole Kshatriya race. It is said that he cleared the earth of Kshatriyas twenty-one times. (See also 'Sahasrabahu'.) As foremost amongst the descendants of Bhrigu, he is also called Bhrigupati, Bhrigunath and Bhrigunayak, 'lord of the Bhrigus'; and Bhrigubar, 'the best of the Bhrigus'. He is also known as Parashudhar, 'he who holds an axe'.

Parvati:	'Of the mountains'. She is the daughter of Himvat (the Himalaya mountains personified), and his wife Maina. She is the consort of Shiv, the reincarnation of his first wife Sati. She is also Shiv's cosmic energy or Shakti. She is worshipped in different forms and is known by different names. Her forms and names invoked by Tulsidas include Ambika, 'the compassionate'; Aparna, 'deprived of leaves'; Bhavani, consort of Bhav (Shiv); Gauri, 'the brilliant goddess'; Girija or Shailaja, 'born of the mountain', and Girinandini, 'daughter of the mountain'. She is also Shakti Shiv's cosmic energy; Shivaa, consort of Shiv; and Uma, 'light' or 'splendour'. In her fierce, demon-slaying form she is called Kalika, or Durga. As the supreme goddess, she is called Jagadamba or Jagadambika, 'mother of the world'.
Patal:	One of the seven subterranean regions, and the abode of the Nagas; hell.
pathin:	A large freshwater fish native to India; it is also known as the pahina or parhina fish.
Payasvini:	'Water-giving'; another name for the River Mandakini.
persuasion, methods of:	There are four methods of persuasion: (i) sama (argument, calm words to win someone over to one's own point of view); (ii) dana (inducement in the form of money or gifts); (iii) danda (punishment, corporal chastisement); (iv) bheda (by causing dissension).
pipal:	The holy fig-tree, *Ficus reliogiosa*.
Prahlad:	The son of the Daitya king Kanakakasipu, and an ardent devotee of Vishnu. Kanakakasipu grew so powerful that he declared that his subjects must

worship him, and him alone. Prahlad refused, and continued to steadfastly worship Vishnu, despite all the punishment that his father heaped upon him. In his fourth avatar, as Narsingh or Narkeshari (half-man, half-lion), Vishnu killed Kanakakasipu, and made Prahlad king of the Daityas as a reward for his devotion. Prahlad was also given a status equal to Indra for his life, and finally united with Vishnu upon death.

Prajapati: 'lord of created beings', the ten mind-born sons of Brahma, from whom all mankind has descended.

Prayag: The modern city of Allahabad, the confluence of the rivers Ganga, Jamuna and the subterranean Sarasvati, and one of the most important places of pilgrimage for Hindus. Krishna, as Madhav, is its presiding deity. Prayag is also supposed to be the site of a banyan tree famous in legend to be imperishable.

Prithuraj: In the Vedas and the Puranas, he is the first consecrated king. He taught men agriculture and to cultivate the earth, and it is from him that the earth derives her name of Prithivi. It is said that he prayed for hearing as sharp as though he had ten thousand ears so that he could hear all of the glory of God.

Priyavrat: A son of Svayambhuva Manu and Satarupa. He was dissatisfied that only half the earth was illuminated by the sun at any one point, and so followed the sun seven times around the earth in his own flaming chariot. The ruts made by the wheels of his chariot became the seven oceans; and so the seven continents were formed.

Pulastya:	One of the Prajapatis or mind-born sons of Brahma, and one of the great Rishis. He was the medium through which the Vishnu Purana was communicated to man. He was the father of Visravas, who, through three handmaidens, became the father of Ravan and Kumbhakaran, of Vibhishan, and of Supnakha; all the Rakshasas are supposed to have sprung from him.
Purana:	Literally, 'old', hence an ancient legend or tale. The Puranas are sacred works comprising the whole body of modern Hindu theology and mythology. The Puranas come much later than the epics, and must be distinguished from them. While the epics tell the stories of heroes as mortal men, the Puranas tell of the deeds of gods. There are eighteen acknowledged Puranas. The Vayu Purana is regarded as the oldest, and dates back to the sixth century CE; other Puranas are considered to be as recent as the thirteenth or even the sixteenth century.
Pushpak:	A self-flying magical chariot, so large that it contains within it a palace or a city. Brahma gave it as a gift to Kuber, but it was carried away by Ravan, who then used it as his chief mode of conveyance. After Ravan had been defeated and killed by Ram, the latter used the Pushpak to carry himself and Sita back to Ayodhya. He then returned it to Kuber.
Raghu:	A prince of the solar dynasty. In Kalidasa's poem *Raghuvansa*, on the ancestry and life of Ram, Raghu is said to be the son of Dilip and the great grandfather of Ram; it is from him that Ram gets the patronymic Raghav, and the title Raghupati, or chief of the dynasty of Raghu.

Rahu: The ascending lunar node in Vedic astrology, and the cause of eclipses. He is also considered as one of the nine planets, the king of meteors and guardian of the south-west quarter. In mythology, Rahu is a Danav who seizes the Sun and the Moon and swallows them, thus causing eclipses. He is the son of Viprachitti and Sinhika, and is known by his metronymic, Sainhikeya. He had four arms, and his lower part ended in a tail. At the churning of the ocean, amongst the many precious objects that were produced was amrit, the nectar of immortality. The gods decided to keep this for themselves, and when it was time to distribute it, the demons were left out. Rahu, assuming a godlike form, seated himself amongst the gods and drank some of the amrit. The Sun and the Moon realized who he was and informed Vishnu, who cut off his head and two of his arms. But, since he had already become immortal by drinking the amrit, he was placed amongst the stars. His upper parts, represented by a dragon's head, being the ascending lunar node, and his lower parts, known as Ketu and represented by a dragon's tail, being the descending node. Since then, Rahu wreaks his vengeance on the Sun and the Moon by occasionally swallowing them. Rahu and Ketu are usually paired together.

Rakshasa; Rakshasi (f.):   A race of demons, of whom Ravan was king. According to some sources, they are the descendants of the sage Pulastya, like Ravana is himself; others say they sprang from the foot of Brahma. They are usually portrayed as huge, ugly, terrifying beings. They are skilled and powerful warriors, with magical powers and the ability to change shape at will. Most of them can fly and many of them are man-eaters who haunt cemeteries, forests and lonely places at night.

They disturb fire-sacrifices, harass pious men and make life difficult for mankind in all sorts of ways. There are good Rakshasas too, such as Ravan's brother, Vibhishan.

Ram; Ramchandra: 'Pleasing, beautiful, charming'; the eldest son of King Dasharath of Avadh, and his chief queen Kaushalya. His wife is Sita, princess of Mithila. He is the seventh avatar of Vishnu, and the protagonist of the Ramayana. As a descendant of the prince Raghu, he is called Raghav or Raghunandan. He is also called Raghunath or Raghupati, lord of the Raghus; Raghunayak, chief of the Raghus; Raghuraj, 'king of the Raghus', Raghubar, 'best of the Raghus'; Raghubir, 'hero of the Raghus'; Raghuchand, 'moon of the dynasty of Raghu'. As Sita's husband, he is also called Sitanath, 'Sita's lord'; Janakinath, 'Janak's lord'. Sita is the incarnation of the goddess Lakshmi, who is also called Ramaa or Shri—as her husband or beloved he is therefore also known as Ramaakant, Ramaaraman, Shrikant, Shriraman. He is also addressed by all the names of Vishnu.

Rambha: An apsara who emerged at the churning of the ocean; she is the epitome of perfect womanhood.

Rantidev: A king of the Lunar dynasty; he was renowned for his piety and generosity. He was a great devotee of Vishnu, and believed that all he had came from him. He was enormously rich and extremely generous, and offered so many cattle in sacrifice that their blood formed the Chambhal river. He saw himself as Vishnu's instrument to serve the poor and needy. According to the Mahabharata, he had 200,000 cooks and had 2000 cattle and as many other animals slaughtered daily for use in his kitchens, and had the meat fed to innumerable poor and needy people. One day, the gods visited

Vishnu in Vaikunth and in casual conversation
asked him, 'Who do you think is your greatest
devotee?' Without hesitation, Vishnu replied that
it was Rantidev. The gods, intrigued, decided
to test Rantidev's devotion, and caused a great
famine to overcome his kingdom. The king, with
his characteristic generosity and piety, opened
the royal granary and treasury to his people. But
the famine continued. The king then opened
his palace to the people, and gave away all that
he possessed. He shared whatever food he had
with them, but soon even that finished. The
people were starving, and, at his wits' end, the
king turned to Vishnu for help. Giving up all
food and drink, he began to meditate on Vishnu.
For forty-eight days he prayed and fasted. On
the forty-ninth day, his ministers persuaded him
to take some food, and brought him water and
a dish made of rice boiled in milk. Just as he
was about to eat the rice and milk, a Brahman
appeared, hungry and starving. The king gave
away part of the food to the Brahman. He was
just about to begin eating again when a poor man
appeared begging for food. The king gave away
another portion of the food to him. Just then, a
Shudra appeared before him, begging for food for
himself and his dogs. The king gave away the rest
of the food to him. He now had only water left,
just enough to slake his thirst. As he was about to
drink the water, a Chandal, an outcast, appeared
and begged for water. The king gave even that
away. The Chandal drank the water, and as he
did so, the king felt refreshed and strengthened.
He opened his eyes in surprise, to see the gods
before him. They acknowledged him as Vishnu's
greatest devotee, and reversed the famine and
its effects, restoring his kingdom to prosperity.
And Vishnu, to honour his devotee, took him
unto himself. Rantidev merged with his Lord,

thus attaining the highest state. An alternative version of the story states that Rantidev, in his generosity, would every now and then hold a great sacrifice and give away all that he possessed. On one occasion, having given away everything he owned, he and his family remained without food or water for forty-eight days. The king accepted his condition, and lived only upon what he received without asking. On the forty-ninth day, as he lay on the ground, starving and semi-conscious, he was given some water and a dish made of rice boiled in milk. As he was about to share this food with his wife and children the gods appeared to test him, in the guise of the Brahman, the Shudra, the low-born man with his dogs and the Chandal.

Rati: 'Love, desire'; the goddess of desire and sexual pleasure, the consort of Kamdev, and daughter of Daksh.

Ravan: The evil and powerful Rakshasa king of Lanka; the son of Vishravas by the Rakshasi Nikasha; grandson of the sage Pulastya. His chief queen was Mandodari. He was the half-brother of Kuber, and as Kuber was king of the Yakshas, Ravan was king of the Rakshasas. Through penance and prayer to Brahma, Ravan received the boon of invulnerability to gods and demons, but was doomed to die because of a woman. He was also able to take any form he pleased. He is described as having ten heads and twenty arms, copper-coloured eyes and teeth as bright as the moon. He was as dark as a cloud, and as enormous as a mountain. His body bore all the marks of royalty, but was marked by the scars of the wounds he had received in his battles against the gods. It was scarred by the thunderbolt of Indra, by the tusks of Indra's elephant, Airavat, and by Vishnu's discus. Tall as a mountain peak, he could stop the sun and the moon in their course across the sky. His strength was so great that he could lift up Mount Kailash in play. He terrorized gods and men with his evil deeds, till at last they appealed to Vishnu for help. Since he had been too arrogant to ask for invincibility against men, Vishnu took birth as Ramchandra, son of Dasharath, for the sole purpose of destroying him; the gods became incarnate as bears and monkeys to help him in this enterprise. For his ten heads, he is called Dashashish. He is also called Dashanan, 'ten-faced'; Dashkandhar or Dashkanth, 'ten-necked'; Dashmukh, 'ten-faced'. As the enemy of the gods, he is known as Surari; as the king of Lanka, he is called Lankesh.

riddhi; Riddhi: Prosperity, affluence, accomplishment. Riddhi is also prosperity, personified as Kuber's wife, or, in some instances, as one of Ganesh's wives. In the plural, the Riddhis refer to some of the attendants of Kuber, and signify riches.

rishi: A sage; the inspired sages to whom the hymns of the Vedas were revealed; also used as a title for the seven great sages, and other wise and learned men.

Rishyamuk: A mountain in the south, near the source of the Pampa river and the lake Pampa, upon which lived the monkey Sugriv and his followers. Ram stayed there for a while with the monkeys.

Sabar; Shabar: A tribal people of southern India.

Sabari; Shabari: A woman of the Sabar tribe (hence her name). The daughter of a hunter, she was a devotee of Ram. She sought salvation upon the death of her guru, the sage, Matanga; just before he died, Matanga assured her that she would indeed attain salvation, and that Ram himself would grant it to her. Sabari waited faithfully for Ram, living for many years as an ascetic in the forest. During his exile, Ram, hearing of her devotion to him, visited her in her hermitage. There, she offered him fruits that she had collected especially for him in the forest, and which she had tasted herself before offering to check their sweetness. Lakshman protested that since she had bitten into the fruit, Ram should not eat them. But Ram saw only her devotion and ate the fruits she offered. He then granted her salvation.

sachchidanand: Literally 'Existence (or being or entity) or truth, thought (or knowledge or consciousness), and happiness (or bliss)'—a name for the Supreme Spirit.

Sagar: A prince of the solar dynasty; king of Avadh. From Sumati, the second of his two wives, he had sixty-thousand sons. During the performance of the Ashvamedha, or horse-sacrifice, the king ordered his sixty-thousand sons to retrieve the sacrificial horse, which had been carried off to the underworld. They dug their way to Patal, where they found the horse grazing and the sage Kapil seated close by in meditation. Thinking him to be the thief, the sons of Sagar began to accuse and threaten him. This so enraged the saint that he reduced all of them to ashes. Their souls were finally liberated by the actions of Bhagirath, who brought the Ganga to earth in order to purify their ashes. Sagar finally completed his sacrifice, and gave the name 'saagar' to the chasm which this sons had dug (saagar means ocean).

sagun: 'With attributes'; possessing a form that has qualities, hence, the incarnate form of the Supreme Spirit.

Sahasrabahu: 'The thousand-armed'; he was king of the Haihaya tribe, and is better known by his patronymic, Kartavirya. As a result of penance and prayer, the divine saint Dattatreya granted him a thousand arms, a golden chariot to take him wherever he wished to go, the power of righting wrongs by dispensing justice, the conquest of the earth and the disposition to rule it righteously, invincibility and finally, death at the hands of a man renowned the whole world over. He ruled wisely and well for 85,000 years. He was a contemporary of Ravan, and when Ravan came to conquer his capital city, Mahishmati, he took him prisoner effortlessly; he let Ravan go on the request of the rishi, Pulastya. One day, when out hunting, Sahasrabahu reached the hermitage of the sage Jamadagni. The sage and the sons were out, but his wife, recognizing the king, treated him with due respect. But instead of acknowledging the hospitality he had received, the king in his arrogance carried off the calf of the sacred cow, Surabhi, which Jamadagni had acquired through penance. When Jamadagni's son, Parashuram, returned and heard what the king had done, he followed the king, cut off his thousand arms with his arrows and killed him. Sahasrabahu's sons, in retaliation, attacked Jamadagni in his hermitage and killed him. When Parashuram found his father's lifeless body, he laid it on a pyre and vowed to wipe out the whole of the Kshatriya race. He killed all the sons of Sahasrabahu, and cleared the earth of Kshatriyas twenty-one times. Sahasrabahu's death at the hands of Parashuram was as per the boon granted him—to be killed by a man renowned the world over.

samadhi: A state of profound meditation restraining the senses and confining the mind to contemplation.

Sampati:

A vulture, the eldest son of Arun, the charioteer of the Sun, and the older brother of the vulture, Jatayu.

Sanak; Sanandan; Sanatan; Sanatkumar:

The four Kumars, the four mind-born sons of Brahma; declining to create progeny, they remained forever boys, and forever pure and innocent. Sanatkumar was the most prominent of them all. They are also known by their patronymic Vaidhatra (from Vidhatra, or Brahma).

Sanjivani:

In mythology, a life-giving herb that is said to restore the dead to life.

sanyasi:

One who has renounced the world, abandoning all attachment; according to Hindu scripture, sannyasa is the last and fourth stage of life for a man.

Saptarishi:

The seven Rishis, the mind-born sons of Brahma. They form, in astronomy, the constellation of the Great Bear.

Sarasvati:

'Watery'. In the Vedas, Sarasvati is primarily a river, as sacred as the Ganga is today. Though now lost, it was the third stream that met the Ganga and the Jamuna at their confluence at Prayag. Sarasvati was also a deity, the personification of the river, and as a river goddess she was the bestower of fertility and wealth. In the Brahmanas and the Mahabharata, she is recognized as Vach, the goddess of speech and eloquence. In later times, she is the goddess of learning, inventor of the Sanskrit language and the Devanagari script, and patron of the arts and sciences. She is also the wife of Brahma. She is represented as a beautiful and graceful young woman, white in colour, wearing a crescent on her brow. She is often shown as holding the vina in

	her hands. Her steed is the swan. In her form as the goddess of speech and eloquence, she is known as Bharati, 'articulate'; Brahmi or Brahmani, 'Brahma's consort'; Gira, 'speech'; Sharada, 'one who bears a vina'; Vani or Bani, literally 'sound, speech, language, voice'. As the consort of Brahma (Vidhatra), she is known as Vidhatri.
Sarju; Sarayu:	A sacred river, that flows past Ram's city of Avadh; it is believed to rise from the sacred Manas lake.
Sati:	A daughter of Daksh, and Shiv's first wife; she killed herself because of her father's anger against Shiv. She was subsequently reincarnated as the goddess Parvati, the daughter of Himvat and Maina.
Savan:	The fifth month of the Hindu calendar, corresponding to July–August.
ser:	A measure of weight, roughly equivalent to a kilogram.
Shachi:	Indra's consort.
Shakti:	Cosmic energy; it denotes the energy or active power of a deity personified as his consort, as Parvati of Shiv, Lakshmi of Vishnu, Sarasvati of Brahma, etc.
Shatanand:	Janak's guru and family priest.
Shatrughna:	'Foe-destroyer'; he is Lakshman's twin and the youngest of Ram's three brothers. He is also called Ripusudan, Ripuhan, 'destroyer of enemies; and Ripudaman or Ripudavan, 'subduer of enemies'.
shehnai:	A wind instrument, somewhat like a clarinet; its sound is considered auspicious and it is especially played at weddings.

Shesh; Sheshnag: Shesh, or Sheshnag, is the king of the Nagas or the serpent race. His kingdom is Patal, abode of the Nagas. He is represented as a serpent with a thousand heads; his coils form the couch upon which Vishnu lies, and his thousand hoods the canopy which shelter him whilst he sleeps during the intervals of creation. He sometimes bears the entire world upon one of his heads. He is also called Anant, 'the endless', and is regarded as the symbol of eternity.

Shibi: Shibi was a pious and generous king, famed for his large-heartedness and his upholding of dharma. One day the gods decided to put him to the test. Agni took on the form of a dove, and Indra that of a hawk, and as the king sat in court one morning, the dove flew into his lap and nestled there. The hawk followed and claimed the dove as its rightful prey. The king refused to give up the dove, since it had sought shelter with him, but he also realized the legitimacy of the hawk's demand. He offered the hawk anything he wanted in place of the dove, but the hawk would be satisfied with nothing except a piece of the king's own flesh, equal in weight to the dove. So the king had a pair of scales brought, and placing the dove on one side, he began hacking off pieces of his own flesh, which he put on the other side. But no matter how much of his own flesh he cut off, the dove was always heavier. At last, he climbed on to the scales himself and would have cut off his own head, but the gods intervened, and Agni and Indra, appearing in their own forms, acknowledged his generosity and made him whole again.

Shiv: Auspicious, propitious, fortunate; the Destroyer, the great and powerful third deity in the Hindu triad; he is described as the destructive power, but his powers and attributes are much wider. As the great god of dissolution, he is called Rudra or

Mahakal; but in Hindu philosophy, dissolution is coupled with regeneration, so as Shiv or Shankar, he is the reproductive power that perpetually restores that which has been destroyed. He is thus also called Ishvar, and Mahadev, 'the great god'. As the restorer, he is worshipped in the form of a linga or phallus, or as the linga combined with a yoni, the female reproductive organ representative of his Shakti, or female energy. He is also the supreme ascetic, the epitome of penance and abstract meditation through which unlimited powers are acquired, the highest spiritual knowledge is gained, and union with the Supreme Absolute achieved. In this form he is represented as a naked ascetic, with matted hair, his body smeared with ashes. He is also the lord of goblins and ghosts, and in this form he wears serpents wound around his neck and a necklace of skulls. He is a handsome man, fair-complexioned, with five faces and four arms, and is usually represented sitting upon a tiger skin in profound meditation. He has a third eye in the middle of his forehead, and surmounted by the crescent moon. His third eye, if opened, has great destructive power—it reduced Kamdev, the god of love, to ashes, and periodically destroys creation in the cycle of destruction and regeneration. His matted locks are coiled upon his head, and within it is held the River Ganga, which he caught and contained as she descended from heaven upon earth (and because of which he is called Gangadhar, 'he who holds the Ganga'). He is often attired in the skin of a tiger, a deer, or an elephant. In his four hands he carries a deer, the bow Ajagav, a damru (small hour-glass–shaped drum) or the Khatwang (a club with a skull at the end), or a cord for binding offenders. He is usually accompanied by his bull, Nandi. His consort is the goddess Parvati. As lord of all creation, he is called Akhileshvar, and as lord of the universe he is called Vishvanath and Jagadish; as the Destroyer, he is also called Har. As lord of Mt Kailash, he is known as Girinath and Girish, 'lord of the mountain'. The city of Kashi is sacred to him; thus he is also called Kashinath, 'lord of Kashi'. As regent of the north-east quarter, he is called Ish or Ishan. For his action of reducing Kamdev, the god of love to ashes, he is known as Anangarati, 'enemy of Anang (Kamdev)'; Kamari, 'the foe or conqueror of Kam'; Kamripu, 'the foe of Kam'. In his androgynous form he is known as Ardhanarishvar, 'the god who is half a woman'. He has a bull (brish) on his banner (ketu), and is therefore also known as Brishketu. When vish or poison was thrown up amongst the treasures retrieved at the churning of the ocean, Shiv swallowed it and held it safely in his throat, which turned blue as a result; from this he is called Nilkanth, 'blue-throated' (See ocean, churning of). As the destroyer of the demon known as Tripurasur, he is also called Purari and Tripurari. An alternative explanation is that he destroyed the triple city known as Tripur, which belonged to a trio of demons collectively called Tripurasur. Since he bears the crescent moon on his brow, he is also called Shashibhushan, 'one who has the moon as his ornament' and Chandramauli, 'the moon-crested one'. For the garland of skulls that he wears around his neck, he is known as Kapali, 'the one who wears a necklace of skulls'. He is also known as Ashutosh, 'he who is quickly pleased'; Bhav, 'existence'; Shambhu, 'one who causes happiness'; Shankar, 'one who causes tranquillity' or 'auspicious'; Mahesh or Mahadev, 'the great god'; Sarv, 'complete, entire, universal'; Sadashiv, 'always happy or prosperous'.

shivaling:	A phallic representation of Shiv.
Shringber; Shringberpur:	The town of Shringber, it lay on the left bank of the Ganga. It was on the border of Koshal with

Bhil country. The area around was inhabited by the Nishad tribe; their chief was Guha. The town has been identified with modern Singraur.

Shringi:

'The deer-horned'; a hermit, and son of the sage Vibhandaka. Shringi or Rishyashringa as he was called, performed the fire-sacrifice that resulted in the birth of Ram and his brothers. One version of his story says that his mother was a doe, and he was therefore born with antlers; another version says that his mother was the apsara, Urvashi, who abandoned her infant son and his father, her lover, after the child's birth. Rishyashringa was brought up by his father in the forest, in complete isolation from all other human beings. He was endowed with magical and mystical powers. Once, when the kingdom of Anga was struck by intense drought, its king, Lomapad, was told that he must hold a sacrifice conducted by a priest who was perfectly chaste. The only such priest that could be found was Rishyashringa, who had grown up with no knowledge of women at all. He was persuaded to come to Anga and perform the sacrifice, which successfully ended the drought in Anga. Rishyashringa then married Shanta, the daughter of Lomapad. (Shanta was actually the adopted daughter of Lomapad; her real father was King Dasharath.)

Shrutakirti:

Sita's cousin, the younger daughter of Janak's younger brother Kushadhvaj (Kushaketu); she was married to Shatrughna.

Shudra:

The fourth, and lowest, of the four castes of Hinduism. This is the servile class, whose duty it was to serve the three higher castes.

Shuk; Shukdev:

An eminent rishi, he was the son of Vyas and the main narrator of the Bhagavat Purana.

Shvapach:	Literally, 'one who eats dog-meat', and thus refers to one belonging to the lowest, most degraded caste.
Siddha:	'Accomplished', a semi-divine being, of great purity and holiness, and said to be specially characterized by the eight siddhis or supernatural faculties, which he acquires by the performance of intense austerities or certain mystical rites or processes. The Siddhas, together with the Munis, and other holy and accomplished beings, inhabit the Bhuvarlok or middle region between the earth and the sun. The term 'Siddha' is also used for a great sage or ascetic who has attained the eight siddhis, usually through intense austerities and yogic practice.
Siddhi; siddhi:	Success or accomplishment personified; one of Ganesh's wives. In northern Indian tradition, Ganesh's two consorts are Siddhi (Success) and Buddhi (Wisdom). In one recounting, they are said to have been born of Brahma's mind, who then offered them to Ganesh as his brides; in another they are regarded as having been summoned by Ganesh himself, and then offered to him by Brahma. Buddhi is also sometimes called Riddhi—she is spiritual success, as opposed to the material success that is her sister Siddhi. In the plural, the siddhis are supernatural faculties. They are usually stated to be eight in number. They are: (i) anima, the faculty of making oneself infinitesimally small; (ii) mahima, the faculty of making oneself infinitely great; (iii) laghima, the faculty of becoming infinitely light; (iv) garima, the faculty of becoming infinitely heavy; (v) prapti, the faculty of obtaining whatever one wishes; (vi) prakamya, the faculty of doing whatever one wishes; (vii) ishitva, the power of absolute supremacy; (viii) vashitva, the power of absolute subjugation.

sindur: Vermilion; applied on the head of a woman
                      it indicates that she is married; it is applied to
                      the head of the bride for the first time by the
                      bridegroom upon the completion of the wedding
                      rites.

sinsupa: The ashok tree.

siris blossom: The flower of the tree Acacia sirissa; the flower
                      is exceptionally fragile and delicate-looking, with
                      pale, slender filament-like petals.

Sita: 'A furrow'; in the Vedas, Sita is the furrow,
                      or farming personified and is worshipped as
                      the goddess of agriculture and fruits. In the
                      Ramayana, she is the daughter of Janak, the
                      king of Videha, and the wife of Ram. Remnants
                      of old Vedic belief can still be seen in the story
                      of her birth. It is related that one day, as King
                      Janak was ploughing the field in preparation for a
                      great fire-sacrifice to obtain children, there sprang
                      from his plough a baby girl, whom he adopted.
                      He named her 'Sita', which means 'furrow', and
                      took her home to his palace, where she grew up
                      as his beloved daughter. From her father, she is
                      known as 'Janaki'. So, from the manner of her
                      birth, Sita is also called Avanikumari, 'daughter of
                      the earth'. She is also known as Vaidehi, 'daughter
                      of Videh, king of Videha' or 'princess of Videha';
                      and Maithili, 'princess of Mithila'.

sixteen ways of   In Hindu tradition, a guest is considered equal
honouring a guest: to a god, and he is honoured by being given the
                      following sixteen things: (i) asana, a seat; (ii)
                      arghya, a libation of water with milk, flowers, etc.;
                      (iii) padya, water to wash the feet; (iv) achamaniya,
                      water to drink; (v) snaniya, water to bathe and for
                      ablutions; (vi) gandhakshak, sandal paste and rice
                      grains; (vii) vastra, fresh clothes; (viii) pushpa,

flowers; (ix) dhupa, incense; (x) dipa, light or lamps; (xi) naivedya, food; (xii) mukhasta jal, water to rinse the mouth with; (xiii) tambula, betel leaves; (xiv) dakshina, a gift; (xv) pradakshina, circumambulation; and (xvi) nirajana, a worship with lighted lamps.

Skand: The god of war, the planet Mars, and the commander of the divine armies. He was born miraculously from the seed of Shiv, for the express purpose of destroying the Asur Tarak. It is said that Shiv cast his seed into fire, and it was afterwards received by the river Ganga. From her waters came forth Skand, in the form of a beautiful baby boy. He was found by the six Krittikas (the Pleiades), and each claimed the baby for herself, and each wanted to nurse him. In order to please them, Skand grew six heads. He is shown as riding on a peacock, with a bow in one hand and an arrow in the other. He is also known as Shanmukh, 'one with six-faces'.

Sone: A river in central India, it is a tributary of the Ganga.

spheres, fourteen: According to Hindu scripture, the universe is divided into fourteen spheres, seven ascending and seven descending. The seven higher spheres, in ascending order, are: Bhuh, Bhuvah, Svah, Mahah, Janah, Tapah and Satyam; the lower sphere, in descending order, are: Atal, Vital, Sutal, Talatal, Mahatal, Rasatal, Patal.

states of being, four: The four states of being are: (i) jagrat or waking; (ii) svapna or sleeping/dreaming; (iii) sushupti or deep repose; and (iv) turiya or the state in which the soul has become one with the Supreme Spirit. These four feminine states are each paired with a male consort; these are: (i) vishva or creation;

	(ii) tejas or power; (iii) pragya or wisdom; and (iv) brahm, the universal Absolute.
Subahu:	A Rakshasa. He defiled and interrupted the fire-sacrifices of the sage Vishvamitra; for this, he was killed by Ram.
Sugriv:	King of the monkeys, and brother of Baali. He is also called Sukanth.
Sukarkhet:	A town, identified with the town of Soron in northern India. It is located on the river Ganga, about thirty-two miles south of modern-day Ayodhya. It is an important place of pilgrimage for Hindus.
Sumantra:	Dasharath's trusted minister and charioteer.
Sumitra:	One of Dasharath's queens, the mother of the twins Lakshman and Shatrughna.
Supnakha; Surpanakha:	Literally, 'having finger-nails like winnowing fans'; a Rakshasi, Ravan's sister.
Surasa:	A goddess, the mother of the Nagas, she was asked by the gods to test Hanuman's strength and courage as he flew across the ocean to Lanka.
Sutikshna:	A hermit who lived in the Dandak forest and met Ram and Sita during their exile. He was a disciple of the sage Agastya.
Svati:	The star Arcturus, as forming the fifteenth nakshatra, or lunar asterism. According to popular belief, the rain that falls under this lunar asterism is endowed with special properties including the attribute that if a drop of it falls into a seashell, it becomes a pearl. The chatak subsists only on the

rain that falls during autumn, under the influence of this nakshatra.

svayamvar: The public ceremony of a young girl or princess selecting a husband of rank from an assembled gathering of suitors; this ceremony is usually restricted to the Kshatriya caste. Sometimes, a task may be set by the bride's family for her suitors to accomplish, as in the case of Sita's svayamvar, where the successful suitor had to string and break Shiv's bow.

tamal: A tree found across India; it has very dark bark and white blossoms.

Tamas; Tamasa: A tributary of the Ganga.

Tara: Wife of Baali, king of the monkeys, and the mother of Angad. After Baali was killed by Ram, she was taken by Baali's younger brother, Sugriv, as his wife.

Tarak: A Daitya, whose austerities made him formidable to the gods, and for whose destruction Shiv's son, Skand, the god of war, was born.

Taraka: The daughter of the Yaksha, Suketu; turned into a Rakshasi by the sage Agastya, she lived in the forest at the confluence of the Ganga and the Sarju and ravaged the surrounding land and terrorized the rishis in the forest. Vishvamitra wanted Ram to kill her, to stop her from doing further harm. But Ram was reluctant to kill a woman. So deciding to deprive her of the power to do harm, he cut off her two arms. Lakshman cut off her nose and ears. But using her magic powers, she pelted Ram and Lakshman with a shower of rocks and boulders, so that finally, at

Vishvamitra's command, Ram killed her with a
single arrow. Her son was the Rakshasa Marich,
who later helped Ravan in his abduction of Sita.

three afflictions or   These are mental and physical distress, distress
the triple fires: caused by the acts of God, and distress caused by
                            others.

tilak: A ceremonial mark made with vermilion or
                            sandalwood paste upon the forehead between the
                            eyebrows upon installation to office, coronation of
                            a king, betrothal, etc.

triveni: 'Triple-braid'; the confluence of the three sacred
                            rivers Ganga, Jamuna and the subterranean
                            Sarasvati at the city of Prayag (modern Allahabad).
                            The waters of the Jamuna are dark, and of the
                            Ganga light. The stream of the Sarasvati is
                            invisible.

Trijata: A Rakshasi who befriended Sita when she was
                            Ravan's prisoner in Lanka. She is also called
                            Dharamagya.

Trishanku: The name given to Satyavrata, a prince of the solar
                            dynasty, and king of Avadh. Satyavrata was a good
                            king, but in his arrogance he decided to ascend to
                            heaven in corporeal form. He therefore asked the
                            sage Vasishtha to perform the sacrifice by means of
                            which he could attain this end. Vasishtha declined
                            to perform the ceremony, declaring that what
                            the king wanted was impossible. Satyavrata then
                            appealed to Vasishtha's sons, who refused, saying
                            that he wanted to make trouble between them and
                            their father and, for his presumption, cursed him
                            to become a Chandal. While in Chandal form,
                            and having nothing to eat one day, Satyavrata
                            killed Vasishtha's cow, the Kamadhenu, and ate
                            her. For these three sins, of pride, making trouble

between father and sons, and killing a cow, Vasishtha gave him the name 'Trishanku' (from *tri* or 'three', and *shanku* or 'sin'). He then turned to Vishvamitra, who agreed to perform the sacrifice and send him to heaven in his current body. The sons of Vasishtha opposed the sacrifice, for which Vishvamitra reduced them all to ashes. He then began the sacrifice, but as Trishanku ascended to heaven, Indra and the other gods opposed his entry and hurled him down to earth. Trishanku fell head first, and hung upside down in the sky, midway between the earth and heaven. It was finally agreed that that is where he should stay. He can still be seen in the sky, as the constellation Trishanku in the southern hemisphere. The saliva that dropped from his mouth is said to be the River Karamnasa, the waters of which, if touched, destroy all religious merit.

Trishira: Literally, 'three-headed'; a Rakshasa, and a brother, son, or friend of Ravan, killed by Ram.

twice-born: A man of any one of the three upper Hindu castes (but particularly a Brahman), whose investiture with the sacred thread upon puberty constitutes, religiously and metaphorically, his second birth.

Udayagiri: This is the eastern mountain from behind which the sun is supposed to rise; it is also called Udayachal.

Urmila: Janak's and Sunayana's daughter, Sita's younger sister; she was married to Lakshman.

Vaikunth: The paradise or heaven of Vishnu; its site is sometimes described as in the Northern Ocean, sometimes it is said to be located on the eastern peak of Mount Meru. Vishnu himself is also sometimes designated by this term.

Valmik; Valmiki: The author of the Sanskrit Ramayana. Regarded
                      as the first, or original poet, he is said to have
                      invented poetry when he began to compose the
                      Ramayana. Tradition maintains that before he
                      became a sage and the author of the Ramayana,
                      Valmiki was the dacoit Ratnakar, who would
                      waylay travellers and then rob and mercilessly
                      kill them. One day, he ran into the sage Narad,
                      who asked him why he did what he did. Ratnakar
                      replied that it was for his family; Narad asked
                      him whether his family appreciated the burden of
                      sin that he was accumulating for their sakes and
                      whether they would share it. Ratnakar staunchly
                      replied that they would, but when he asked his wife
                      and children, they refused to accept the burden
                      of his crimes. Ratnakar realized the folly of his
                      ways and begged for forgiveness. Narad then gave
                      him the mantra of Ram's name, but since this was
                      a mantra that could not be given to thieves and
                      murderers, Narad told him to recite it backwards.
                      Ratnakar did so, and meditated on the name,
                      sitting so still and for so long that anthills grew
                      around him. He continued his penance for many
                      long years, till finally a divine voice declared him
                      to be free of the guilt of his crimes, and renamed
                      him Valmiki, or 'the one born of anthills'.

Vamdev: A prominent rishi, attached to Dasharath's court.

Varun: Amongst the oldest of the Vedic gods, Varun is
                      the personification of the sky, the maker of earth
                      and heaven. He is described as being furnished
                      with snares and nooses, with which he seizes
                      and binds evildoers. No mortal can escape from
                      Varun's snares.

Vasishtha: A celebrated Vedic sage, to whom many hymns
                      are ascribed. According to the Vishnu Purana, he
                      was the family priest of the house of Ishkvaku; he

was contemporary not only with Ishkvaku himself, but with his descendants down to the sixty-first generation, including Dasharath and Ram.

Veda; Vedas: From *vid*, 'know'; hence 'divine knowledge'. The Vedas, composed in verse in an ancient form of Sanskrit some time between 1500 and 1000 BCE (though opinions vary considerably about their age, and many scholars believe that they can be pushed back at least another thousand years), are the foundation of Hindu belief and practice. It is believed that the Vedas emanated as the breath of the Supreme Being. It is agreed that they were revealed orally to the sages whose names they bear, and thus the whole body of the Veda—the entire body of divine knowledge—is known as 'Sruti' or 'what was heard'. The Vedas are four in number: Rig, Yajur, Sama, Atharva. The Rig Veda is the oldest; in fact, it is the original Veda, from which the Yajur and Sama Vedas are mostly derived. The Atharva Veda was composed much later.

Vedant: 'End of the Veda'; name of the complete Veda; name of a certain system of philosophy and theology based particularly on the Upanishads; and of works concerning this philosophy and in support of it.

Vedashira: One of the seven great rishis (Saptarishi), associated with the fourth Manwantara. (See Manu.)

vedi: A quadrangular space, with the sacred fire in the centre, where wedding rites are conducted.

vedika: Ground prepared for a sacrifice or ceremony, usually consisting of a raised floor or platform and covered with a roof supported by pillars.

Vena: Son of Anga by his queen, Sunita, and a descendant
                 of Manu Swayambhuva. Vena grew up to be a
                 cruel and vicious man, so much so that his father,
                 unable to bear his atrocities, left the kingdom
                 and disappeared, no one knew where. Seeing the
                 kingdom without a king, the sages decided to put
                 Vena upon the throne. Royal power made him
                 worse, and in his arrogance, he banned offerings
                 and performance of sacrifices to the gods, declaring
                 that he alone was worthy of such worship. The
                 sages reasoned with him, but he refused to listen;
                 they admonished him more strongly, but he would
                 not change his mind. Finally, they killed him with
                 blades of consecrated grass. After his death, the
                 sages saw clouds of dust in the distance, and were
                 told that these were raised by men who had begun
                 to loot and plunder because the country was now
                 without a king. Since Vena was childless, the sages
                 rubbed his left thigh to produce a son; from this
                 arose a short, dark man with a flat nose. He was
                 asked to sit, 'nishida'; he did so and thus became a
                 Nishad, from which sprang the tribe living in the
                 Vindhya mountains. The sages then rubbed the
                 right hand of Vena, and from this came forth his
                 son Prithu. (See Prithuraj.) Vena's story is told a
                 little differently in the Padma Purana. This states
                 that Vena was a good king at the start of his rule,
                 but soon turned to the teachings of the Jains. For
                 this heresy, the sages attacked and beat him, till
                 from his left thigh came forth the Nishad tribe, and
                 from his right arm came Prithu. Being freed of sin
                 by the birth of the Nishad, he gave up his kingdom
                 and retired to an ashram on the Narmada, where
                 he engaged in penance. For this, Vishnu forgave
                 him and made him one with himself.

Vibhishan: 'The terrible'; a younger brother of Ravan, and
                 ally of Ram. He was raised to the throne of Lanka
                 by Ram after the defeat and death of Ravan.

Videh:	'Bodiless'; the title born by the kings of the kingdom of Videha, including King Janak, Sita's father.
Videha:	The kingdom of King Janak, Sita's father. Its capital city was the city of Mithila.
vina:	An ancient multi-stringed musical instrument; it is supposed to have been invented by Narad.
Vinata:	A daughter of Daksh, one of the thirteen wives of the sage Kashyap, and mother of Garud. From her were born all the birds.
Viradh:	Also known as Tumburu, he was a Gandharva cursed by Kuber to become a horrible, man-eating Rakshasa. He is described as being as tall as a mountain peak, deformed, of dreadful aspect, clad in a tiger's skin, smeared with fat, soaked in blood, like death with an open mouth, bearing three lions, four tigers, two wolves, ten deer and the great head of an elephant with tusks on the point of an iron pike. He had obtained from Brahma the boon of invulnerability. Ram, with Lakshman and Sita, encountered him in the Dandak forest. (This incident is told in detail in Valmiki's Ramayana.) Viradh cursed and taunted the brothers, and grabbed Sita. Ram and Lakshman shot him with their arrows, proving that he was not invulnerable. But he caught them and throwing them over his shoulder, ran off with them as easily as if they had been children. They broke both his arms, beat him with their fists and threw him to the ground, but they could not kill him. So they dug a deep hole and buried him alive. Then there arose from the earth a beautiful form, who said he was a Gandharva cursed by Kuber to take on the form of a Rakshasa. Ram released him from the curse and sent him back to his own realm.

Vishnu: From *vish*, to pervade. The preserver and
                      restorer, he is the second of the Hindu triad. He
                      is also called Hari. In the Rig Veda, Vishnu is
                      the manifestation of solar energy, and does not
                      have the importance he acquired later as the
                      great preserver of the universe. In the Puranas
                      and the Mahabharata, he is the embodiment of
                      mercy and goodness, which manifests itself as
                      the preserving power, which is self-existent and
                      all-pervading. He is therefore associated with
                      water, which was everywhere before the creation
                      of the world. He is represented in human form
                      as reclining upon the serpent Shesh, and floating
                      upon the Ocean of Milk. He is therefore also
                      called Narayan or 'floating upon the waters'. His
                      consort is Lakshmi, the goddess of wealth and
                      beauty. The river Ganga is said to spring from his
                      toe. Vishnu is represented with four hands; one
                      holds the Panchajanya, a shankha or conch-shell;
                      the second the Sudarshan or Vajranabha, which
                      is a chakra or discus; the third holds Kaumodaki,
                      a gada or club; and the fourth holds a Padma,
                      or lotus. As the husband of Lakshmi (who is
                      also known as Shri, Ramaa and Kamla), he is
                      known as Shripati, Ramapati and Kamlapati; as
                      the one who dwells with Lakshmi, he is known
                      as Shrinivas, Ramanivas and Ramaniket. He is
                      also known as Sarangpani, 'the one who bears the
                      bow called Sarang'. As the slayer of the demon
                      Khar in his incarnation as Ramchandra, he is
                      known as Kharari, 'enemy of Khar'; as the slayer
                      of the demons Madhu and Kaitabh he is known
                      as Madhusudan and Kaitabhajit respectively. As
                      the giver of liberation, he is called Mukund. He
                      is also known as Anant, 'the infinite'. Vishnu
                      has 'descended' to earth, or taken incarnate form
                      several times. His 'descents', or avatars, are usually
                      said to be ten in number, though the Bhagavata
                      Purana says that they are twenty-two, or

innumerable. Vishnu's ten avatars are as follows: (i) Matsya, 'the fish': this avatar is connected with the Hindu legend of the flood. The objective was to save Vaivaswata, the seventh Manu, who became the progenitor of all mankind. One day Manu found in the water he used for his ablutions a little fish which spoke to him and warned him of a great flood that was coming which would destroy all living creatures, and said that it would save him. The fish grew and grew till it was so huge that it had to be put into the ocean. The fish then instructed Manu to build a ship, and to take refuge in it when the flood came. Manu did so, and when the flood came, Manu embarked in the ship. The fish then swam to Manu, who, using the serpent Sheshnag tied the ship to the fish's horn, and was towed to safety; (ii) Kurma, 'the tortoise': when the great flood subsided, the gods realized that many valuable things had been lost at the bottom of the ocean. So Vishnu appeared as a tortoise, and placed himself at the bottom of the Ocean of Milk, and took upon his back the mountain Mandar. The gods and demons wound the serpent Vasuki around the mountain. The gods took one end of the serpent, the demons the other, and in this way they churned the ocean until they recovered the lost objects; (iii) Varah, 'the boar': a Daitya called Hataklochan had dragged the earth to the bottom of the sea. In order to recover the earth, Vishnu took the form of a boar, and after a battle that lasted a thousand years, he killed the Daitya and carried the earth back to the surface on his tusks; (iv) Narsingh, Narhari, or Narkeshari 'the man-lion': Vishnu took on the form of half-lion, half-man to deliver the world from the Daitya Kanakakasipu. Kananakasipu's son, Prahlad, was a devotee of Vishnu, and refused to obey his father's order that he should worship him and not Vishnu. When

Prahlad declared that Vishnu was all-pervading
and everywhere, Kanakakasipu demanded to
know if he was present even in the stone pillar in
the hall of his palace. At this, to avenge Prahlad,
Vishnu appeared out of the pillar in the form
of Narsingh, half-man, half lion, and therefore
neither man nor beast, and killed Kanakakasipu.
The first four avatars are said to have taken place
during the Satyayug, the first age of the world; (v)
Vaman, 'the dwarf': in the Tretayug (the second
age of the world), the Daitya king Bali became so
powerful that he became king of the three worlds.
The gods asked Vishnu to help them, so that
may once again regain their pre-eminence in the
world. So Vishnu descended to earth as a dwarf,
and the son of Kashyap and Aditi. The dwarf
begged Bali to give him as much land as he could
cover in three strides. Bali, with his characteristic
generosity, agreed. The dwarf took two strides by
which he covered heaven and earth. Recognizing
Bali's virtue, he refrained from taking the third
step, and left Patal, or the underworld to Bali. This
avatar is also known as Tribikram or Trivikrama,
literally 'three strides'; (vi) Parashuram, 'Ram
with the axe': he was born in the Tretayug, as
the son of the Brahman Jamadagni, and his wife,
Renuka. From his father's side he was descended
from Bhrigu. He appeared in the world for
repressing the tyranny and violence of the
Kshatriya or warrior caste. Though he appeared
in this world before Ramchandra, Vishnu's
seventh avatar and the hero of the Ramayana,
they were both living in this world at the same
time. His weapon was the parashu or axe; (vii)
Ram, or Ramchandra, the hero of the Ramayana
and of Tulsi's *Ramcharitmanas*, he was born in
the Tretayug to destroy the demon Ravan. He
was the son of Dasharath, king of Ayodhya;
(viii) Krishna, 'the dark': he is considered to be

the most perfect of all of Vishnu's avatars. He is often regarded not as an avatar, but as Vishnu himself, when his elder brother Balram takes his place as the eighth avatar; (ix) Buddha: Buddha's far-reaching influence as a religious leader caused the Hindu Brahmins to adopt him as an avatar of Vishnu, who encourages wicked men to disregard the Vedas and the gods, and so bring about their own destruction. In eastern India, the ninth avatar is Jagannath, 'lord of the world', a form of Krishna; (x) Kalki, 'the white horse': the last and tenth avatar is yet to come. Vishnu will appear at the end of the Kaliyug, the last and fourth age, mounted on a white horse, and carrying a fiery sword. He will finally destroy the wicked and rid the world of evil, and the cycle of creation will begin again with piety restored.

Vishvakarma: A son of Brahma, and the chief architect and artist of the gods.

Vishvamitra: A celebrated sage, and the companion and counsellor of the young Ram. He was born a Kshatriya, and was the king of Kanauj, but through long and intense austerities, successfully elevated himself to the caste of Brahman and became one of the seven great Rishis. According to the Rig Veda, he was the son of a king named Kushika, because of which he is called Kaushik. Later sources make him the son of Gadhi, king of Kanyakubja and a descendant of Puru. He is therefore also called Gadhij, 'born of Gadhi' or, Gadhinandan, 'Gadhi's son'.

Vyas: Literally, 'an arranger', this title is common to many ancient authors, but is especially applied to Veda Vyas, the arranger of the Vedas. The name is also given to the compiler of the Mahabharata, and the arranger of the Puranas.

Yaksha:

Yakshas are semi-divine beings who protect forests and other wild places, and are generally harmless, though they may, on rare occasions, be evil. They are the attendants of the god of wealth, Kuber.

Yayati:

Son of Nahush, and the fifth king of the Lunar dynasty. He had two wives, Devyani and Sarmishtha. From Devyani was born his son Yadu, and from Sarmishtha his son Puru, the respective founders of the Yadavas and the Pauravas. In all he had five sons, the three others being Druhyu, Turvasu and Anu. Yayati was fond of women, and for his infidelity to Devyani, he was cursed with old age and infirmity by her father, Shukra. This curse Shukra consented to transfer to any of his sons who would agree to bear it. All refused, except Puru, who gave up his youth to his father and took on his curse of decrepitude. Yayati spent a thousand years enjoying the pleasures of the senses, after which he restored his youth to Puru and made him his successor. This story is told in the Mahabharata, as well as in the Vishnu Purana. The version in the Padma Purana is different. Yayati was invited to heaven by Indra, who sent his charioteer Matali to fetch him. On the way, they had a philosophical discussion, which had such an impact on Yayati that when he returned to earth, he, by his virtuous rule, made all his subjects free from passion and decay. Yama, the god of Death, complained that men no longer died. So Indra sent Kamdev, the god of love, and his daughter, Asruvindumati, to tempt Yayati with desire. They succeeded, and Yayati, deeply enamoured of the youthful Asruvindumati and in order to become a fit husband for her, asked each of his sons to exchange their youth for his old age. All refused, except Puru, who gave his manly vigour to his father and assumed his decrepitude. After some time, Asruvindumati persuaded Yayati to return to heaven, and he then gave Puru back his youth. According to the Mahabharata, King Yayati, at the end of his life, gave up his throne to Puru and retired to the forest to lead the life of an ascetic. There, the king lived on fruits and roots for some time, and practised austerities, attaining complete control of his mind and his senses. He also performed fire sacrifices to honour his ancestors and the gods, and followed every prescribed rite and tradition for one in the third or forest-dwelling stage of life (See four stages of life). He then lived on scattered seeds that he gathered for a thousand years, and then for another year observing the vow of silence and living upon air alone and without sleep. He passed another year practising the most severe austerities, with four fires burning around him and the sun above, and then, living upon air alone, stood upon one leg for six months. These austerities earned him a place in heaven. He lived in heaven for a long time, where he was held in great reverence by the gods and other celestial beings. One day, Yayati went to meet Indra, the king of the gods, and in the course of conversation, Indra asked him to whom he was equal in the austerities he had practised. Yayati's boastful answer, that he did not, in the matter of austerities, behold any who was his equal amongst men, gods, Gandharvas and rishis, led to a diminishing of his virtues, and he was hurled from the heavens back into the world of men.

yojan: A measure of distance, equivalent to 4 kos or about 9 miles.

Acknowledgements

Many people have stood by me in the five long years it has taken to complete this translation. Of these, my thanks first and foremost to R. Sivapriya, who made this project possible, and to Ambar Sahil Chatterjee, who has seen this through from the very beginning to the end. My gratitude also, to Shantanu Rai Chaudhuri, for his patient and meticulous editing.

I would also like to thank my teacher, Mrs Chandrakanta Chandra, who first introduced me to the literary genius of Tulsidas and the wonders of medieval Hindi literature in school, and whose help, in resolving nuances of language or understanding points of Tulsi's philosophy or ideology, has been invaluable to me on this journey of discovery and translation.

As always, my profound thanks to Dr Rupert Snell, my guru and guide, without whose encouragement I may not have had the courage to take up this project, and who has been ever present with help, advice, and support every step of the way.

My very special thanks to my daughters, Vipasha Bansal and Vidisha Jain, who bore the brunt of my obsession with this work. Vipasha patiently rescued me from innumerable tangles of grammar and syntax, and Vidisha was unfailing in her encouragement and support.

And finally, to my long-suffering family and friends—in particular Usha Bubna, Dr Asha Maheshwari, Anil Ratti and Shaiontoni Bose—for their patience and support, my undying gratitude.

Notes

Introduction

1. Though even at the time that Valmiki composed his epic, two other, very different, tellings of the Ram story existed—one was the Buddhist *Dasaratha Jataka*, in which Ram and Sita are brother and sister and rule as consorts, and the other the Jain *Paumchariya* by Vimalasuri, who sets the story in the court of the historical king Srinika and depicts the Rakshasas not as demons, but as normal human beings.

2. This reference to Tulsi is found in the *Bhaktamal*, a collection of short biographies composed by Nabhadas, possibly around 1585.

3. For a detailed discussion on the spread and circulation of the *Ramcharitmanas*, see Philip Lutgendorf, 'The Quest for the Legendary Tulsidas', *According to Tradition: Hagiographical Writing in India*, edited by Winand M. Callewaert and Rupert Snell.

4. For a discussion on available biographies of Tulsidas, see Philip Lutgendorf, 'The Quest for the Legendary Tulsidas', *According to Tradition: Hagiographical Writing in India*, edited by Winand M. Callewaert and Rupert Snell.

5. *Balkand*, 34.

6. *Balkand*, 30A, 31.

7. *Balkand*, 14D.

8. *Balkand*, Mangalacharan 7.

9. The relevant passages are contained in Book 3, *Aranyakand*, 24, where Sita conceals herself in the fire and substitutes her shadow; and in Book 6, *Lankakand*, 108–09, where the shadow Sita is destroyed and the real Sita steps forth out of the fire.

10. *Balkand*, 16.
11. *Balkand*, 14.
12. *Balkand*, 227–36.
13. Philip Lutgendorf, *The Life of a Text: Performing the* Ramcaritmanas *of Tulsidas*, University of California Press, 1991, p. 7.
14. *Aranyakand*, 34–36.
15. *Balkand*, 30.
16. *Balkand*, 124A.
17. For a more detailed discussion on the title, see Philip Lutgendorf, *The Life of a Text: Performing the* Ramcaritmanas *of Tulsidas*, University of California Press, 1991, pp. 19–20.
18. *Balkand*, 35–36.
19. *Balkand*, 36–37.
20. As an example, see *Uttarkand*, 113.
21. *Ayodhyakand*, 0; this doha, numbered 0, is the first doha after the Sanskrit mangalacharan; from this the Avadhi text of the second book begins.

Book II: AYODHYAKAND (AYODHYA)

1. Ram's dismay at the king's decision to choose him as heir-apparent silences the critics who may otherwise have said that he took advantage of Bharat's absence from Avadh to grab this title, which should be Bharat's as per an old promise made by Dasharath to Kaikeyi's kin as the condition of he marrying her.
2. Kadru and Vinata were two of the thirteen wives of the sage Kashyap, who, say the Puranas, was the progenitor of all living creatures through his various wives. From Kadru were born the serpents, and from Vinata the birds. One day, an argument broke out between the two women about the colour of Uchchaihsravas, the white horse of Indra. Kadru insisted that it was black, while Vinata said that it was white. They agreed that whoever was wrong would serve the other as a servant all her life. When Kadru realized that the horse was indeed white, she fastened one of her black serpent sons on to the horse's back, and Vinata, mistaking it to be the tail, conceded that the horse was black. Vinata then had to serve Kadru for many years, suffering great indignities and torment, till she was set free by her son, Garud.
3. Dasharath was once engaged in battle with the Daitya, Sambara, who had revolted against Indra, the king of the gods. Dasharath was severely wounded and fell unconscious, as did his charioteer. The king would have

died had not Kaikeyi, who had accompanied him into battle, rescued him and driven his chariot to safety. When the king regained consciousness and realized how his queen had saved him, he granted her any two boons that she might desire. Another version of the story (in the *Adhyatma Ramayan*), says that once, when the king was engaged in battle with the demons, the axle of his chariot broke, and the king's chariot would have been overturned and the king killed had not Kaikeyi, who was with him, noticed this and inserted her own arm in place of the axle and kept it there till the king had defeated his enemy. In gratitude, the king had promised to grant her any two requests she might make. Kaikeyi, however, had not asked for anything at the time, so that the two boons were still outstanding.

4. This was the kop-griha, a room a woman would retire into when feeling angry or offended or insulted.

5. King Shibi cut off his own flesh to equal the weight of a dove that had sought his protection against a hawk. No matter how much of his own flesh he cut off to give the hawk, the dove was always heavier. At last, he climbed on to the scales himself and would have cut off his own head— but the gods intervened, and acknowledged his generosity and made him whole again. The rishi Dadhichi gave up his life so that the gods could fashioned Indra's thunderbolt and other weapons from his bones to slay the demon Vritra and his army. The Daitya king, Bali, had become so powerful through devotion and penance that he had defeated Indra, and extended his rule over the three worlds. Vishnu, taking on the form of a dwarf (his fifth avatar), asked the generous Bali for three steps of land. Vishnu then stepped over the earth with his first step, the heavens with his second, and when he asked where he should put his foot for the third step, Bali offered his own head. Out of respect for Bali's goodness and generosity, Vishnu stopped short and gave him the infernal region of Patal to rule. (Also see Glossary.)

6. Keeping watch in a cremation ground refers to a tantric ritual to call up a spirit or ghost and bind it in one's power.

7. The staunchly Buddhist kingdom of Magadh came to be regarded as impure by conservative Hindus, though it contained many Hindu pilgrimage sites like Gaya which they continued to visit.

8. A legendary king of Ayodhya, Harishchandra gave away his kingdom and all he possessed, selling even his wife and son, to fulfil a promise he had made to the sage Vishvamitra. (Also see Glossary.)

9. The foam (maja, or manja) that appears on the surface of ponds and rivers with the first showers of the rainy season is believed to cause madness

in fish. An alternative interpretation offered is that the word maja here means 'bait'—in which case the line could be translated as 'Like a fish that flails and flounders upon swallowing the fisherman's bait'.

10. It is believed that if a snake catches a muskrat instead of an ordinary rat, it can neither swallow it nor disgorge it. If it swallows the muskrat, it dies, and if it brings it up, the muskrat will blind the snake.

11. Galav, a pupil of Rishi Vishvamitra, insisted upon giving him guru dakshina, the fee due to a teacher, even though the rishi said he did not want it. Annoyed by his persistence, Vishvamitra asked for a thousand white horses with one black ear. This caused Galav a lifetime of hardship. Nahush, a wise and virtuous king, was asked to reign temporarily in Indra's stead. Overcome by pride, he coveted Indra's wife, Shachi, and in order to win her, insisted that he be taken to her in a palanquin carried by sages. Rishi Agastya, angered by his disrespect, cursed him to be born as a python upon earth. (Also see Glossary.)

12. By referring to Lakshman as his Lord, Tulsi reminds his audience of Lakshman's divine status as partial avatar of Vishnu.

13. Ram's departure for the forest leaves Avadh bereft of her king, but sets in motion the events that lead up to the abduction of Sita, the downfall and death of Ravan and the ultimate fulfilment of the purpose of the gods— hence the ill omens in Lanka, the grief in Avadh and the mixed sorrow and joy in heaven.

14. They cursed themselves and praised the fishes, for fish die as soon as they are deprived of water, whilst they were still alive though separated from Ram.

15. King Rantidev was a devotee of Vishnu and known for his generosity. Once the gods decided to test his faith and generosity and caused a great famine in his land. The king gave away all he possessed to his people. When even that did not help, he gave up all food and drink and devoted himself to Vishnu. After weeks of fasting, his ministers persuaded him to take some food, and brought him water and a dish made of rice boiled in milk. Just as he was about to eat the rice and milk, the gods appeared disguised as people of different castes begging for food. The king gave away all his food, including his last sip of water to an outcast. At this, the gods acknowledged his great faith and generosity and restored his kingdom to prosperity. (Also see Glossary.)

16. This refers to the story of King Bali and Vishnu's fifth avatar as the dwarf.

17. Ram's acceptance of the boatman's request to wash his feet before he climbed aboard his boat had confused and mystified Ganga, for how

could Ram thus give in to a boatman's rough and rude instruction? But upon seeing his toenails, her doubt and bewilderment vanished, for she recognized him as the true Lord, the source of her waters, for it is from his feet that the stream of the divine river springs (see Balkand, 211). She realized that the Lord's acceptance of the boatman's request was part of the Lord's divine play, in accordance with his assumption of human form, and she rejoiced to think of the touch of his divine feet.

18. The following several lines about this mysterious young ascetic have no bearing on the main narrative. But they are found in many of the manuscripts, including the Gita Press version that I have used as the basis for my translation, and most commentators seem to agree that they have been written by Tulsidas. I have therefore retained these lines, mysterious though they are. The most puzzling and ambiguous phrase in the description of this ascetic is 'kabi alakhita gati'—literally, 'poet invisible state'. Some commentators interpret these lines to mean that the identity of the ascetic is unknown to the poet, and hence the ascetic is Hanuman or Agni, the fire-god, or another divinity in disguise; others take these lines to mean that the ascetic is an unknown poet, a reference by Tulsidas to himself, in his youth. I prefer the latter interpretation.

19. Lilies open in the moonlight, so the others of the solar clan respond in the same way to Ram. Hence Ram is the moon to the lilies (i.e., the other heroes) of the solar dynasty.

20. Rohini, the fourth lunar asterism, is the favourite wife of the moon god; the planet Mercury (Budh), is his son.

21. Sita walks timidly or fearfully along the path because she did not want to place her feet upon Ram's footprints and thus erase them; Lakshman is careful not to tread on their footprints, and keeps them to his right in the tradition of honouring deities by keeping them to one's right.

22. Anasuya was the wife of the Rishi Atri. Intense penance and austerities had given her miraculous powers. She lived with her husband in a hermitage in the forest south of Chitrakut. Once, no rain fell in Chitrakut for ten years, resulting in a great famine. There was no food left for the sages who lived there, or the birds and animals. Anasuya, through the power of her penance, brought the river Mandakini down to Chitrakut from heaven and the area grew green and lush again. Here, Tulsi also plays on the name of the river, Mandakini, calling it a 'dakini', a witch whose evil eye causes miscarriages and who devours babies and young children.

23. Since Chitrakut is one of the peaks of the Vindhya range of mountains, its glory is shared by the entire range—and so the joy of the Vindhya mountains.

24. Basav is another name for Indra, whose capital is the city of Amarpur or Amaravati; Shachi is his consort, and Jayant is his son.

25. Though Sumantra is displaying all the signs of one about to die, his life-breath refuses to depart in the hope of seeing Ram again at the end of his exile.

26. In Hindu tradition, it is believed that a soul condemned to hell is given a special body which can endure every torment and does not perish till the condemned soul has made full reparation for its sins.

27. The moon is believed to contain amrit, the nectar of immortality.

28. Yayati was the son of Nahusha, and the fifth king of the lunar dynasty. At the end of his life, King Yayati gave up his throne to his son and retired to the forest to lead the life of an ascetic. His austerities earned him a place in heaven where he lived for a long time. One day, he went to meet Indra, the king of the gods, and in the course of conversation, Indra asked him to whom he was equal in the austerities he had practised. Yayati's boastful answer, that he did not, in the matter of austerities, behold any who was his equal amongst men, gods, Gandharvas and rishis, led to a diminishing of his virtues, and he was hurled from the heavens back into the world of men. (Also see Glossary.)

29. Sampati was the eldest son of Arun, the charioteer of the Sun, and the older brother of the vulture, Jatayu. In their youth, the brothers used to compete as to who could fly higher in the sky. Once, Jatayu flew so high that he was in danger of getting burnt by the sun. But Sampati flew higher, and spreading his wings, protected his younger brother from the sun's fierce flames. Jatayu was saved, but Sampati's wings were burnt, and he fell to the ground from the sky. He lived the rest of his life without wings. He plays an important role later on in the story, when he gives Ram's monkey allies the important information that Ravan has carried Sita off to Lanka. His story is also related at that point in the epic.

30. This incident is related in detail in Valmiki's Ramayana. As a young man, Dasharath had been renowned for his skill as an archer and his ability to shoot by sound alone. One evening (whilst he was still only the heir-apparent and before he had met or married Kaushalya), he seized his bow and arrows and in his arrogance, set off in his chariot along the banks of the Sarayu in search of an elephant, tiger or buffalo to shoot—in the dark, by sound. As he waited by the river in the deep darkness of the

night, he heard a gurgling sound, and believing it to be an elephant come down to the river to drink, he fitted an arrow to his bow and let it fly. A cry of pain rent the darkness, and Dasharath realized with dismay that he had shot a human being. He threw down his bow and arrows and ran as fast as he could towards the cry, to find a young boy lying by the river, mortally wounded by his arrow. The boy was dressed in hermit's robes, with matted hair—and the sound that the king had mistaken for an elephant's had been made by the young hermit filling a pitcher of water for his blind and aged parents. Dasharath realized he could not save the boy. As he stood there helplessly, the boy begged him to pull out the arrow that had so wounded him, and told him how to find his parents, who were waiting for him to return with water to slake their thirst. The boy implored the prince to go to his parents and tell them how their son had died, and counselled him to ask their forgiveness, lest their wrath destroy him forever. Dasharath stayed by the boy, aghast at what he had done. With his last breath, the boy assured him that he had not committed the sin of killing a Brahman, for though a hermit, he was born of a Vaishya father and a Shudra mother, and therefore not of the twice-born. As the boy drew nearer and nearer to death, Dasharath gently pulled his arrow out, and waited by his side till he died. Then, picking up the pitcher the boy had dropped, he filled it with water from the stream, and following the directions the boy had given, made his way to his parents' hut. There, he found the old couple waiting anxiously for their son's return. Hearing his footsteps, the father called out to him, believing him to be his son. Dasharath drew closer, and with tears in his eyes, told the old couple the sad story of their son's death. The parents begged him to take them to their son's body, and after performing the last rites for their son, the father turned to Dasharath and cursed him that just as he had deprived him of his son, so would Dasharath one day mourn a son, and of that suffering, die. But since he had killed his son unwittingly, the curse would take effect at a time far distant and not at once. Moreover, since he had voluntarily confessed his crime, he was spared an immediate death—else he and all his descendants would have perished forever. The name of the hermit boy killed by Dasharath was Shravan Kumar, and he is held as the epitome of filial devotion in India, even today.

31. That is, Bharat persuaded them not to climb on to the king's funeral pyre and perish with him as satis.

32. Offering of sesame seeds—a handful (or double handful) of black sesame seeds mixed with water is offered to the deceased by his son (or by the

person who has performed the funeral rites) after the cremation; it signifies the severing of all ties with the deceased.

33. This refers to the dashagatra rites, performed over ten days after a cremation. Ten pindas, small balls of cooked rice mixed with sesame seeds, are offered to the deceased, one for each part of the body. This helps the deceased soul to build a new body, and cast off its connections with the old.

34. Shiv often visits the homes of householders in the form of a beggar or a wandering ascetic; and so all such people must be received with courtesy as part of the worship of Shiv.

35. The Mahabharata relates that, at the command of his father, Parashuram cut off his mother's head. His obedience pleased his father so much that he told him to ask a boon. Parashuram asked that his mother be restored to life, and that he himself become invincible in combat and enjoy a long life. (See also Glossary, and Balkand, Stanza 276, endnote 81.)

36. For being unfaithful to his wife, King Yayati was cursed with premature old age and infirmity by her father, Shukra. This curse Shukra consented to transfer to any of his five sons who would agree to bear it. His youngest son, Puru, gave up his youth to his father and took on his curse of decrepitude. Yayati spent a thousand years enjoying the pleasures of the senses, after which he restored his youth to Puru and made him his successor. (See also Glossary.)

37. The thunderbolt was fashioned from the bones of the sage Dadhichi. (See also stanza 30 and Glossary.)

38. Here, Tulsi uses a folk saying—'to hold the sweets of bliss in both hands' derives from the custom of placing a laddu (a sweetmeat made of chickpea, lentil, or flour with sugar and ghee, and shaped like a small ball) in each hand of a faithful wife who dies before her husband; the laddus indicate her success in this world (where, by dying before her husband, she did not have to face widowhood) and her success in the next (where she attains bliss for her fidelity). In Guha's case, if he wins against Bharat, he would have served Ram's cause, if he is killed, he will attain eternal bliss for dying in the service of the Lord.

39. These are forest tribes and other groups despised by traditional Hindus as ignorant, base and uncivilized and regarded as outcasts from upper-caste Hindu society.

40. So that his right side was always, as prescribed by ritual, towards the object of reverence (in this case the grass mat).

41. The waters of the Jamuna are dark, and of the Ganga light. (The stream of the Sarasvati is invisible.)

42. Bharat's own dharma could refer to Kshatriya dharma, which allows only giving and never begging for anything from anyone, or it could refer to his dharma of devotion only to Ram, from which he swerves by praying to another deity.

43. Soma, the Moon-god once became so arrogant that he carried off Tara, the wife of Brihaspati, guru of the gods, and refused to give her back, disregarding the entreaties of her husband as well as Brahma's command. Soma was supported by the Daityas and Danavas and other enemies of the gods, while Indra and most of the other gods supported Brihaspati. The battle that ensued was so fierce that it shook the earth. At last, Brahma stepped in and stopped the quarrel and forced the Moon to return Tara to Brihaspati. Tara soon gave birth to a child, whom she declared to be the son of the Moon. The child was named Budh (regent of Mercury), and from him sprung the lunar dynasty. The Moon bears on his face the blemishes put their by Brihaspati in his anger. Another version of the story states that Brihaspati, returning from bathing in the Ganga, found the Moon with his wife, and threw his dripping garments at his face in anger, and this caused the blemishes on the Moon's face.

44. The Riddhis are attendants of the god of wealth, Kuber, and are wealth personified; the Siddhis are supernatural powers of which anima (the ability to make oneself infinitesimally small) is one. (Also see Glossary).

45. The people are overcome with conflicting emotions—joy at the delights available to them, but dismay too, given their grief over their separation from Ram. (In Valmiki's Ramayana, though, the people are so delighted by the wonders they see that they are ready to give up their search for Ram.)

46. Brihaspati is referring to the use of divine maya earlier, when Sarasvati confused Manthara's mind.

47. The story is told in the Puranas: the sage Durvasa, known for his fiery temper and regarded by some as an emanation of Shiv, once visited king Ambarish, a devoted follower of Vishnu. The king welcomed him and invited him to dine with him. The sage agreed and went down to the river to bathe before the meal. Now it happened to be dvadashi, the twelfth day of the lunar fortnight. The king had fasted the day before, and ritual demanded he break his fast while it was still dvadashi. The king waited for the sage to return from the river, but the sage was taking his time. The king did not wish to eat without his guest, but it was necessary he break his fast within the prescribed time. His advisors suggested he take a sip of the water in which the feet of the Lord's image had been washed—that way

he would have broken his fast in time, yet not be guilty of disrespecting his guest by eating before him. The king did so, and just then the sage returned from the river. When Durvasa realised that the king had already broken his fast without waiting for him, he flew into a rage, and pulling out a hair from his head, turned into the Rakshasa Kritya, who rushed at the king to devour him. But Ambarish, who had dedicated himself to Vishnu, did not flinch. He did not run, nor did he make any attempt to defend himself. Vishnu, who was watching, then sent his own discus, Sudarshan, to help the king. After killing the Rakshasa, the discus turned upon Durvasa, chasing him all over the world for an entire year. No one gave the sage shelter, and even the gods refused to help, saying that nothing could be done for him until he went back to Ambarish and asked his forgiveness. Meanwhile, the king had been fasting since the sage left, and taking pity on his plight, prayed to Vishnu's weapon to spare the sage. Sudarshan heard his prayer and returned to Vishnu. Durvasa now realised the king's greatness, and fell at his feet in remorse. The king forgave him, and then, paying him every respect, entertained him to a lavish feast before seeing him on his way.

48. Tulsi is probably referring to Kamadgiri, 'the mountain that fulfils all desires'. In Chitrakut, the hill is regarded as a sacred site by Hindus even today.

49. King Vena banned offerings and performance of sacrifices to the gods and the giving of gifts to Brahmans, declaring that he alone was worthy of receiving offerings. (See also Glossary.)

50. Sahasrabahu, the 'thousand-armed', was king of the Haihaya tribe. In return for hospitality, he carried off the sage Jamadagni's cow. For this offence, he was killed by Jamadagni's son, Parashuram. Indra, king of the gods, seduced Ahalya, the wife of the sage Gautam. Trishanku, a king of Ayodhya, tried to ascend to heaven in his corporeal form. (See also Glossary.)

51. The chatak subsists only on the drops of rain that fall in autumn, and loves the raincloud; the fish loves water and cannot survive without it.

52. A complete or fourfold (chaturanga) army consists of infantry, cavalry, elephants and chariots.

53. As explained elsewhere, Videh is the title of Janak, king of the kingdom of Videha. It also means 'bodiless' or 'disembodied'. His title, Videh, is untrue in these circumstances of overwhelming grief because had he been truly 'videh' or bodiless (i.e., detached), he would not have felt the grief he did.

54. Or a face that pleases all his devotees, according to their inclination and what they seek in him.

55. As per Indian tradition, it is not appropriate to accept food, particularly grains or cereals of any kind and in any form, in a married daughter's home. So it would not have been appropriate for Janak to eat any grain-based food at the hermitage. Moreover, Ram is living as an ascetic, on roots and wild fruits.

56. Once, Lord Vishnu, moved by his austerities, appeared before the sage Markandeya and offered to grant him a boon of his choosing. The muni asked that he be allowed to witness the glory of Vishnu's maya. Vishnu disappeared, with the assurance that his wish would be fulfilled. One evening, as the muni was engaged in penance by the Pushpabhadra river, it began to rain. It rained so hard that the rivers, the seas and the oceans overflowed, and the land disappeared. The muni, though an enlightened soul, grew alarmed and afraid as he was tossed about in the seething flood. Carried along by the flood, he saw at last a tree rising above the waters. This was the imperishable banyan tree of Prayag. In its topmost branches, the muni saw an infant, contentedly sucking its big toe. This was, of course, none other than Vishnu himself. At this sight, the muni's fear and exhaustion disappeared, and he regained his equanimity of mind. The divine child then vouchsafed to the muni a vision of the whole universe, after which the infant, as well as the flood vanished, leaving the muni as he was before.

57. The three places are Haridwar (where the Ganga enters the plains), Prayag (the confluence of the Ganga with the Jamuna and the Sarasvati), and Gangasagar (the mouth of the Ganga, where the river meets the sea).

58. Once, the Vindhya mountains asked the Sun, who goes around Mt Meru every day, to revolve around it as well. The Sun refused, saying that his course had been determined by the Lord of the Universe. Enraged by the Sun's refusal, the Vindhyas grew taller and taller every day, so that it became difficult for the Sun to cross it every day in his passage from east to west. Alarmed, the gods asked the sage Agastya for help. Agastya approached the mountain range and asked it to bend down so he could cross over to the south. The Vindhyas did so, and the sage crossed over, but made the mountain range promise that it would remain in that position till he crossed back to the north. The sage has still not crossed back, and so the Vindhays remain in that position.

59. The Daitya Kanakalochan (also known as Hataklochan) had dragged the earth to the bottom of the sea. In order to recover the earth, Vishnu took

the form of a boar (Varah, his third avatar), and after a battle that lasted a thousand years, he killed the Daitya and carried the earth back to the surface on his tusks.

60. Commentators differ on what the two loves may be—some say it is the love of her parents and her mothers-in-law, others that it is the love of her parents and her husband.

61. Their realms had been taken over by Ravan.

62. It is said that bees shun the flowers of the champak tree despite their sweet and heady fragrance.

Book III: ARANYAKAND (THE FOREST)

1. Shachi is the consort of Indra, king of the gods. The reference here is to Vishnu's fifth avatar, the dwarf Vaman, who, born as the son of Aditi and Kashyap, was thus the younger brother of Indra.

2. 'To attain one's own eternal form' is to become one with the divine, for the Supreme Spirit pervades all, and every being is but a manifestation of the Absolute.

3. Tulsi was born as Vrinda, the daughter of the Asur Kalnemi. As Vrinda, she was the wife of the powerful Asur king, Jalandhar. Vrinda was a devotee of Vishnu, and because of her intense devotion to him, she was endowed with enormous yogic powers. She was also a chaste and faithful wife, and her prayers to Vishnu for his well-being further strengthened the already strong Jalandhar. Ultimately, Jalandhar became so powerful that he was crowned king of the Asurs. Very soon, Jalandhar had defeated every king on earth. Now, with the whole earth under his sway, he set about conquering the gods and defeated them easily. The gods realized that his invincibility came from his wife's faithfulness. So, as Vrinda prayed for her husband's success on the battlefield, Vishnu appeared before her in the guise of her husband. Vrinda was completely taken in by Vishnu, and overjoyed at seeing him safe and sound. She stopped praying and embraced Vishnu, as a result of which her power was broken, and consequently, her husband's. At that very instant, Shiv killed the Asur king. Vrinda felt that something was wrong, and Vishnu, abandoning his disguise, appeared before her as himself. Angry and grief-stricken, Vrinda cursed Vishnu to be separated from his wife. It is for this reason that he had to take form as Ram, and suffer separation from Sita. The heart-broken Vrinda then died. Vishnu, grieving for his devotee, then transformed her into the tulsi plant (some versions of the story say that Shiv transformed her into the tulsi plant).

No prayer to Vishnu is complete without an offering of tulsi leaves. (Vrinda and Jalandhar's story is also referred to in Balkand, Stanza 123.)

4. Here, the muni wants the boon of eternal devotion to Hari. He does not wish to become one with him—for if he becomes one with him, he cannot adore him. Therefore the boon of 'separation and devotion'.

5. The great muni referred to here is Shukracharya, the guru of the Asurs. The story of his curse is related in the Uttarakand of Valmiki's Ramayana. Danda, the youngest son of Ikshvaku, founder of the solar dynasty, was cruel and wrathful. Ishkvaku, unhappy with his behaviour, banished him from his kingdom of Ayodhya. Danda left, taking with him some of his father's wealth and subjects, and accompanied by Shukracharya, founded his own kingdom, called Dandak, in the south. There, with Shukracharya's help, he ruled for a thousand years and was a just and righteous king. Then one day, while Shukracharya was away, Danda saw his beautiful daughter, Abja. She rejected his advances, but Danda, overcome by lust, raped her. When Shukracharya returned in the evening, his daughter told him what had happened, and in his wrath, he called forth a storm that destroyed Danda and his entire kingdom, and reduced it to a wilderness. In place of the kingdom, there grew a dense forest, full of Rakshasas and wild beasts, and which only hermits and munis dared enter.

6. This meeting is described at great length by Valmiki. It is at this meeting that Jatayu promises to protect Sita, a promise which later costs him his life.

7. In Hindu belief, all creation, and all that happens around us, is the Lord's lila, his sport or pastime.

8. Hindus believe that a class of demons knows as Mandeha surround the rising sun every morning, and are dispersed only by the drops of water scattered into the air during the performance of pre-dawn prayers by the twice-born.

9. Ram put on a show of concern in accordance with the play he had set in motion. However, he was not worried, for he knew that the real Sita was safe within the fire, and that all that was happening was his lila, his sport, in order to accomplish the gods' purpose, viz., the death of Ravan.

10. The birds, animals, fruits, flowers and other objects listed here by Ram are the ones used by poets to describe the characteristics of a beautiful woman: her flashing eyes are compared to the wagtail and to fish, her shapely nose to a parrot's beak, her neck to that of a pigeon's, her dark, curling hair to a swarm of bees, her eyes to those of a doe, her voice to the sweet and tuneful singing of the kokil, her teeth to jasmine buds and pomegranate

seeds, the radiance of her skin and complexion to lightning, her eyes, face, hands and feet to the lotus, her radiant face to the autumn moon, her long, braided hair to a serpent, her captivating smile as impossible to break free from as Varun's snares, her curving brows to Kamdev's bow, her graceful gait to that of the swan and the elephant, her slender waist to that of a lion's, her firm, round breasts to the fruit of the wood-apple tree, and her smooth, firm thighs to golden bananas. All of these were overshadowed by Sita's incomparable beauty. Now that Sita is no longer there, all these were once again able to hear their own praise, and so, in her absence, rejoiced.

11. Kabandh was originally a Gandharva, and had been cursed by the sage Durvasa to become a hideous Rakshasa. When mortally wounded, he asked Ram to burn his body, and from that fire, he came out in his original form as a Gandharva. (See also Glossary.)

12. Sabari was a tribal woman, devoted to the worship of Ram. Her guru, the muni Matanga, had predicted before his death that the Lord would visit her. She lived in the forest as an ascetic for many years, waiting for Ram.

13. These are lust, anger, greed, attachment, pride and envy.